Modern Critical Views

Edward Albee
African American
    Poets Volume I
American and
    Canadian Women
    Poets, 1930–present
American Women
    Poets, 1650–1950
Maya Angelou
Asian-American
    Writers
Margaret Atwood
Jane Austen
James Baldwin
Samuel Beckett
Saul Bellow
The Bible
William Blake
Jorge Luis Borges
Ray Bradbury
The Brontës
Gwendolyn Brooks
Elizabeth Barrett
    Browning
Robert Browning
Italo Calvino
Albert Camus
Lewis Carroll
Willa Cather
Cervantes
Geoffrey Chaucer
Anton Chekhov
Kate Chopin
Agatha Christie
Samuel Taylor
    Coleridge
Joseph Conrad
Contemporary Poets
Stephen Crane
Dante
Daniel Defoe
Charles Dickens
Emily Dickinson

John Donne and the
    17th-Century Poets
Fyodor Dostoevsky
W.E.B. Du Bois
George Eliot
T. S. Eliot
Ralph Ellison
Ralph Waldo Emerson
William Faulkner
F. Scott Fitzgerald
Sigmund Freud
Robert Frost
George Gordon, Lord
    Byron
Graham Greene
Thomas Hardy
Nathaniel Hawthorne
Ernest Hemingway
Hispanic-American
    Writers
Homer
Langston Hughes
Zora Neale Hurston
Henrik Ibsen
John Irving
Henry James
James Joyce
Franz Kafka
John Keats
Jamaica Kincaid
Stephen King
Rudyard Kipling
D. H. Lawrence
Ursula K. Le Guin
Sinclair Lewis
Bernard Malamud
Christopher Marlowe
Gabriel García
    Márquez
Cormac McCarthy
Carson McCullers
Herman Melville
Molière

Arthur Miller
John Milton
Molière
Toni Morrison
Native-American
    Writers
Joyce Carol Oates
Flannery O'Connor
Eugene O'Neill
George Orwell
Octavio Paz
Sylvia Plath
Edgar Allan Poe
Katherine Anne
    Porter
J. D. Salinger
Jean-Paul Sartre
William Shakespeare:
    Histories and
    Poems
William Shakespeare:
    Romances
William Shakespeare:
    The Comedies
William Shakespeare:
    The Tragedies
George Bernard Shaw
Mary Wollstonecraft
    Shelley
Percy Bysshe Shelley
Alexander
    Solzhenitsyn
Sophocles
John Steinbeck
Tom Stoppard
Jonathan Swift
Amy Tan
Alfred, Lord Tennyson
Henry David Thoreau
J. R. R. Tolkien
Leo Tolstoy
Mark Twain
John Updike

Modern Critical Views

Modern Critical Views

AMERICAN AND CANADIAN WOMEN POETS 1930–PRESENT

Edited and with an introduction by
Harold Bloom
Sterling Professor of the Humanities
Yale University

CHELSEA HOUSE PUBLISHERS
Philadelphia

©2002 by Chelsea House Publishers, a subsidiary of
Haights Cross Communications.

Introduction © 2002 by Harold Bloom.

Printed and bound in the United States of America
10 9 8 7 6 5 4 3 2 1

Library of Congress Cataloging-in-Publication Data

American and Canadian women poets, 1930-present / edited and
with an introduction by Harold Bloom.
        p. cm. -- (Modern critical views)
    Includes bibliographical references (p.   ) and index.
    ISBN 0-7910-6331-3
    1. American poetry--Women authors--History and criticism.
  2. Women and literature--United States--History--20th
  century. 3. Canadian poetry--Women authors--History and
  criticism. 4. Women and literature--Canada--History--20th
  century. 5. Canadian poetry--20th century--History and
  criticism. 6. American poetry--20th century--History and
  criticism. I. Bloom, Harold. II. Series.

PS151 .A43 2002
811'.5099287'0973--dc21
                                        2002003535

Chelsea House Publishers
1974 Sproul Road, Suite 400
Broomall, PA 19008-0914

http://www.chelseahouse.com

Contents

Editor's Note

This volume gathers together what in its editor's judgment represents the best criticism yet published upon the principal American and Canadian women poets, from Elizabeth Bishop to the present moment. The editor is grateful to Karin Cope for her erudition and insight, which helped him in locating and choosing the essays included here. Two essays each have been devoted to Elizabeth Bishop, and Jay Macpherson. The remaining poets each receive one essay in criticism.

Elizabeth Bishop, the principal American poet after Dickinson, receives an illuminating overview from Helen Vendler, who ponders the intricate balance of the familiar and the uncanny in Bishop's poetry. Lee Edelman, in a detailed explication of Bishop's "In the Waiting Room," demonstrates a way in which the poem indisputably does involve us in the question of "female textuality."

Richard Howard gives an eloquent appreciation of an extraordinary poet, May Swenson, who in the editor's judgment is, in proportion to her merits, the most undervalued woman poet of our own or any other time. Howard celebrates her as being both magician and naturalistic dramatist, and sees the two modes as being unified in her later work.

The noted black poet Gwendolyn Brooks is sensitively discussed by Gary Smith, who sees her as exposing and combating the mythologies to which black women have been subjected. Paul A. Lacey's essay on Denise Levertov emphasizes her contribution to an enlarged social consciousness, in a kind of countermovement towards mythologizing.

J. D. McClatchy's tribute to Anne Sexton praises her for honesty and courage, qualities also ascribed to Adrienne Rich in an analysis of Rich's ideological stance by Margaret Homans. In an appreciation parallel to these, Barbara Hardy sees Sylvia Plath as having created a persona in her poems capable of "resisting narcissism and closure, right to the death." R. B. Stepto's high estimate of Audre Lorde also discourses on a poet's courage but refreshingly emphasizes Lorde's apt knowledge of West African culture and religion.

Richard Howard, reviewing Amy Clampitt's elegant *The Kingfisher*, salutes it as the best "first book" of American poems since A. R. Ammons, while noting Clampitt's precision throughout. John Hollander, in a similar review of Vicki Hearne's first book, *Nervous Horses*, emphasizes this young poet's remarkable combination of fresh *materia poetica* and profound philosophical insight.

The remainder of this book is devoted to the two leading Canadian women poets, Jay Macpherson and Anne Carson. Macpherson is described by the great critic Northrop Frye as an authentic mythological poet, very much in Blake's tradition. Margaret Atwood, in an overview of Macpherson's work, usefully compares her to Coleridge, another of this poet's authentic precursors. My essay on Anne Carson, first published here, is an appreciation of a great poet's full emergence.

Introduction

I

A tradition of poets that includes Emily Dickinson, Marianne Moore, and Elizabeth Bishop has a palpable distinction, but it may be too soon to speak or write of a canon of "American Women Poets." The sixteen American and two Canadian poets studied in these two volumes are not chosen arbitrarily, yet considerations of the books' lengths as well as of the poets' canonical probability have entered into my selection. I regret the omission of Léonie Adams, Muriel Rukeyser, Sandra McPherson, Grace Schulman, Josephine Miles, Maxine Kumin, Mona Van Duyn, and several others, while various critics and readers might have included Amy Lowell, Sara Teasdale, Elinor Wylie, Edna St. Vincent Millay, and a large group of our contemporaries. But the eighteen poets studied here do seem a central grouping, and the canonical process is always an ongoing one anyway. Future editions of these books may be relied upon to correct emphases and clarify choices.

Two distinguished critics of literature by women, Sandra M. Gilbert and Susan Gubar, have taught us to speak of "the tradition in English," yet with characteristic fairness they quote the great poet Elizabeth Bishop's denial of such a tradition:

> Undoubtedly gender does play an important part in the making of any art, but art is art and to separate writings, paintings, musical compositions, etc., into two sexes is to emphasize values in them that are not art.

Bishop, a subtle intellect, makes clear that gender is a source of values in the genesis of art, but asserts that such values are not in themselves aesthetic. Though my inclination is to agree with her, I am wary of arguing against the tendency of origins to turn into ends or aims in the genealogy of imagination. Since I myself am frequently misunderstood on this point by feminist critics (though never, I am happy to say, by Gilbert and Gubar) I have a certain desire to illuminate the matter. Most Western poetry has been what Gertrude Stein called "patriarchal poetry," and most Western criticism necessarily has been patriarchal also. If Dr. Samuel Johnson, William Hazlitt, Ralph Waldo Emerson, and Dr. Sigmund Freud are to be considered patriarchal, then I as their ephebe presumably must be patriarchal also. So be it. But such a coloring or troping of critical stance is descriptive rather than prescriptive. Most strong Western poets, for whatever reasons, have been male: Homer and the Yahwist presumably, and certainly Virgil, Lucretius, Horace, on through Dante, Petrarch, and Chaucer to Shakespeare, Spenser, Milton, Pope, Wordsworth, Goethe, Shelley, Leopardi, Hugo, Whitman, Baudelaire, Browning, Yeats, Rilke, Stevens, and so many more. To this day, the only woman poet in English of that stature is Dickinson. Not every poet studied in these books seems to me of proven achievement; I have grave reservations about Plath and one or two others. Moore and Bishop, while hardly comparable to Dickinson, seem to me beyond dispute, and so do Jay Macpherson, May Swenson, and Vicki Hearne, but there are problematic aspects to many of the others.

However, there are values also, in nearly all the others, that seem to me rather different from the qualities of their strongest male contemporaries, and some of those differences do ensue from a vision, an experiential and rhetorical stance, that has its origin in sexual difference. To locate the differences in stance seems to me the admirable enterprise of the best feminist literary criticism. That polemic and ideology should be so overt in much feminist literary criticism is understandable, and unfortunately aesthetic considerations sometimes are submerged in political and programmatic designs, but nothing is got for nothing, and I foresee that the emphases of feminist criticism will be modified by the success of that criticism. Though I will attempt to isolate differences in vision from male precursors in Elizabeth Bishop in this introduction, I am aware that I am a patriarchal critic, and I will not attempt to mask my own sense of the dilemmas confronted by women poets and poetry in what follows.

II

Dickinson sets a standard that no twentieth-century American poet, man or woman, not even Stevens or Frost or Hart Crane, can endure as measurement. Her influence upon our century's women poets is profound and more than a little dangerous. Rather than trace it from poet to poet, I want to observe it at play in the most powerful of Dickinson's descendants, Elizabeth Bishop, who engagingly employed Dickinson as a countervailing force and presence against Wallace Stevens, a more immediate influence upon Bishop's work. There are many instances of this beautiful interplay in Bishop, but perhaps the most remarkable is in the final verse paragraph of her magnificent and very American shore-ode, "The End of March":

> On the way back our faces froze on the other side.
> The sun came out for just a minute.
> For just a minute, set in their bezels of sand,
> the drab, damp, scattered stones
> were multi-colored,
> and all those high enough threw out long shadows,
> individual shadows, then pulled them in again.
> They could have been teasing the lion sun,
> except that now he was behind them
> —a sun who'd walked the beach the last low tide,
> making those big, majestic paw-prints,
> who perhaps had batted a kite out of the sky to play with.

The lion sun is Stevens's, and in some sense represents Stevens here, while the long shadows are Dickinson's, and represent her teasing and gentling effect upon the Stevensian trope of the lion. Bishop intends us to remember Dickinson's lyric 764:

> Presentiment—is that long Shadow—on the Lawn—
> Indicative that Suns go down—
>
> The Notice to the startled Grass
> That Darkness—is about to pass—

We are to remember also several Stevensian intertwinings of sun, lion, and male poet or Stevens, and perhaps these in particular among them, though there are others:

> it is
> For that the poet is always in the sun,
>
> Patches the moon together in his room,

To his Virgilian cadences, up down,
Up down.

    The lion sleeps in the sun.
    Its nose is on its paws.
    It can kill a man.

In the metaphysical streets of the physical town
We remember the lion of Juda and we save
The phrase . . . Say of each lion of the spirit

It is a cat of a sleek transparency
That shines with a nocturnal shine alone.
The great cat must stand potent in the sun.

The second of these passages is from a poem candidly entitled "Poetry is a Destructive Force." Perhaps it is and must be, to and by men; I do not know. Dickinson valued the presentiment of mortality over even the lion sun of male poetic tradition. Bishop's high, momentarily multicolored stones throw out Dickinsonian long shadows of presentiment that are also the individual shadows of female poetic temperaments, say of Dickinson and Marianne Moore and of Bishop herself. Indeed they could have been teasing the lion sun, Stevens, that great cat standing always potent in the light of imagination, not the mere sun of common day. Except that Bishop, nearly as subtle as Dickinson, gently intimates that even so great a male precursor has at last been evaded, if not overcome: "except that now he was behind them." In a loving trope of closure, Bishop reminds us that, in how they play, all men are different from women:

    —a sun who'd walked the beach the last low tide,
    making those big, majestic paw-prints,
    who perhaps had batted a kite out of the sky to play with.

Even great poets, when they are men, play as if they were children again. In the teasing shadows of presentiment, Bishop gives us a mode of play that belongs to women poets, a mode that is neither childish nor childlike. Like Dickinson, Bishop teaches us that the strongest women poets can possess: "Another way—to see."

HELEN VENDLER

Elizabeth Bishop: Domestication, Domesticity, and the Otherworldly

Elizabeth Bishop's poems in *Geography III* put into relief the continuing vibration of her work between two frequencies—the domestic and the strange. In another poet the alternation might seem a debate, but Bishop drifts rather than divides, gazes rather than chooses. Though the exotic is frequent in her poems of travel, it is not only the exotic that is strange and not only the local that is domestic. (It is more exact to speak, with regard to Bishop, of the domestic rather than the familiar, because what is familiar is always named, in her poetry, in terms of a house, a family, someone beloved, home. And it is truer to speak of the strange rather than of the exotic, because the strange can occur even in the bosom of the familiar, even, most unnervingly, at the domestic hearth.)

To show the interpenetration of the domestic and the strange at their most inseparable, it is necessary to glance back at some poems printed in *Questions of Travel.* In one, "Sestina," the components are almost entirely innocent—a house, a grandmother, a child, a Little Marvel Stove, and an almanac. The strange component, which finally renders the whole house unnatural, is tears. Although the grandmother hides her tears and says only "It's time for tea now," the child senses the tears unshed and displaces them everywhere—into the dancing waterdrops from the teakettle, into the rain on the roof, into the tea in the grandmother's cup.

From *World Literature Today* 51, no. 1 (Winter 1977). © 1977 by the University of Oklahoma Press.

> the child
> is watching the teakettle's small hard tears
> dance like mad on the hot black stove
> the way the rain must dance on the house . . .
>
>   the almanac
> hovers half open above the child,
> hovers above the old grandmother
> and her teacup full of dark brown tears.

The child's sense of the world is expressed only in the rigid house she draws (I say "she," but the child, in the folk-order of the poem, is of indeterminate sex). The child must translate the tears she has felt, and so she "puts . . . a man with buttons like tears" into her drawing, while

> the little moons fall down like tears
> from between the pages of the almanac
> into the flower bed the child
> has carefully placed in the front of the house.

The tercet ending the sestina draws together all the elements of the collage:

> *Time to plant tears*, says the almanac.
> The grandmother sings to the marvellous stove
> and the child draws another inscrutable house.

The absence of the child's parents is the unspoken cause of those tears, so unconcealable though so concealed. For all the efforts of the grandmother, for all the silence of the child, for all the brave cheer of the Little Marvel Stove, the house remains frozen, and the blank center stands for the definitive presence of the unnatural in the child's domestic experience—*especially* in the child's domestic experience. Of all the things that should not be inscrutable, one's house comes first. The fact that one's house always is inscrutable, that nothing is more enigmatic than the heart of the domestic scene, offers Bishop one of her recurrent subjects.

The centrality of the domestic provokes as well one of Bishop's most characteristic forms of expression. When she is not actually representing herself as a child, she is, often, sounding like one. The sestina, which borrows from the eternally childlike diction of the folktale, is a case in point. Not only the diction of the folktale, but also its fixity of relation appears in the poem, especially in its processional close, which places the almanac, the grandmother, and the child in an arrangement as unmoving as those found in medieval painting, with the almanac representing the overarching Divine Necessity, the grandmother as the elder principle, and the child as the principle of youth. The voice speaking the last three lines dispassionately records the coincident presence of grief, song, necessity, and the marvelous; but in spite of the "equal" placing of the last three lines, the ultimate weight on inscrutability, even in the heart of the domestic, draws this poem into the orbit of the strange.

A poem close by in *Questions of Travel* tips the balance in the other direction, toward the domestic. The filling station which gives its name to the poem seems at first the antithesis of beauty, at least in the eye of the beholder who speaks the poem. The station is dirty, oil-soaked, oil-permeated; the father's suit is dirty; his sons are greasy; all is "quite thoroughly dirty"; there is even "a dirty dog." The speaker, though filled with "a horror so refined," is unable to look away from the proliferating detail which, though this is a filling station, becomes ever more relentlessly domestic. "Do they live in the station?" wonders the speaker, and notes incredulously a porch, "a set of crushed and grease-/ impregnated wickerwork," the dog "quite comfy" on the wicker sofa, comics, a taboret covered by a doily, and "a big hirsute begonia." The domestic, we perceive, becomes a compulsion that we take with us even to the most unpromising locations, where we busy ourselves establishing domestic tranquility as a demonstration of meaningfulness, as a proof of "love." Is our theology only a reflection of our nesting habits?

> Why the extraneous plant?
> Why the taboret?
> Why, oh why, the doily? . . .
>
> Somebody embroidered the doily.
> Somebody waters the plant,
> or oils it, maybe. Somebody
> arranges the rows of cans
> so that they softly say:
> *ESSO-SO-SO-SO*
> to high-strung automobiles.
> Somebody loves us all.

In this parody of metaphysical questioning and the theological argument from design, the "awful but cheerful" activities of the world include the acts by which man domesticates his surroundings, even if those surroundings are purely mechanical, like the filling station or the truck in Brazil painted with "throbbing rosebuds."

The existence of the domestic is most imperiled by death. By definition, the domestic is the conjoined intimate: in American literature the quintessential poem of domesticity is "Snowbound." When death intrudes on the domestic circle, the laying-out of the corpse at home, in the old fashion, forces domesticity to its ultimate powers of accommodation. Stevens's "Emperor of Ice-Cream" places the cold and dumb corpse at the home wake in grotesque conjunction with the funeral baked meats, so to speak, which are being confected in the kitchen, as the primitive impulse to feast over the dead is seen surviving, instinctive and barbaric, even in our "civilized" society. Bishop's "First Death in Nova Scotia" places the poet as a child in a familiar parlor transfixed in perception by the presence of a coffin containing "little cousin Arthur":

> In the cold, cold parlor
> my mother laid out Arthur
> beneath the chromographs:
> Edward, Prince of Wales,
> with Princess Alexandra,
> and King George with Queen Mary.
> Below them on the table
> stood a stuffed loon
> shot and stuffed by Uncle
> Arthur, Arthur's father.

All of these details are immemorially known to the child. But focused by the coffin, the familiar becomes unreal: the stuffed loon becomes alive, his taciturnity seems voluntary, his red glass eyes can see.

> Since Uncle Arthur fired
> a bullet into him,
> he hadn't said a word.
> He kept his own counsel . . .
>
> Arthur's coffin was
> a little frosted cake,
> and the red-eyed loon eyed it
> from his white, frozen lake.

The adults conspire in a fantasy of communication still possible, as the child is told, "say good-bye / to your little cousin Arthur" and given a lily of the valley to put in the hand of the corpse. The child joins in the fantasy, first by imagining that the chill in the parlor makes it the domain of Jack Frost, who has painted Arthur's red hair as he paints the Maple Leaf of Canada, and next by imagining that "the gracious royal couples" in the chromographs have "invited Arthur to be / the smallest page at court." The constrained effort by all in the parlor to encompass Arthur's death in the domestic scene culminates in the child's effort to make a gestalt of parlor, coffin, corpse, chromographs, loon, Jack Frost, the Maple Leaf Forever, and the lily. But the strain is too great for the child, who allows doubt and dismay to creep in—not as to ultimate destiny, oh no, for Arthur is sure to become "the smallest page" at court, that confusing place of grander domesticity, half-palace, half-heaven; but rather displaced onto means.

> But how could Arthur go,
> clutching his tiny lily,
> with his eyes shut up so tight
> and the roads deep in snow?

Domesticity is frail, and it is shaken by the final strangeness of death. Until death, and even after it, the work of domestication of the unfamiliar goes on, all of it a substitute for some assurance of transcendent domesticity, some belief that we are truly, in this world, in our mother's house, that "somebody loves us all." After a loss that destroys one form of domesticity, the effort to reconstitute it in another form begins. The definition of death in certain of Bishop's poems is to have given up on domesticating the world and reestablishing yet once more some form of intimacy. Conversely, the definition of life in the conversion of the strange to the familial, of the unexplored to the knowable, of the alien to the beloved.

No domesticity is entirely safe. As in the midst of life we are in death, so, in Bishop's poetry, in the midst of the familiar, and most especially there, we feel the familiar as the unknowable. This guerrilla attack of the alien, springing from the very bulwarks of the familiar, is the subject of "In the Waiting Room." It is 1918, and a child, almost seven, waits, reading the *National Geographic*, while her aunt is being treated in the dentist's office. The scene is unremarkable: "grown-up people, / arctics and overcoats, / lamps and magazines," but two things unnerve the child. The first is a picture in the magazine: "black, naked women with necks / wound round and round with wire / like the necks of light bulbs. / Their breasts were horrifying"; and the second is "an *oh!* of pain /—Aunt Consuelo's voice" from inside. The child is attacked by vertigo, feels the cry to be her own uttered in "the family voice" and knows at once her separateness and her identity as one of the human group.

> But I felt: you are an I,
> you are an *Elizabeth*,
> you are one of *them*.
> *Why* should you be one too?
>
> . . . .
>
> What similarities—
> boots, hands, the family voice
> I felt in my throat, or even
> the *National Geographic*
> and those awful hanging breasts—
> held us all together
> or made us all just one?

In "There Was a Child Went Forth" Whitman speaks of a comparable first moment of metaphysical doubt:

> the sense of what is real, the thought if after all it should
>   prove unreal,
> The doubts of day-time and the doubts of night-time, the curious
>   whether and how,
> Whether that which appears so is so, or is it all flashes and specks?
> Men and women crowding fast in the streets, if they are not flashes
>   and specks what are they?

It is typical of Whitman that after his momentary vertigo he should tether himself to the natural world of sea and sky. It is equally typical of Bishop, after the waiting room slides "beneath a big black wave, / another, and another," to return to the sober certainty of waking fact, though with a selection of fact dictated by feeling.

> The War was on. Outside,
> in Worcester, Massachusetts,
> were night and slush and cold,
> and it was still the fifth
> of February, 1918.

The child's compulsion to include in her world even the most unfamiliar data, to couple the exotica of the *National Geographic* with the knees and trousers and skirts of her neighbors in the waiting room, brings together the strange at its most horrifying with the quintessence of the familiar—oneself, one's aunt, the "family voice." In the end, will the savage be domesticated or oneself rendered unknowable? The child cannot bear the conjunction and faints. Language fails the six-year-old. "How—I didn't know any / word for it—how 'unlikely.'"

That understatement, so common in Bishop, gives words their full weight. As the fact of her own contingency strikes the child, "familiar" and "strange" become concepts which have lost all meaning. "Mrs. Anderson's Swedish baby," says Stevens, "might well have been German or Spanish." Carlos Drummond de Andrade (whose rhythms perhaps suggested the trimeters of "In the Waiting Room") says in a poem translated by Bishop:

> Mundo mundo vasto mundo,
> se eu me chamasse Raimundo
> seria uma rima, não seria uma soluçãdo.

If one's name rhymed with the name of the cosmos, as "Raimundo" rhymes with "mundo," there would appear to be a congruence between self and world, and domestication of the world to man's dimensions would seem possible. But, says Drummond, that would be a rhyme, not a solution. The child of "In the Waiting Room" discovers that she is in no intelligible relation to her world, and, too young yet to conceive of domination of the world by will or domestication of the world by love, she slides into an abyss of darkness.

In "Poem" ("About the size of an old-style dollar bill") the poet gazes idly at a small painting done by her great-uncle and begins yet another meditation on the domestication of the world. She gazes idly—that is, until she realizes that the painting is of a place she has lived: "Heavens, I recognize the place, I know it!" In a beautiful tour de force "the place" is described three times. The first time it is rendered visually, exactly, interestedly, appreciatively, and so on: such, we realize, is pure visual pleasure touched with relatively impersonal recognition ("It must be Nova Scotia; only there / does one see gabled wooden houses / painted that awful shade of brown"). Here is the painting as first seen:

> Elm trees, low hills, a thin church steeple
> —that gray-blue wisp—or is it? In the foreground
> a water meadow with some tiny cows,

two brushstrokes each, but confidently cows;
two minuscule white geese in the blue water,
back-to-back, feeding, and a slanting stick.
Up closer, a wild iris, white and yellow,
fresh-squiggled from the tube.
The air is fresh and cold; cold early spring
clear as gray glass; a half inch of blue sky
below the steel-gray storm clouds.

Then the recognition—"Heavens, I know it!"—intervenes, and with it a double transfiguration occurs: the mind enlarges the picture beyond the limits of the frame, placing the painted scene in a larger, remembered landscape, and the items in the picture are given a local habitation and a name.

Heavens, I recognize the place, I know it!
It's behind—I can almost remember the farmer's name.
His barn backed on that meadow. There it is,
titanium white, one dab. The hint of steeple,
filaments of brush-hairs, barely there,
must be the Presbyterian church.
Would that be Miss Gillespie's house?
Those particular geese and cows
are naturally before my time.

In spite of the connection between self and picture, the painting remains a painting, described by someone recognizing its means—a dab of titanium white here, some fine brushwork there. And the scene is set back in time—those geese and cows belong to another era. But by the end of the poem the poet has united herself with the artist. They have both loved this unimportant corner of the earth; it has existed in their lives, in their memories and in their art.

Art "copying from life" and life itself,
life and the memory of it so compressed
they're turned into each other. Which is which?
Life and the memory of it cramped,
dim, on a piece of Bristol board,
dim, but how live, how touching in detail
—the little that we get for free,
the little of our earthly trust. Not much.

Out of the world a small piece is lived in, domesticated, remembered, memorialized, even immortalized. Immortalized because the third time that the painting is described, it is seen not by the eye—whether the eye of the connoisseur or the eye of the local inhabitant contemplating a past era—but by the heart, touched into participation. There is no longer any mention of tube or brushstrokes or paint colors or Bristol board; we are in the scene itself.

> Not much.
> About the size of our abidance
> along with theirs, the munching cows,
> the iris, crisp and shivering, the water
> still standing from spring freshets,
> the yet-to-be dismantled elms, the geese.

Though the effect of being in the landscape arises in part from the present participles (the munching cows, the shivering iris, the standing water), it comes as well from the repetition of nouns from earlier passages (cows, iris), now denuded of their "paint" modifiers ("two brushstrokes each," "squiggled from the tube"), from the replication of the twice-repeated early "fresh" in "freshets" and most of all from the prophecy of the "yet-to-be-dismantled" elms. As lightly as possible, the word "dismantled" then refutes the whole illusion of entire absorption in the memorial scene; the world of the child who was once the poet now seems the scenery arranged for a drama with only too brief a tenure on the stage—the play once over, the set is dismantled, the illusion gone. The poem, having taken the reader through the process that we name domestication and by which a strange terrain becomes first recognizable, then familiar, and then beloved, releases the reader at last from the intimacy it has induced. Domestication is followed, almost inevitably, by that dismantling which is, in its acute form, disaster, the "One Art" of another poem:

> I lost my mother's watch. And look! my last, or
> next-to-last of three loved houses went . . .
>
> I lost two cities, lovely ones. And, vaster,
> some realms I owned, two rivers, a continent . . .
>
> the art of losing's not too hard to master
> though it may look like (*Write* it!) like disaster.

That is the tone of disaster confronted, with whatever irony.

A more straightforward account of the whole cycle of domestication and loss can be seen in the long monologue, "Crusoe in England." Crusoe is safely back in England, and his long autobiographical retrospect exposes in full clarity the imperfection of the domestication of nature so long as love is missing, the exhaustion of solitary colonization.

> I'd have
> nightmares of other islands
> stretching away from mine, infinities
> of islands, islands spawning islands,
> like frogs' eggs turning into polliwogs
> of islands, knowing that I had to live
> on each and every one, eventually
> for ages, registering their flora,
> their fauna, their geography.

Crusoe's efforts at the domestication of nature (making a flute, distilling home brew, even devising a dye out of red berries) create a certain degree of pleasure ("I felt a deep affection for / the smallest of my island industries"), and yet the lack of any society except that of turtles and goats and waterspouts ("sacerdotal beings of glass . . . / Beautiful, yes, but not much company") causes both self-pity and a barely admitted hope. Crusoe, in a metaphysical moment, christens one volcano *"Mont d'Espoir* or *Mount Despair,"* mirroring both his desolation and his expectancy. The island landscape has been domesticated, "home-made," and yet domestication can turn to domesticity only with the arrival of Friday: "Just when I thought I couldn't stand it / another minute longer, Friday came." Speechless with joy, Crusoe can speak only in the most vacant and consequently the most comprehensive of words.

> Friday was nice.
> Friday was nice, and we were friends.
> . . . he had a pretty body.

Love escapes language. Crusoe could describe with the precision of a geographer the exact appearances of volcanoes, turtles, clouds, lava, goats, and waterspouts and waves, but he is reduced to gesture and sketch before the reality of domesticity.

In the final, recapitulatory movement of the poem Bishop first reiterates the conferral of meaning implicit in the domestication of the universe and then contemplates the loss of meaning once the arena of domestication is abandoned.

> The knife there on the shelf—
> it reeked of meaning, like a crucifix.
> It lived . . .
> I knew each nick and scratch by heart . . .
> Now it won't look at me at all.
> The living soul has dribbled away.
> My eyes rest on it and pass on.

Unlike the meanings of domestication, which repose in presence and use, the meaning of domesticity is mysterious and permanent. The monologue ends:

> The local museum's asked me to
> leave everything to them:
> the flute, the knife, the shrivelled shoes . . .
> How can anyone want such things?
> —And Friday, my dear Friday, died of measles
> seventeen years ago come March.

The ultimate locus of domestication is the heart, which, once cultivated, retains its "living soul" forever.

This dream of eternal and undismantled fidelity in domesticity, unaffected even by death, is one extreme reached by Bishop's imagination as it turns round its theme. But more profound, I think, is the version of life's experience recounted in "The Moose," a poem in which no lasting exclusive companionship between human beings is envisaged, but in which a series of deep and inexplicable satisfactions unroll in sequence, each of them precious. Domestication of the land is one, domesticity of the affections is another, and the contemplation of the sublimity of the nonhuman world is the third.

In the first half of the poem one of the geographies of the world is given an ineffable beauty, both plain and luxurious. Nova Scotia's tides, sunsets, villages, fog, flora, fauna, and people are all summoned quietly into the verse, as if for a last farewell, as the speaker journeys away to Boston. The verse, like the landscape, is "old-fashioned."

> The bus starts. The light
> is deepening; the fog
> shifting, salty, thin,
> comes closing in.
>
> Its cold, round crystals
> form and slide and settle

in the white hens' feathers,
in gray glazed cabbages,
on the cabbage roses
and lupins like apostles;

the sweet peas cling
to wet white string
on the whitewashed fences;
bumblebees creep
inside the foxgloves,
and evening commences.

The exquisitely noticed modulations of whiteness, the evening harmony of settling and clinging and closing and creeping, the delicate touch of each clause, the valedictory air of the whole, the momentary identification with hens, sweet peas, and bumblebees all speak of the attentive and yielding soul through which the landscape is being articulated.

As darkness settles, the awakened soul is slowly lulled into "a dreamy divagation / . . . / a gentle, auditory, slow hallucination." This central passage embodies a regression into childhood, as the speaker imagines that the muffled noises in the bus are the tones of "an old conversation":

Grandparents' voices

uninterruptedly
talking, in Eternity:
names being mentioned,
things cleared up finally . . .
Talking the way they talked
in the old featherbed,
peacefully, on and on . . .

Now, it's all right now
even to fall asleep
just as on all those nights.

Life, in the world of this poem, has so far only two components: a beloved landscape and beloved people, that which can be domesticated and those who have joined in domesticity. The grandparents' voices have mulled over *all* the human concerns of the village:

what he said, what she said,
who got pensioned;

deaths, deaths and sicknesses;
the year he re-married;
the year (something) happened.
She died in childbirth.
That was the son lost
when the schooner foundered.

He took to drink. Yes.
She went to the bad.
When Amos began to pray
even in the store and
finally the family had
to put him away.

"Yes . . ." that peculiar
affirmative. "Yes . . ."
A sharp, indrawn breath,
half-groan, half-acceptance.

In this passage, so plainly different in its rural talk and sorrow from the ravishing aestheticism of the earlier descriptive passage, Bishop joins herself to the Wordsworth of the *Lyrical Ballads*. The domestic affections become, for a moment, all there is. Amos who went mad, the son lost at sea, the mother who died, the girl gone to the bad—these could all have figured in poems like "Michael" or "The Thorn." The litany of names evoking the bonds of domestic sympathy becomes one form of poetry, and the views of the "meadows, hills, and groves" of Nova Scotia is another. What this surrounding world looks like, we know; that "Life's like that" (as the sighed "Yes" implies), we also know. The poem might seem complete. But just as the speaker is about to drowse almost beyond consciousness, there is a jolt, and the bus stops in the moonlight, because "A moose has come out of / the impenetrable wood." This moose, looming "high as a church, / homely as a house," strikes wonder in the passengers, who "exclaim in whispers, / childishly, softly." The moose remains.

Taking her time,
she looks the bus over,
grand, other-worldly.

> Why, why do we feel
> (we all feel) this sweet
> sensation of joy?

What is this joy?

In "The Most of It" Frost uses a variant of this fable. There, as in Bishop's poem, a creature emerges from "the impenetrable wood" and is beheld. But Frost's beast disappoints expectation. The poet had wanted "counter-love, original response," but the "embodiment that crashed" proves to be not "human," not "someone else additional to him," but rather a large buck, which disappears as it came. Frost's beast is male, Bishop's female; Frost's a symbol of brute force, Bishop's a creature "safe as houses"; Frost's a challenge, Bishop's a reassurance. The presence approaching from the wood plays, in both these poems, the role that a god would play in a pre-Wordsworthian poem and the role that a human being—a leech-gatherer, an ancient soldier, a beggar—would play in Wordsworth. These human beings, when they appear in Wordsworth's poetry, are partly iconic, partly subhuman, as the Leech-Gatherer is part statue, part sea-beast, and as the old man in "Animal Tranquillity and Decay" is "insensibly subdued" to a state of peace more animal than human. "I think I could turn and live with animals," says Whitman, foreshadowing a modernity that finds the alternative to the human not in the divine but in the animal. Animal life is pure presence, with its own grandeur. It assures the poet of the inexhaustibility of being. Bishop's moose is at once maternal, inscrutable, and mild. If the occupants of the bus are bound, in their human vehicle, to the world of village catastrophe and pained acknowledgment, they feel a releasing joy in glimpsing some large, grand solidity, even a vaguely grotesque one, which exists outside their tales and sighs, which is entirely "otherworldly." "The darkness drops again," as the bus moves on; the "dim smell of moose" fades in comparison to "the acrid smell of gasoline."

"The Moose" is such a purely linear poem, following as it does the journey of the bus, that an effort of will is required to gaze at it whole. The immediacy of each separate section—as we see the landscape, then the people, then the moose—blots out what has gone before. But the temptation—felt when the poem is contemplated entire—to say something global, something almost allegorical, suggests that something in the sequence is more than purely arbitrary. The poem passes from adult observation of a familiar landscape to the unending ritual, first glimpsed in childhood, of human sorrow and narration, to a final joy in the otherworldly, in whatever lies within the impenetrable wood and from time to time allows itself to be beheld. Beyond or behind the familiar, whether the visual or the human familiar, lies the perpetually strange and mysterious. It is that mystery which causes those whispered exclamations alternating with the pained "Yes" provoked by human vicissitude. It guarantees the poet more to do. On it depends all the impulse to domestication. Though the human effort is bent to the elimination of the wild, nothing is more restorative than to know that earth's being is larger than our human enclosures. Elizabeth Bishop's poetry of domestication and domesticity depends, in the last analysis, on her equal apprehension of the reserves of mystery which give, in their own way, a joy more strange than the familiar blessings of the world made human.

LEE EDELMAN

The Geography of Gender: Elizabeth Bishop's "In the Waiting Room"

I always tell the truth in my poems. *With* The
Fish, *that's* exactly *how it happened. It was in Key
West, and I did* catch it just as the poem says. *That
was in 1938. Oh, but I did change* one *thing . . .*
—ELIZABETH BISHOP

T ime and again in discussing her poetry Elizabeth Bishop insists on its
fidelity to literal reality. "It was all true," she affirms of "The Moose," "it was
all exactly the way I described it except that I say 'seven relatives.' Well, they
weren't really relatives, they were various stepsons and so on, but that's the
only thing that isn't quite true." In her attempts to "place" her poetry by
means of such comments, Bishop reproduces a central gesture of the poetry
itself. For that poetry, in Bishop's master-trope, takes place beneath the aegis
of "geography," a study of places that leads her, invariably, to the question of
poetic positioning—a question that converges, in turn, with the quest for,
and the questioning of, poetic authority. Even in the casual remarks cited
above, Bishop undertakes to authenticate her work, and she does so, tellingly,
by fixing its origin on the solid ground of literality—a literality that Bishop
repeatedly identifies as "truth."

From *Contemporary Literature* 26, no. 2 (Summer 1985). © 1985 by the Board of Regents of the
University of Wisconsin System. University of Wisconsin Press, 1984.

But what does it mean to assert that a poem is "true," is somehow literal? Is it, in fact, ever possible to read such an assertion literally? Or, to put it another way, for what is such an appeal to literality a figure? Against what does it defend? These questions must color any reading of Bishop's poetry precisely because that poetry insists on the figural subtlety with which it represents the world. "More delicate than the historians, are the mapmakers' colors," Bishop writes in "The Map," the poem she placed first in her first book of poems. And that poem provides a key to the landscape of her poetry by directing attention to issues of textuality and trope. The truth that interests Bishop from the outset is not the truth of history or fact *per se*, but the more "delicate" matter of representation, the finely discriminated "colors" that lead back to the functioning of poetic coloration, or trope. If Bishop, as map-maker, "colors" her world, she has less in common with the sort of Stevensian literalist of the first idea as she presents herself at times, than she does with Stevens's sublimely solipsistic Hoon, who calls forth a world from within himself to find himself "more truly and more strange."

To make such a claim about Bishop's work, however, is to displace truth from its relation to literality. To link the ability to see "truly" to the ability to make reality "more strange" is to make truth itself a stranger term—and one more problematic. For truth now comes into alignment with trope, literal and figurative effectively change places. Bishop's remarks about the literal origins of her poetry become significant, in this light, less for their assertions than for their qualifications: "that's *exactly* how it happened . . . Oh, but I did change *one* thing"; "it was all exactly the way I described it . . . Well, they weren't really relatives." Like the poetry itself, Bishop's characterizations of that poetry question the relationship between literal and figurative, observation and invention, perception and vision. All of which is to say that Bishop's is a poetry conscious of the difficulty and the necessity of reading, conscious of the inevitable mediations of selfhood, the intrusions of the "I," that make direct contact with any literality—with any "truth"—an impossibility.

But critics, for the most part, have refrained from seriously reading Bishop's readings of reading. They have cited her work, instead, as exemplary of precise observation and accurate detail, presenting us with an Elizabeth Bishop who seems startlingly like some latterday "gentle Jane." David Kalstone suggests something of the problem when he notes that "critics have praised her descriptive powers and treated her as something of a miniaturist. As mistakenly as with the work of Marianne Moore, they have sometimes asked if Bishop's is poetry at all." It is indeed significant that Moore and Bishop, two of the most widely praised female American poets of the century, have been championed for their careful observation, their scrupulous particularity, their characteristic restraint. As Sandra Gilbert and Susan Gubar point out in *The Madwoman in the Attic*, these are qualities less often associated with lyric poetry than with prose fiction. They define the skills necessary for success in a genre that historically has been more hospitable to women, perhaps because its conventions, themselves more social and domestic, rely upon powers of perception and narration that coincide with traditional perspectives on women as analysts of emotion, on the one hand, and as busybodies or gossips, on the other. If few would reduce Bishop to the status of a gossip, many have noted the distinct and engaging quality of the voice that seems to emanate from her work—a voice described by John Ashbery as speaking in "a pleasant, chatty vernacular tone . . . calmly and unpoetically." It is this "unpoetic" voice—Robert Lowell called it "unrhetorical"—in combination with her alert and disciplined eye, that has led critics to read Bishop's poetry, in John Hollander's words, "almost as if she were a novelist." Viewing it as a species of moral anecdote, even admirers of Bishop's work have tended to ignore the rigor of her intellect, the range of her allusiveness, the complexity of her tropes. Instead, they imply what Anne Stevenson, in her book on Bishop's life and work, asserts: "Whatever ideas emerge have not been arrived at over a period of time but perceived, it would seem, in passing. They are the by-products of her meticulous observations."

Bishop, of course, has encouraged such misreadings by characterizing her poetry as "just description" and by emphasizing its grounding in the literal. I have suggested that this assertion of literality must itself be interpreted as a figure, that it defines for Bishop a strategy of evasion the sources of which this paper will attempt, in part, to trace. But the critical reception of Bishop, with its complicity in her reductive self-definition, with its acceptance of her willful evasions and its misprisions of her irony, exemplifies an interpretive blindness, which is to say, an ideological blindness, that enacts the very problems of reading on which Bishop's poetry frequently dwells. Readings that appropriate Bishop either to the company of poetic observers and reporters or to the ranks of moral fabulists, readings that place her in a clear relation to the literal reality her work is said to register, have the odd effect of seeming, instead, to be already placed or inscribed within that work, within her meditations on the way in which questions of placement and appropriation necessarily inform the very act of reading. No text better demonstrates the intricate connections among these concerns, or better locates the uncanny nature of her poetry's anticipation of its own misreadings, than does "In the Waiting Room," the poem with which Bishop introduced her last published volume, *Geography III. A* reading of that poem, which is a poem about reading, and a reading that interrogates the various readings of the poem, may suggest something of what is at stake in Bishop's reading of reading and show how "In the Waiting Room" effectively positions itself to read its readers.

> First, however, . . . I shall read very carefully (or try to read, since they may be partly obliterated, or in a foreign language) the inscriptions already there. Then I shall adapt my own compositions, in order that they may not conflict with those written by the prisoner before me. The voice of a new inmate will be noticeable, but there will be no contradictions or criticisms of what has already been laid down, rather a "commentary."
>
> (Elizabeth Bishop)

Commentaries on "In the Waiting Room" tend to agree that the poem presents a young girl's moment of awakening to the separations and the bonds among human beings, to the forces that shape individual identity through the interrelated recognitions of community and isolation. More remarkable than this unaccustomed critical consensus, however, is the degree to which its readers concur in identifying the poem's narrative or "plot" as the locus of the interpretive issues raised by the text. It is significant, in consequence, that critics have felt themselves both able and obliged to summarize the "story," to rehearse the events on which the poem's act of recognition hinges. Helen Vendler, for example, recapitulates the plot as follows: "waiting in a dentist's office, reading the *National Geographic*, feeling horrified at pictures of savages, hearing her aunt cry out in pain from inside the dentist's room, the child feels vertigo." Michael Wood directs attention to this same central episode when he describes "In the Waiting Room" as a poem in which "an almost-seven-year-old Elizabeth Bishop is horrified by the hanging breasts of African women seen in a copy of the *National Geographic*, and hears her own voice when her aunt cries out in pain." Similarly, Sybil Estess focuses on this narrative relationship when she writes that the child's "encounter with the strange pictures in the *National Geographic* is simultaneous with hearing her aunt's muffled cry of suffering."

These redactions would seem to rule out the possibility of hidden textual complications by the uniformity with which they define the poem's critical events. Yet when I suggest that there is something unusual and telling about the uniformity of these summaries, I anticipate that some will wonder why it should be considered odd that accounts of the same text should focus on the same significant episodes. What, one might ask, is so strange about critical agreement on the literal events that take place within the poem?

One response to such a question might begin by observing that the text itself seems to undermine the stability of the literal. Certainly the poem appears to appropriate—and to ground itself in—the particulars of a literal reality or truth. Bishop takes pains, for instance, to describe the contents of the magazine read by the young girl in the waiting room. Not only does she evoke in detail its pictures of volcanoes and of "black, naked women," but she specifies the particular issue of the magazine, identifying it as the *National Geographic* of February, 1918. But Bishop, as Jerome Mazzaro puts it, "tampers with the actual contents." While that issue of the magazine does indeed contain an article on volcanoes—lavishly titled "The Valley of Ten Thousand Smokes: An Account of the Discovery and Exploration of the Most Wonderful Volcanic Region in the World"—it offers no images of "Babies with pointed heads," no pictures of "black, naked women with necks/ wound round and round with wire." In an interview with George Starbuck, Bishop, responding to the critics who noticed the factual "error" in her text, declared: "My memory had confused two 1918 issues of the *Geographic*. Not having seen them since then, I checked it out in the New York Public Library. In the February issue there was an article, 'The Valley of 10,000 Smokes,' about Alaska that I'd remembered, too. But the African things, it turned out, were in the *next* issue, in March." Bishop's clarification only underscores her insistence on literal origins—and her wariness of her own imaginative powers. For the curious reader will discover what might have been suspected all along: the "African things" are not to be found in the March issue of the *National Geographic*, either. In fact, that issue has no essay about Africa at all.

With this in mind we are prepared for the warning that Alfred Corn offers the unsuspecting reader. He notes that, just as the picture essay Bishop describes "is not to be found in the February 1918 *National Geographic*," so "Anyone checking to see whether Miss Bishop's aunt was named Consuelo probably ought to be prepared for a similar thwarting of curiosity." In the face of this, one might well pose the question that Corn then frames: "If the facts are 'wrong,' why did Bishop make such a point of them in the poem?" Or, to put the question another way, toward what end does Bishop attempt to appropriate a literal grounding for her poem if that poem insists on fracturing the literality on which it positions itself? Whatever answer one might posit in response to such a question, the very fact that the poem invites us to ask it, the very fact that the poem revises simplistic conceptions of "fact" or literality may answer objections to my remark that there is something strange about the critics' agreement on the literal events that take place within the text.

But a new objection will surely be raised, accusing me of conflating two different senses of the "literal," or even of using "literal" in a way that is itself not strictly literal. While there may be questions, the objectors will insist, about the text's fidelity to the facts outside of it—questions, that is, about the literal truth of the text—those questions do not prevent us from articulating literally what happens within that text. Whether or not Bishop had a real Aunt Consuelo, there can be no doubt, they will argue, that Vendler and Estess and Wood are correct in asserting that, literally, within the poem, and as one of its crucial events, Aunt Consuelo cries out in pain from inside the dentist's office. And yet I intend not only to cast doubt upon that central event, but to suggest that the poem itself is less interested in the event than in the doubts about it, and that the critics' certainties distort the poem's insistence on confusion.

My own comments, of course, must repeat the error of attempted clarification. So I will approach this episode at the center of the text by way of my own brief summary of what occurs before it. The young girl, sitting outside in the waiting room while her aunt is in the dentist's office, reads the *National Geographic* "straight through," from cover to cover, and then, having closed the magazine, she begins to inspect the cover itself.

> Suddenly, from inside,
> came an *oh!* of pain
> —Aunt Consuelo's voice—
> not very loud or long.
> I wasn't at all surprised;
> even then I knew she was
> a foolish, timid woman.
> I might have been embarrassed,
> but wasn't. What took *me*
> completely by surprise
> was that it was *me*:
> my voice, in my mouth.
> Without thinking at all
> I was my foolish aunt,
> I—we—were falling, falling,
> our eyes glued to the cover
> of the *National Geographic*,
> February, 1918.

To gloss this passage as the young girl hearing "her aunt cry out in pain" is surely to ignore the real problem that both the girl and the text experience here: the problem of determining the place from which this voice originates. Since the poem asserts that it comes from "inside," the meanings of "inside" and "outside" must be determined, their geographical relation, as it were, must be mapped. The difficulty of making such determinations, however, springs from the overdetermination of meaning in this passage. The voice that cries out and, in so doing, sends the young girl—later identified as "Elizabeth"—plunging into the abyss that constitutes identity, disorients not by any lack of specification, but by the undecidable doubleness with which it is specified. The child recognizes the voice at once as Aunt Consuelo's and as her own. Any attempt to fix a clear relationship between these two alternatives, to label one as the ground upon which the other appears as figure, must presuppose an ability to penetrate the text, to get inside of it and thereby determine what it signifies by "inside." The critical consensus that attributes the cry of pain to Aunt Consuelo does, of course, precisely that. It refers the literal sense of "inside" to Aunt Consuelo's situation inside the dentist's office and thereby implies an interpretive model that rests upon an ability to distinguish the inside from the outside, the literal from the figurative. It suggests, moreover, that the literal is the textual "inside" on which the figural "outside" depends, and, therefore, that critical understanding must proceed by piercing or reading through the confusions of figuration in order to recover the literal ground that not only enables us to "place" the figural, but also allows us, by so doing, to keep the figural in its place.

Bishop's geography, however, persistently refuses the consolations of hierarchy or placement; instead, it defines itself as the questioning of places—a project emblematized by the way in which Bishop tropes upon the volume's epigraph from a geography textbook of 1884. She appends to its confident litany of answers to questions about the world (*"What is the Earth? / The planet or body on which we live. / What is the shape of the Earth? / Round, like a ball"*) a series of inquiries that seek to evade the reductive literalism of such an Idiot Questioner:

> *In what direction is the Volcano? The*
> *Cape? The Bay? The Lake? The Strait?*
> *The Mountains? The Isthmus?*
> *What is in the East? In the West? In the*
> *South? In the North? In the Northwest?*
> *In the Southeast? In the Northeast?*
> *In the Southwest?*

Given Bishop's insistent questioning of places, we can say that in a very real sense those commentators who put themselves in a position to identify

Aunt Consuelo as the source of the cry of pain in "In the Waiting Room" take the words out of Bishop's mouth in taking the cry out of "Elizabeth's". Their need to locate the place from which the cry or voice originates places the question of the voice's origination at the origin of the textual problem in the poem. That is to say, it locates the poem as an effect of the voice's origination, enabling them to read it as a fable of humanization through identification, a lesson in the sort of Wordsworthian "primal sympathy" that shapes "the human heart by which we live."

But within the poem itself the voice is contextually located, and since the logic of poetry allows some truth to *post hoc ergo propter hoc*, this location determines the voice itself as an effect—as, specifically, a reading effect. The cry that the text tells us comes "Suddenly, from inside," comes, within the text, after "Elizabeth" has finished reading the *National Geographic* and is scrutinizing its cover. To understand that cry, then, and the meaning of its place—or, more precisely of its displacement—requires a more careful study of the scene of reading that comes before it and, in some sense, calls it forth.

Evoking herself as an almost-seven-year-old child sitting in the dentist's waiting room, the "Elizabeth" whose memory constitutes the poem offers off-handedly, in a parenthetical aside, the assertion that governs the whole of the passage preceding the cry: "(I could read)." However casually the parentheses introduce this simple statement, both the statement itself and the simplicity with which it is presented identify a claim to authority. For the child, that authority derives from her mastery of the mystery of written language and from her concomitant access to the documents of culture, the inscriptions of society. Just as she has mastered reading, and as reading allows for a mastery of culture, so reading itself, for the young "Elizabeth," is understood as an exercise of mastery. The child of whose ability to read we are assured implicitly assumes the readability of texts, since reading for her is a process of perceiving the real and stable relationships that exist between word and image, past and present, cause and effect. The juxtaposition of photographs and captions, therefore, is transparently meaningful for "Elizabeth." From her position as a reader, outside of the text, she can readily decipher the fixed relationships that are delineated within it.

But the critical moment in the poem is precipitated at just the point when this model of reading as mastery comes undone, when the division between inside and outside breaks down and, as a result, the determinacy of textual relationships is called into question. Though only in the course of reading the magazine does "Elizabeth" perceive the inadequacy of her positioning as a reader, Bishop's text implies from the outset the insufficiency of any mode of interpretation that claims to release the meaning it locates "inside" a text by asserting its own ability to speak from a position of mastery "outside" of it. For this reason everything that "Elizabeth" encounters in the pages of the *National Geographic* serves to disturb the stability of a binary opposition. The first photographs that she recalls looking at, for instance, strategically define a sequential process:

> the inside of a volcano,
> black, and full of ashes;
> then it was spilling over
> in rivulets of fire.

Not only do these images undo the central distinction between inside and outside, but they do so by positing an excess of interiority that displaces itself onto the exterior. In other words, the inside here obtrudes upon the outside and thereby asserts its claim to mastery by transforming the landscape and showing how the exterior, how the landscape itself, is composed of interior matter.

The inside/outside dichotomy is reversed and discredited at once, and the effect of this maneuver on the theory of reading is to imply that the textual inside masters the reader outside of it far more than the reader can ever master the text. Or, more precisely, the very distinction between reader and text is untenable: the reader finds herself read by the text in which she is already inscribed and in which she reinscribes herself in the process of performing her reading. Since "Elizabeth" asserts that she "carefully studied" these photographs, it is worth noting, too, that not only do they disrupt the opposition between inside and outside, but also, insofar as the "ashes" in the first picture produce the "rivulets of fire" in the second, they disrupt the natural or logical relationship ascribed to cause and effect.

Inasmuch as Bishop's version of the *National Geographic* for February, 1918 corresponds to the actual issue of that magazine only in that both include images of volcanoes, her imagined periodical must function as a sort of exemplary text contrived to instruct young "Elizabeth," and us, in the difficulty of reading. Toward this end the photograph of Osa and Martin Johnson, though it seems less violently subversive than Bishop's Dickinsonian volcanoes, plays a significant part. The Johnsons, in the first decades of this century, achieved fame as a husband and wife team of explorers and naturalists, and in her autobiography, *I Married Adventure*, Osa Johnson provides information that may have inspired, and certainly sheds light on, the rest of the items that Bishop chooses to include in her magazine. But the photograph of the Johnsons themselves does more than allude to one of Bishop's likely sources. Her portrait of husband and wife focuses attention on the particulars of their clothing, and the most significant aspect of their clothing is the fact that it is identical. Both appear "dressed in riding breeches, / laced boots, and pith helmets." (I might add that there is a picture of Osa and Martin Johnson in which she appears in such a costume, but her husband, interestingly enough, does not wear an identical outfit.) In terms of Osa's autobiography, this image metonymically represents her trans-formation from a typical Kansas girl of sixteen, dreaming of weddings and weeping "with all the persecuted little picture heroines of the day," into an adventurer able to hold her own in a world of cannibals and headhunters. Osa underscores this transformation precisely in terms of clothing in two passages from *I Married Adventure.* The first time that her future husband calls on her at home, Osa's brother causes her to "burst out crying" by telling her that Mr. Johnson has joined with cannibals in eating missionaries. When her caller arrives, Osa is still upstairs crying and, as she tells us, "With women's clothes as complicated as they were in that day, even with Mama's help, it was nearly half an hour before I could get downstairs." Later, after they are married and she has agreed to join Martin on expeditions into the realm of the cannibals, he describes to her the sort of clothing that they will need to take along:

> "And some denim overalls and huck shirts," Martin said,
> following me into the kitchen.
> "For me?" I asked.
> "For both of us," he replied.

The identical outfits in which Bishop envisions the Johnsons in her photograph, then, point emblematically toward the subversion of the hierarchical opposition of male and female, an opposition into the nature of which Osa Johnson will peer when, like Lévi-Strauss, she confronts the role of women in "primitive" cultures as linguistic and economic objects of circulation and exchange. The structural anthropologist's insight offers a valuable point of reference here because "Elizabeth," after perusing the picture of the Johnsons, encounters in her text disturbing images that illuminate *la pensée sauvage.* (It is important to note, moreover, if only parenthetically, that "Elizabeth," for whom reading is at once a discipline of mastery and a mode of mastering her culture, occupies herself in reading a magazine devoted to geography and ethnology—discourses that imply a troubling relationship between the reading of cultures and the assertion of an ethnocentric form of cultural mastery.)

Bishop now presents the young "Elizabeth" with a textual impasse that resists appropriation by her system of reading as mastery and in so doing challenges her confidence in the very readability of texts: "A dead man slung on a pole /—'Long Pig,' the caption said." Dividing image and caption, picture and text not only by means of the linear break, but also by the dash—a mark of punctuation that dialectically connects and separates at once—Bishop emphasizes the apparently absolute undecidability of the relationship here. Some element of error seems necessarily to have entered into the working of the text. Has "Elizabeth" mistakenly interpreted the photograph of a pig as that of a human corpse? Has an editor carelessly transposed captions so that the photograph of a corpse has been identified as that of a pig? What "Elizabeth" faces here, of course, is the fundamental "error" of figurative language that creates the difficulty in trying to locate the literal as the ground from which the figural can be construed. The pole on which the dead object—be it corpse or pig—is slung serves as the axis of meaning on which the trope itself seems to turn. Like a dash, or like the slash that marks a fraction or a mathematical ratio, the pole establishes the polarities that it also brings together. For "Elizabeth" only the discrepancy matters, the difference that cannot be mastered or read. But anthropologists—or those familiar with Osa Johnson's autobiography—will be able to read this figural relationship more easily than does "Elizabeth," since they will recognize what the phrase "Long Pig" metaphorically connotes.

Describing her first expedition into a "savage" society, Osa recalls that she and her husband were warned that "'those fellows on Vao still bury their old people alive and eat long pig'." And later, remembering the dismay of the captain who, at their insistence, ferried her husband and herself to Vao despite such admonitions, Osa writes, "If we were reckless enough to risk being served up as 'long pig' by the savages of Malekula, that was our lookout, not his." "Long Pig," then, names man when he ceases to be human, when he enters into a system of signification which he no longer masters from an external position of privileged subjectivity, but into which he himself enters as an object of circulation. The metaphoric labelling of a "dead man" as "long pig" has the effect of exposing the metaphoricity of the apparently literal or natural category of humanity itself. Far from being a presence controlling language from without, humanity is understood to be figural, another product of the linguistic system.

Though Bishop's text, then, has challenged the stability of distinctions between inside and outside, male and female, literal and figurative, human and bestial, young "Elizabeth" reads on from her own position of limnality in the waiting room until she confronts, at last, an image of women and their infants:

> Babies with pointed heads
> wound round and round with string;

> black, naked women with necks
> wound round and round with wire
> like the necks of light bulbs.

Osa Johnson may again have provided Bishop with the material that she
incorporates here into their imagined magazine. In her autobiography Mrs.
Johnson refers to the Malekulan practice of elongating the head: "This was
done by binding soft, oiled coconut fiber around the skulls of infants shortly
after birth and leaving them there for something over a year. The narrower
and longer the head when the basket contrivance was removed, the greater
the pride of the mother. That her baby had cried almost without ceasing
during this period of distortion was of no concern whatsoever." The
autobiography, however, does not refer to the elongation of the women's
necks, and in the photograph that Osa Johnson includes of a Malekulan
woman and her infant—a photograph in which the child's head is indeed
"wound round and round with string"—the mother does not wear the rings
of wire that are used to stretch women's necks in some tribal cultures. Bishop
willfully introduces the symmetry that characterizes her images of women
and children so that both here suffer physical distortion by objects "wound
round and round" their bodies. This assimilation of women to the status of
children takes place simultaneously with the recognition made by the young
"Elizabeth" of her own destined status as a woman, of her own inevitable
role, therefore, in the sexual economy of her culture. She reads the burden
of female sexuality here as the inescapability of distortion, as the enforced
awareness of one's body as a malleable object. Anatomy itself loses the
authority of any natural or literal grounding; instead, it becomes one more
figure in the language of the culture.

As woman is reduced to a figure trapped in the linguistic circuit, so her
body becomes a text on which her figural status is inscribed. The culturally
sanctioned, which is to say, the patriarchally determined, markings of female
sexuality are thus understood as diacritical marks, and Bishop, significantly,
evokes these linguistic markings, these metonyms of woman as erotic
signifier, specifically in terms of constraint. Moreover, her particular vision
of constriction as the patriarchal writing of woman's sexuality on her body
takes the form of a wire wound about the woman's neck, an image that
conjures the garrote—an instrument of strangulation that prevents the
victim from uttering any cry at all. If the necks of the women in the
photograph are bound by these wires "like the necks of light bulbs," then
what they illuminate for "Elizabeth" is her fate as a woman, her necessary
implication in the system of signs she had thought to master by being able to
read. Now, for the first time, she reacts to the text, acknowledging an

emotional response to the naked women: "Their breasts," she says, "were horrifying."

The horror that "Elizabeth" feels betokens her perception of the monstrosity, the abnormality that informs the given or "norm" of sexuality. Sexuality itself, she has discovered, is always constituted as a system of signs that must operate through the substitution of figures; consequently, it is neither a "natural" system nor an inevitable one. Yet within the patriarchal system the "normal" figurations of female sexuality take the form of literal disfigurations. Woman herself becomes a creation of man since, as Simone de Beauvoir recognized years ago, one is not born a woman: as a linguistic construct who figures through disfiguration, woman is the monstrous creation of the patriarchy. And what most horrifies "Elizabeth" as she focuses on the breasts of these disfigured or monstrous women is her recognition of the fundamental affinity she shares with them. In a sense they speak to her in the words that Mary Shelley gave to the monster that she imagined as the product of a wholly masculine gestation: "my form is a filthy type of yours, more horrid even from the very resemblance." It is finally this resemblance, which is to say, the relationship of metaphoric interchangeability, that horrifies "Elizabeth." At last she must recognize fully what is at stake in the dismantling of binary oppositions, for the reader and what she reads collapse into one another as "Elizabeth" finds herself located *by* the text, *inside* the text, and as a text.

Yet in neutral, uninflected tones she continues:

> I read it right straight through.
> I was too shy to stop.
> And then I looked at the cover:
> the yellow margins, the date.

The very blandness of this account, following her admission of horror, testifies to an effort of denial or repression as "Elizabeth" seeks to master herself by affirming her difference from the text and, thus, her ability to master it through reading. She studies the cover, the margins, and the date in order to construct a frame for her reading experience that will circumscribe or contain it. The burden of her task here is the desperate need to contextualize the text so as to prevent her suffocation, her strangulation within it. The "yellow margins" that she focuses on represent her margin of security to the extent that they define a border, a yellow or cautionary zone distinguishing the inside from the outside. But the security of such a reading of the margin falls within the margin of error as soon as one recognizes the complex dynamic involved in the positing of such a frame. In a brilliant analysis of these problems in her essay "The Frame of Reference: Poe, Lacan, Derrida," Barbara Johnson cites Derrida's contention that "frames are always framed." What this means in terms of "Elizabeth" and her reading of the *National Geographic is* that the act of framing arises as a response to her disturbing recognition that the text refuses to be delimited or framed. Thus her framing of the text is itself framed by her terrifying awareness of the text's unframability. As Barbara Johnson comments in her analysis of Derrida, therefore, "the frame thus becomes not the borderline between the inside and the outside, but precisely what subverts the applicability of the inside/ outside polarity to the act of interpretation."

One subversive aspect of "Elizabeth's" response to the photograph of the women remains to be considered. The breasts that "Elizabeth" describes as horrifying may horrify not only because they link her to the disfigurations and constraint that mark female sexuality in patriarchal cultures; they may horrify as well because they evoke an eroticism that undermines the institution of heterosexuality—the institution that determines sexual difference as well as its inscriptions. Adrienne Rich has recently discussed Bishop in terms of "the lesbian writing under the false universal of heterosexuality," but here in "In the Waiting Room," and at the other crucial points throughout her career, Bishop covertly discredits that "false universal" and its ideology. After acknowledging her emotional reaction to the breasts of the naked women—in an earlier draft they are said not to horrify her, but rather to fill her with awe—"Elizabeth" explains that she continued reading because she was "too shy to stop." This shyness surely corresponds to the fearful embarrassment that expresses desire in the very act of trying to veil it. Too shy, then—which is to say, too inhibited or constrained—to stop or to linger over these pictures, "Elizabeth" reads the magazine "straight through" because doing so, in a sense, marks her reading as "straight." It prevents the embarrassing discovery of her emotional investment in the "naked women" and of her unsettling response to their breasts—a response that shifts between horror and awe.

But by silencing the voice of her own sexuality, by succumbing to the constraint of shyness and framing the text in order to distance herself from the desire that it unleashes, she locates herself, paradoxically, inside the text once more. For her constraining shyness merely reenacts the cultural inscriptions of female sexuality that the magazine has presented to her in terms of silencing and constraint. Because her reading has alerted her to the patriarchal and heterosexual foundation on which the ideology of binary oppositions rests, and because it has suggested to her the inevitability of her reduction to the status of a figure in that cultural system or text, "Elizabeth" directs her attention to the magazine's cover in an obvious effort to cover up, to deny or suppress the insights that her reading has uncovered. In the act of foregrounding the cover she undertakes to frame the text as a literary object, to reduce its provenance by underscoring the literary status of its discourse. Such a framing has the same effect as the framing achieved by the bracketing of a word or phrase by quotation marks: it produces the detachment of irony. But the irony of "Elizabeth's" attempt here to position herself ironically with relation to the text is that irony introduces once more the elements of subversion and indeterminacy that are precisely the elements of the text that she fears and from which she seeks to detach herself.

This, then, is "Elizabeth's" situation after her exercise in reading: sitting in the dentist's office while her aunt receives treatment inside, she looks at the cover of the *National Geographic* and tries to hold on to the solid ground of literality outside the abyss of textuality she has discovered within it. In doing so, she silences the voice of her own internal desire and conforms to the socially determined role that her shyness forces her to play. At the same time, however, she recognizes, as a result of her reading, the inadequacy of the inside/outside polarity that underlies each of her tensions—tensions that mount until they no longer admit of repression or constraint: "Suddenly, from inside, / came an oh! of pain."

With this we come back to where we began—back to the question of the voice and the question of the place from which the voice originates. But we return with a difference to the extent that the critical desire to locate or to define or to frame any literal "inside" for that voice to emerge from has been discredited as an ideological blindness, a hierarchical gesture. There is no inside in this poem that can be distinguished from its outside: the cry emanates from inside the dentist's office, and from inside the waiting room, and from inside the *National Geographic,* and from inside "In the Waiting Room." It is a cry that cries out against any attempt to clarify its confusions because it is a female cry—a cry of the female—that recognizes the attempts to clarify it as attempts to put it in its place. It is an *"oh!"* that refuses to be readily deciphered because it knows that if it is read it must always be read as a cipher—as a zero, a void, or a figure in some predetermined social text. Those critics, then, who read the poem by trying to place the cry, effect, instead, a denial of that cry which is a cry of displacement—a cry of the female refusal of position in favor of dis-position. As a figural subversion, it wages war against the reduction of woman to the status of a literal figure, an oxymoronic entity constrained to be interpreted within the patriarchal text. It is against that text that the cry wages war, becomes a war cry to unleash the textuality that rips the fabric of the cultural text. To conclude, then, is only to urge a beginning, to urge that we attend to this cry as a cry of female textuality, a cry that links "Elizabeth" to her "foolish" aunt and to the tormented mother in Bishop's story, "In the Village." In this way we can approach the poem's cry, in Stevens's words, as the "cry of its occasion" and begin to engage the issues of gender and constraint that are so deeply involved in Bishop's story of *"oh!"*

May Swenson:
"Turned Back to the Wild by Love"

When May Swenson, speaking in her thaumaturgical fashion of poetry, says that "attention to the silence in between is the amulet that makes it work," we are reminded, while on other occasions in her work we are reassured, that there is a kind of poetry, as there used to be a kind of love, which dares not speak its name. Indeed, it was in the latter's heyday (1891, when Mallarmé thanked Oscar Wilde for *The Picture of Dorian Gray*, "one of the only books that can move me, for its commotion proceeds from an essential reverie, and from the strangest silences of the soul"), that the former's program was devised, by the thanker: "to *name* an object is to suppress three-quarters of our pleasure in the poem, a pleasure which consists in gradually divining . . . ; to *suggest*, that is the ideal. That is making perfect use of the kind of mystery which constitutes the symbol." Of course, there is a complementary impulse to *identify* in this reluctance to call a spade a spade; it is an impulse implicit in the very paradox supported by the word *identification*, which we use both to select an object in all its singularity, and to dissolve that "identical" object into its likeness with another. The refusal, or the reluctance, to *name* in order that she may the more truly *identify is* what we notice first about May Swenson's poetry—though she does not proceed so strictly with the enterprise as Mallarmé, for whom the designation of a flower enforced its *absence* from any bouquet. When Miss

From *Alone with America: Essays on the Art of Poetry in the United States since 1950*. © 1980 by Richard Howard. Enlarged edition, Atheneum, 1980.

Swenson says:

> beautiful each Shape
> to see
> wonderful each Thing
> to name

she means the kind of ascertaining of Existence Hölderlin meant when he said that poetry was a naming of the Gods—and for such an appeal (such an appellation), the ordinary labels do not suffice. Miss Swenson would not be so extreme about her magic as the symbolists, but she is plainly aware of the numbing power of proper names; as the story of Rumpelstiltskin demonstrates, there is an awful mastery in knowing what a being is called, and in so calling him—indeed such mastery suggests, to May Swenson at least, a corresponding lack of attention to the quality of being itself, a failure, by the wielding of nomination's "mace petrific," to encounter, to espouse form as it *becomes* what it is.

It is an old kind of poetry, then, that this poet resumes in her quest for "my face in the rock, my name on the wildest tree," a poetry that goes back to Orpheus, probably, and moves forward through Blake and Emily Dickinson, whom May Swenson specifically echoes, I think, in her eagerness to see Being wherever she looks:

> Any Object before the Eye
> can fill the space can occupy
> the supple frame of eternity
>
> my Hand before me such
> tangents reaches into Much
> root and twig extremes can touch
>
> any Hour can be the all
> expanding like a cunning Ball
> to a Vast from very small
>
> any Single becomes the More
> multiples sprout from alpha's core
> from Vase of legend vessels of lore . . .

It is the poetry which comes into existence whenever the need is felt (as by Valéry most recently, most magisterially) to *charm*, to *enchant*, to *bind by spells* an existence otherwise apprehended as inaccessibly other. For as Valéry says of Orpheus, it was only by his songs that trees knew the full horror of dancing. Similarly, in May Swenson's kennings, their method "a parliament of overlappings" and their goal "an assuaging singleness," we find that the hand in her lap, the cat on the sill, the cloud in the sky become, before we have a chance to adjust our sights and to enslave our other senses as well to what we *know*, fables of unlabelled Being:

> For each path leads both out and in
> I come while going   No to and from
> There is only here   And here
> is as well as there   Wherever
> I am led I move within the care
> of the season
> hidden in the creases of her skirts
> of green or brown or beaded red
> And when they are white
> I am not lost   I am not lost then
> only covered for the night

Evidently, Miss Swenson's effort has been to discover runes, the conjurations by which she cannot only apostrophize the hand, the cat and the cloud in their innominate otherness, but by which she can, in some essential and relieving way, *become them*, leave her own impinging selfhood in the paralyzed region where names are assigned, and assume instead the energies of natural process.

From the first—in 1954 came *her* first collection, the significantly titled *Another Animal*—May Swenson has practiced, in riddles, chants, hex-signs and a whole panoply of invented *sortilege* unwonted in Western poetry since the Witch of Endor brought up Samuel, the ways not only of summoning Being into her grasp, but of getting herself out of that grasp and into alien shapes, into those emblems of power most often identified with the sexual:

> on this ball   oh to Endure
> half dark   like the stone
> half light   sufficient
> i walk Upright   to itself alone
> i lie Prone
> within the night   or Reincarnate
>   like the tree
> the longing   be born each spring

> that i know   to greenery
> is in the Stone also
> it must be   or like the lion
> the same that rises   without law
> in the Tree   to roam the Wild
> the longing   on velvet paw . . .
> in the Lion's call
> speaks for all

Consider the array of instruments in this fragment of the first poem from that first book, "Evolution": the incantatory use of rhyme; the rhythms of the spell; the typography that lines up the first column to stand not only pat but put, as it were, against the outer verticality of the second column, so that the poem on the page articulates, by the space it leaves as by the form it takes, a regular *passage* through which the forces can move to their completion; the lower-casing of the first-person pronoun, and the capitalization of the three Entities addressed, then their relegation to lower-case too, and the assumption of capital status by the two crucial verbs, "Reincarnate" and "Endure," and by the hypostatized adjective "Wild"; the irregular little stanzas content to exhibit, in loving complacency, a single word as an entire line; the rejection of punctuation as an unnecessary artifice in this organum of being. Evidently, this poet is engaged, and more than engaged, is elated, by the responsibilities of form. In subsequent poems in *Another Animal,* as in her other books, Miss Swenson exhibits a very determined attitude toward *contrivance;* aware, I suppose, of the danger inherent in her own siren-songs, with their obsessive reliance on the devices of incantation, she is more than eager to cast off the blasphemies of "Satanic Form":

> Things metallic or glass
> frozen twisted flattened
> stretched to agonized bubbles
> bricks beams receptacles vehicles
> forced through fire hatched to unwilling form

—and to assume in their place the "blessed" and organic avatars it is her art to invoke, not so much to counterfeit as to conjure:

> flower and stone not cursed with symmetry
> cloud and shadow not doomed to shape and fixity
> the intricate body of many without rivet or nail
> O love the juice in the green stem growing . . .

Contraption, like naming, is seen as the wrong version of experience. The paradox of the riddling poet is that she must identify without naming, make without artifice, "a model of time, a map of space." Miss Swenson is engaged in the Higher Fabrication, that *poesis* which is the true baptism; when she fails to devise charms that capture Being in their toils, she becomes, like Dickinson, again, merely charming; the appeal is no more, at times, than appealing, when it needed to be a summons:

> I lived by magic
> A little bag in my chest held a whirling stone
> so hot it was past burning
> so radiant it was blinding
>
> When the moon rose worn and broken
> her face like a coin endlessly exchanged
> in the hands of the sea
> her ray fell upon the doors which opened
> and I walked in the living wood . . .

Throughout this book, as the title itself suggests, and in the course of the collections to come, May Swenson has found a figure which allows her to escape the difficulties of both nomination and mechanism; it is the figure of the centaur, which cannot be merely named for it is imaginary, and which cannot be merely artificial for it is alive. She begins, in the title poem:

> Another animal imagine moving
>   in his rippling hide
>   down the track of the centaur . . .

the shaped verses undulate down the page in a first presentment of "dappled animals with hooves and human knees"; in "To Confirm a Thing," the figure is moralized a little:

> In the equal Night where oracular beasts
>   the planets depose
> and our Selves assume their orbits . . .
> My thighs made marble-hard
>   uncouple only to the Archer
> with his diametrical bow
>   who prances in the South
> himself a part of his horse . . .

Then let me by these signs
                                    maintain my magnitude
as the candid Centaur his dynasty upholds
                                    And in the Ecliptic Year
our sweet rebellions
                                    shall not be occulted but remain
coronals in heaven's Wheel.

And finally, in "Question," the same figure, which has become perhaps too cosmic, too "mechanical" in its astronomic implications, is returned to its erotic energies, the self addressed in that animal form where, by a certain incantation, Miss Swenson best finds her being in its highest range:

Body my house
my horse may hound
what will I do
when you are fallen

Where will I sleep
How will I ride
What will I hunt
Where can I go
without my mount
all eager and quick . . .

With cloud for shift
how will I hide?

May Swenson's second book was published in 1958; *A Cage of Spines*, garlanded with praise by Elizabeth Bishop, Richard Wilbur and Robert Lowell, among others; of these, only Howard Moss seems taken with the notion that in Swenson's "world," Being is illuminated so that "whatever she describes is not only more itself but more than itself." The strategies and devices, the shamanism and sorcery this poet deploys have become, in this larger, luminous collection, more elaborate, more convinced, and deserve further attention; their accommodation of the mystery that only when a thing is apprehended as something else can it be known as itself is fierce and full in *A Cage of Spines*. But we must note, first, an interesting development, from implication to statement, of the Centaur theme, the projection of energies and erotics into animal form, so that the poet may ask, "to what beast's intent / are we the fodder and nourishment?" The new note sounded occurs at the very start of the book, in a poem explicit enough to be called "The Centaur." For the first time, Swenson evokes life—her life—in the chatty, novelistic mode previously judged "too effusive in design for our analyses":

> The summer that I was ten—
> Can it be there was only one
> summer that I was ten? It must
>
> have been a long one then—

Looking down the prospect of her imagination, the poet reports how she would ride her willow branch all morning:

> I was the horse and the rider,
> and the leather I slapped to his rump
> spanked my own behind . . .

and come inside, after an exhausting morning's riding (and being ridden):

> *Where have you been?* said my mother.
> *Been riding,* I said from the sink,
> and filled me a glass of water . . .
> *Go tie back your hair,* said my mother,
> and *Why is your mouth all green?*
> *Rob Roy, he pulled some clover*
> *as we crossed the field,* I told her.

Here not by incantation but by exactitude in narrative, Miss Swenson gets across the doubleness in being she strives for throughout. It is a method she will resume in the book after this one, but the rest of *A Cage of Spines is* dedicated to the means of witchcraft. By riddles and charms, the poet aspires to a more resonant being than the life grudgingly acknowledged in her own body:

> I would be inheritor
> of the lamb's way and the deer's,
> my thrust take from the ground
> I tread or lie on. In thighs of trees,
> in recumbent stones, in the loins
> of beasts is found

> that line my own nakedness carried.
>   Here, in an Eden of the mind,
> I would remain among my kind,
>   to lake and hill, to tree and beast married.

Not only the shaped poems, the compulsive rhymes and puns ("what seams is only art"), the riddles and agnominations ("the shape of this box keels me oval / Heels feel its bottom / Nape knocks its top"—from the conundrum about eggs), but the discovery of the secret messages hidden within ordinary speech, as Being is concealed by Labels, excite Miss Swenson to poems of an almost frantic hermeticism: in two homages to writers, she extends her method to a kind of esoteric dalliance. First in "Frontispiece," which appears to describe a picture of Virginia Woolf in terms of the circumstances that led her to suicide, we realize from an odd, ominous resonance the lines have, that not only the names of the writer herself ("your chaste-fierce name") but the titles of all her books have been braided into the verse; thus the "frontispiece" is a compendium of names indeed, only disguised, worked back into the texture of Being and used not as nominations but proof:

> The waves carve your hearse and tomb
> and toll your voyage out again again.

The second poem of dedication is even more curious, for in it not merely names but all words are susceptible of disintegration into their secret content; what we are offered is ostensibly a description of Frost ("R. F., His Hand Against a Tree") but the account is continually breaking down as Miss Swenson discovers, like Nabokov (whose English is so often a matter of perpetual inside jokes), that she can say more about her subject by letting the language speak for itself, merely doing a little pruning and spacing to let the sense in:

> Lots of trees in the fo
>   rest but this one's an O
>   a K that's plan
>   ted hims elf and nob
>   oddy has k nots of that hand
>   some polish or the knarl
>   edge of ear th or the obs
>   tiny ate servation his blueyes
>   make or the tr easures his sent
>   ient t humb les find.

These are, as she calls them, "glyphs of a daring alphabet" indeed, and "hide what they depend on." There are other diableries in this book likely to exasperate as well as to exalt; chiefly a poem called "Parade of Painters" in which 36 painters are "assigned" first a characteristic color, then a texture ("Manet porcelain, Matisse thistles," etc.), then a shape. Then the whole thing is assembled in a litany of 36 lines which reads something like a dada catalogue, save that Swenson has shown us her method and its underlying logic: we cannot fault it, but we may fail to be *charmed* by the procession, as it passes, of painter, shape, texture and color:

> Delacroix mouth viscera iris
> Degas witchmoth birch clay
> Pissaro dhow privet marble
> Seurat hourglass linen popular
> Dufy glove pearl azure
> Rouault mummy serge blood . . .

Much more characteristic of Swenson's excellence, I think, is "News from the Cabin," in which all her impulses congregate joyously around a less arbitrary theme: visits from four creatures, none named but all identified by the characteristic textures, rhythms, and vocabulary we should associate with a woodpecker, a squirrel, a jay, and a snake, if we were to *become* them by the power of our *recital* (rather like the interludes young Arthur experiences, in T. H. White's books, as he serves his apprenticeship to fish, hawks, even hedgehogs in order to learn how to be a man). Consider the sound of this from "Hairy":

> Cried *peek*! Beaked it—chiselled the drupe.
> His nostril I saw, slit in a slate whistle,
> White-black dominoes clicked in his wings.
> Bunched beneath the dangle he heckled with holes,
>   bellysack soft, eye a brad, a red-flecked
>   mallet his ball-peen head, his neck its haft.

and the movement of the end of "Scurry":

> Sat put, pert, neat, in his suit and his seat, for a minute
>   a frown between snub ears, bulb-eyed head
>   toward me sideways, chewed.
> Rocked, squeaked. Stored the stone in his cheek.
> Finished, fell to all fours, a little roan couch;

> flurried paws loped him off, prone-bodied,
>   tail turned torch, sail, scarf.

In these extraordinary poems, animal life is invoked, is actually *acquired* for
the conjurer's purposes (extended energy, a generalized erotic awareness) by
the haptic qualities of language itself, even more than by the riddling process
so programmatically set up in the other pieces. The generosity, the
abundance of Swenson's means may allow her, on the one hand, to speak
somewhat sentimentally in "East River" of Brooklyn seen across the water as
"a shelf of old shoes, needing repair, but clean knots of smoke are being tied
and untied," and thereby we see, though both are patronized, Brooklyn *and*
the shoes; but in "News from the Cabin," on the other, she also commands,
as in the last section, "Supple," an utterance whose imagery is assimilated
without condescension to its very movement, a diction so wedded to
appearances that the speaker "leaves the spot" enriched with an access of
being, an increment which comes only when life has been enchanted to its
own understanding:

> I followed that elastic: loose
>   unicolored knot, a noose he made as if unconscious.
> Until my shadow touched him; half his curd
>   shuddered, the rest lay chill.
> I stirred: the ribbon raised a loop;
>   its end stretched, then cringed like an udder;
>   a bifid tongue, his only rapid, whirred
>   in the vent; vertical pupils lit his hood.
> That part, a groping finger, hinged, stayed upright.
> Indicated what? That I stood
>   in his light? I left the spot.

In 1963, a large group of poems from Miss Swenson's first two volumes,
with some fifty new poems, was published under the general title *To Mix with
Time*, a phrase which in its own context reiterates her project: "One must
work a magic to mix with time / in order to become old." Here the very
compression, the proliferation *inward* of the new abracadabras seem to have
enabled the poet to be elsewhere quite explicit about her undertaking:

> There unraveled
> from a file in my mind a magic motion
> I, too, used to play with: from chosen words a potion
> could be wrung; pickings of them, eaten, could make

you fly, walk
on water, be somebody else, do or undo anything, go back
or forward on belts of time . . .

It is good to have it spelled out, for there are here many poems of a specifically esoteric quality, whose organization on the page, as in the ear, suggests the location of a mystery in Being which the poet would attain to only by a ritual, a litany of participles and lattices of space:

There is a	Swaddled Thing
There is a	*Swaddled Thing*
There is a	Rocking Box
There is a	*Covered Box*
The	Unwrapping
the	Ripening
Then the	Loosening
the	Spoiling
The	Stiffening
then the	Wrapping
The	Softening
but the long long	Drying
The	Wrapping
the	Wrapping
the	Straightening
and	Wrapping
The rigid	Rolling
the gilded	Scrolling
The	Wrapping
and	Wrapping
and careful	Rewrapping
The	Thinning
and	Drying
but the	Wrapping
and	Fattening
There is the worm	Coiled
and the straw	Straightened
There is the	Plank
and the glaucous	Bundle
the paper	Skull
and the charred	Hair

the linen	Lip
and the leather	Eyelid
There is a	Person
of flesh that is *a rocking*	*Box*
There is a	Box
of wood that is *a painte*	*Person*

To which the poet, her own exegete, adds this "Note from a diary: I remembered Giotto's fresco, 'Birth of the Virgin' in a cloister in Florence: the 'Mother of God' was a swaddled infant held upright, like a board or plaque, by her nurse . . . and I remembered a mummy in the Vatican Museum in Rome; in her sarcophagus shaped and painted like herself, an Egyptian girl 2000 years old lay unwrapped to the waist." The notation, in the poem, of identities between the infant and the mummy, and the enactment of vital, or mortal, differences that reaches the climax of the last four lines, with their paradoxical reversals, dramatizes the kind of formal extremes May Swenson is ready to risk. "The idea," she says in "Out of my Head," the first poem in this book, "is to make a vehicle out of it." To employ, that is, the spell in order to be taken somewhere; or as she says in another place, and in her most orphic cadences:

> we weave asleep
> a body
> and awake unravel
> the same veins
> we travel

The unravelling of those travelled veins is undertaken, of course, in other ways besides such necromantic ones. There is a group of poems, in *To Mix with Time*, written in France, Italy and Spain and concerned with the reporting of surfaces, not the casting of spells. As in the earlier "Centaur," the poet appears sufficiently possessed of her identity to feel no need of commanding her surround by voodoo. She can trust her sensibility, in these new old places, to do its work, and oblige the *genius loci* to give. up its own ghost:

> Gondola-slim
> above the bridge, a new moon held a dim
> circle of charcoal between its points.
> Bats played in the greenish air,
> their wing-joints

soft as moths' against the bone-gray palazzi where
not a window was alight . . .

These are secular poems, then, rarely moralized or magicked, but left to
speak for themselves, in the descriptive mode of Elizabeth Bishop, though
there are exceptions, occurring (as we might expect) in the case of the
"Fountains of Aix," where the word "water" is disjoined fifteen times from
the lines and made to slide down the side of a stanza:

> A goddess is driving a chariot through   water.
>   Her reins and whips are tight white   water.
>   Bronze hooves of horses wrangle with   water.
>   Faces with mossy lips unlocked
>   always uttering   water
>   Water
>
>   wearing their features blank,
>   their ears deaf, their eyes mad
>   or patient or blind or astonished at   water
>   always uttered out of their mouths . . .

and again in a poem about death, "The Alyscamps at Arles," in which the
words "bodies," "bones," "died," "stones," and "flesh" are isolated in a
central column, set off like tombs in each line, and recurring some two dozen
times. Europe, we take it, is sacred ground, and the mere fact of treading it
is enough, almost, for Miss Swenson's genius to speak low to her. The
conjugation, in this book, of a temporal response to earth and a runic
riddling of it is indeed "to mix with time;" there is a relaxation of need,
somehow, as if the poet had come to find things enthralling enough in
themselves:

> In any random, sprawling, decomposing thing
> is the charming string
> of its history—and what it will be next . . .

Like "Evolution," her first poem in her first book, her last one here, "The
Exchange," recapitulates her enterprise—to get out of herself and into those
larger, warmer energies of earth, and to do so by liturgical means ("Words?
Let their / mutations work / toward the escape / of object into the nearest
next / shape, motion, assembly, temporal context"):

Populous and mixed is mind.
Earth take thought,
my mouth be moss . . .
Wind be motion,
birds be passion,
water invite me to your bed.

Things Taking Place was the working title May Swenson had originally given *To Mix with Time,* and its suggestion of a larger interest in a secular world where events occur, where life "happens," and a lessening concern with the cosmic energies of "mere" Being, is even more applicable to the poet's latest work, published in 1967 in a long book called *Half Sun Half Sleep.* Not that Miss Swenson is any less interested in the energies, the powers that drive the stars in their courses, or in the measurements and movements responsible for that formal echo of dune and wave, beach and tide—rather, the largest impulses which often she could *handle,* precisely, as abstractions only, are now accommodated into the observed intercourse of her body and its environment, her life and its limits. There are charms here too, but they are *secular* charms, and the fact that so many of the rhyme words are tucked away in the "wrong" parts of the line suggests the profane intentions of these cunning incantations—if Miss Swenson has designs on life, they are subordinated to a surface she prefers unruly:

Well, do they sing? If so, I *expect* their
note is extreme. Not something one *hears,*
but must watch the cat's *ears* to *detect* . . . [emphasis mine]

she furthers, too, her old mistrust, even her outright distaste for the exemplars of "Satanic Form," which she finds in most of our modern enclosures, elevator cages, Pullman cars and airplane bellies, and specifically in our satellites and space missiles. One of the most brilliant pieces in the new book is "August 19, Pad 19," a jeering, nerve-end journal of an astronaut "positioned for either breach birth / or urn burial." Reminiscent of her other entrapped forms—the mummy and the swaddled infant—the astronaut is prepared:

. . . Never so helpless, so choked with power.
Never so impotent, so important.
So naked, wrapped, equipped, and immobile,
cared for by 5000 nurses.
Let them siphon my urine to the nearest star.
Let it flare and spin like a Catherine.

> . . . T minus 10 . . . The click of countdown stops.
> My pram and mummy case, this trap's
> tumescent tube's still locked to wet,
> magnetic, unpredictable earth.
> All my system's go, but oh,
> an anger of the air won't let me go.
> On the screen the blip is *MISSION SCRUBBED* . . .

and the poem's ultimate irony is to oblige this sequestered consciousness, furious in its failure, to feel "out on the dome some innocent drops of rain." The titles suggest the poet's preferences: "On Handling Some Small Shells from the Windward Islands," "A Basin of Eggs," "Drawing the Cat," "On Seeing Rocks Cropping out of a Hill in Central Park" and—quintessentially— "Things in Common." There is of course a certain trust in her old ways of working, call them weapons even, the sharp-edged, riddling means of tricking us into the poem; the book itself is arranged with the titles in alphabetical order, and there are a number of shaped poems, of spells and counting-rhymes, for as she says in "The Truth," a poem about a snake that is snake-shaped,

> Speculations about shape amount to a counting
> of the coils.

But there is a moving away from the kind of hermetic indication that cannot show loss as well as gain. There is the sense, recorded in a poem about two trees leaning together, "All That Time," that our interpretations of phenomena may be cruelly aberrant:

> And where their tops tangled
> it looked like he was crying
> on her shoulder.
> On the other hand, maybe he
>
> had been trying to weaken her,
> break her, or at least
> make her bend
> over backwards for him . . .

and that we must devise a form that will account for "strange abrasions zodiacal wounds." The important thing, she says, is

> To be the instrument
> and the wound of feeling.

As the book's title suggests, the balance between sacred and profane, ritual and report, with its implication of the balance between seeing and dreaming, speech and somnambulism, is carefully tended:

> The tug of the void
> the will of the world
> together . . .

These poems are exuberant in their hocus-pocus, surely, but they are also a little rueful about the facility to which one can trust in the hope of getting out of the self ("One must be a cloud to occupy a house of cloud . . . refusing the fixture of a solid soul"); also they are not so explicit in exploring "the suck of the sea's dark mind": if Swenson still asks, in a poem called "The Lightning" through which a diagonal gutter of space jabs through her twenty lines to the word "entrails," "When will I grope my way clear of the entrails of intellect?" she is nonetheless prepared to use the mementoes of that gutted intellect to deal with the sea's dark mind, referring to the "ancient diary the waves are murmuring" and accounting in terms of gains as well as losses for her existence as a rational animal:

> When I was a sea worm
> I never saw the sun,
>
> but flowed, a salty germ,
> in the bloodstream of the sea.
> There I left an alphabet
>
> but it grew dim to me.
> Something caught me in its net,
> took me from the deep
>
> book of the ocean, weaned me,
> put fin and wing to sleep,
> made me stand and made me
>
> face the sun's dry eye.
> On the shore of intellect
> I forgot how to fly . . .

In brightness I lost track
of my underworld
of ultraviolet wisdom.

My fiery head furled
up its cool kingdom
and put night away.

These are no longer nor even want to be the poems of a small furry animal
("the page my acre") nor of a selfless demiurge ("They founded the sun./
When the sun found them / it undertook its path and aim . . . / The air first
heard itself / called glory in their lungs"); they are the witty resigned poems
of a woman "hunting clarities of Being," asking

Have I arrived from
     left or
     right to hover here
in the clear permission of my
     temperature? Is my
     flow a fading
     up or
     down—my glow
     going? Or is my flush
     rushing to a rose of ripe
     explosion?

a woman eager still to manipulate the phenomenal world by magic, but so
possessed, now, of the means of her identity that the ritual, spellbinding,
litaneutical elements of her art have grown consistent, even coincident, with
her temporal, conditioned, suffering experience and seem—to pay her the
highest compliment May Swenson could care to receive—no more than
natural.

GARY SMITH

Gwendolyn Brooks's A Street in Bronzeville, *the Harlem Renaissance and the Mythologies of Black Women*

When Gwendolyn Brooks published her first collection of poetry *A Street in Bronzeville* (1945) with Harper and Brothers, she already enjoyed a substantial reputation in the literary circles of Chicago. Nearly a decade earlier, her mother Keziah Brooks, had arranged meetings between her daughter and James Weldon Johnson and Langston Hughes, two of the most distinguished Black writers of America's Harlem Renaissance. Determined to mold Gwendolyn into a *lady Paul Laurence Dunbar*, Mrs. Brooks proffered poems for the famous writers to read. While Johnson's advice to the young poet was abrupt, eventually he exerted an incisive influence on her later work. In a letter and a marginal note included on the returned poems, addressed to her on 30 August 1937, Johnson praised Brooks's obvious talent and pointed her in the direction of Modernist poetry:

> My dear Miss Brooks: I have read the poems you sent me last. Of them I especially liked *Reunion* and *Myself*. Reunion is very good, and *Myself* is good. You should, by all means, continue you[r] study and work. I shall always be glad to give you any assistance that I can. Sincerely yours. James Weldon Johnson.

From *MELUS: The Journal of the Society for the Study of the Multi-Ethnic Literature of the United States 10*, no. 3 (Fall 1983). © 1983 by MELUS.

> Dear Miss Brooks—You have an unquestionable talent and feeling for poetry. Continue to write—at the same time, study carefully the work of the best modern poets—not to imitate them, but to help cultivate the highest possible standards of self-criticism. Sincerely, James Weldon Johnson.

Of course, the irony in Johnson's advice, addressed as it is to the future *lady* Dunbar, is that he actually began his own career by conspicuously imitating Dunbar's dialect poems, *Lyrics of a Lowly Life;* yet he encourages Brooks to study the work of the "best Modern poets." He was, perhaps, reacting to the latent elements of modernism already found in her poetry; but the effect was to turn Brooks momentarily away from the Black aesthetic of Hughes's *Weary Blues* (1926) and Countee Cullen's *Color* (1925) toward the Modernist aesthetics of T. S. Eliot, Ezra Pound, and e. e. cummings. It is interesting to note, however, that, even though Johnson's second letter admonishes Brooks to study the Modernist poets, he cautions her "not to imitate them," but to read them with the intent of cultivating the "highest possible standards of self-criticism." Flattered by the older poet's attention and advice, Brooks embarked upon a serious attempt to absorb as much Modernist poetry as she could carry from the public library.

If Johnson played the part of literary mentor, Brooks's relationship with Hughes was more personal, warmer, and longer lasting. She was already on familiar terms with *Weary Blues,* so their first meeting was particularly inspirational. Brooks showed Hughes a packet of her poems, and he praised her talent and encouraged her to continue to write. Years later, after Brooks's reputation was firmly established by a Pulitzer Prize for Annie Allen (1949), her relationship with Hughes blossomed into mutual admiration. Hughes dedicated his collection of short stories, *Something in Common* (1963), to her. While Hughes's poetic style had an immeasurable influence on Brooks's poetry, she also respected his personal values and lifestyle. As she noted in her autobiography [*Report*], Hughes was her idol:

> Langston Hughes! The words and deeds of Langston Hughes were rooted in kindness, and in pride. His point of departure was always a clear pride in his race. Race pride may be craft, art, or a music that combines the best of jazz and hymn. Langston frolicked and chanted to the measure of his own race-reverence.

> He was an easy man. You could rest in his company. No one possessed a more serious understanding of life's immensities. No one was firmer in recognition of the horrors man imposes upon

man, in hardy insistence on reckonings. But when those who
knew him remember him the memory inevitably will include
laughter of an unusually warm and tender kind. The wise man,
he knew, will take some juice out of this one life that is his gift.

Mightily did he use the street. He found its multiple heart, its
tastes, smells, alarms, formulas, flowers, garbage and convul-
sions. He brought them all to his table-top. He crushed them to
a writing paste. He himself became the pen.

In other words, while Johnson encouraged Brooks to find "standards for
self-criticism" in Modernism, Hughes underscored the value of cultivating
the ground upon which she stood. In Hughes, in both the poet and man,
Brooks found standards for living: he was a model of witty candor and
friendly unpretentiousness and, most importantly, a literary success. Hughes
convinced Brooks that a Black poet need not travel outside the realm of his
own experiences to create a poetic vision and write successful poetry. Unlike
the Modernist Eliot who gathered much of his poetic material from the
drawingrooms and salons of London, Hughes found his material in the
coldwater flats and backstreets of Harlem. And Brooks, as is self-evident in
nearly all her poetry, learned Hughes's example by heart.

II

The critical reception of *A Street in Bronzeville* contained, in embryo, many
of the central issues in the scholarly debate that continues to engage Brooks's
poetry. As in the following quotation from *The New York Times Book Review*,
most reviewers were able to recognize Brooks's versatility and craft as a poet:

If the idiom is colloquial, the language is universal. Brooks
commands both the colloquial and more austere rhythms. She
can vary manner and tone. In form, she demonstrates a wide
range: quatrains, free verse, ballads, and sonnets—all
appropriately controlled. The longer line suits her better than
the short, but she is not verbose. In some of the sonnets, she uses
an abruptness of address that is highly individual.

Yet, while noting her stylistic successes, not many critics fully understood her
achievement in her first book. This difficulty was not only characteristic of
critics who examined the formal aspects of prosody in her work, but also of

critics who addressed themselves to the social realism in her poetry. Moreover, what Brooks gained at the hands of critics who focused on her technique, she lost to critics who chose to emphasize the exotic, Negro features of the book, as the following quote illustrates:

> *A Street in Bronzeville* ranges from blues ballads and funeral chants to verse in high humor. With both clarity and insight, it mirrors the impressions of life in an urban Negro community. The best poem is "The Sundays of Satin-Legs Smith," a poignant and hour-by-hour page out of a zoot-suiter's life. A subtle change of pace proves Brooks' facility in a variety of poetic forms.

The poems in *A Street in Bronzeville* actually served notice that Brooks had learned her craft well enough to combine successfully themes and styles from both the Harlem Renaissance and Modernist poetry. She even achieves some of her more interesting effects in the book by parodying the two traditions. She juggles the pessimism of Modernist poetry with the general optimism of the Harlem Renaissance. Three of her more notable achievements, "kitchenette building," "the mother," and "Sundays of Satin-Legs Smith," are parodic challenges to T. S. Eliot's dispirited anti-hero J. Alfred Prufrock. "[K]itchenette building" begins with Eliot-like emphasis on the dry infertility of modern life: "We are things of dry hours and the involuntary plan." The poem concludes with the humored optimism that "Since Number 5 is out of the bathroom / we think of lukewarm water, we hope to get in it." Another example is the alienated, seemingly disaffected narrator of "the mother" who laments the loss of her children but with the resurgent, hopeful voice that closes the poem: "Believe me, I loved you all." Finally a comparison could be made between the elaborate, self-assertive manner with which Satin-legs Smith dresses himself for his largely purposeless Sunday outing and the tentative efforts of his counterpart, J. Alfred Prufrock.

Because of the affinities *A Street in Bronzeville* shares with Modernist poetry and the Harlem Renaissance, Brooks was initiated not only into the vanguard of American literature, but also into what had been the inner circle of Harlem writers. Two of the Renaissance's leading poets, Claude McKay and Countee Cullen, addressed letters to her to mark the publication of *A Street in Bronzeville*. McKay welcomed her into a dubious but potentially rewarding career:

> I want to congratulate you again on the publication of 'A Street in Bronzeville' [sic] and welcome you among the band of hard

working poets who do have something to say. It is a pretty rough road we have to travel, but I suppose much compensation is derived from the joy of being able to sing. Yours sincerely, Claude McKay. (October 10, 1945.)

Cullen pinpointed her dual place in American literature:

I have just finished reading, 'A Street in Bronzeville' [sic] and want you to know that I enjoyed it thoroughly. There can be no doubt that you are a poet, a good one, with every indication of becoming a better. I am glad to be able to say 'welcome' to you to that too small group of Negro poets, and to the larger group of American ones. No one can deny you your place there. (August 24, 1945.)

The immediate interest in these letters is how both poets touch upon the nerve ends of the critical debate that surrounded *A Street in Bronzeville*. For McKay, while Brooks has "something to say," she can also "sing"; and for Cullen, she belongs not only to the minority of Negro poets, but also to the majority of American ones. Nonetheless, the critical question for both poets might well have been Brooks's relationship to the Harlem Renaissance. What had she absorbed of the important tenets of the Black aesthetic as expressed during the New Negro Movement? And how had she addressed herself, as a poet, to the literary movement's assertion of the folk and African culture, and its promotion of the arts as the agent to define racial integrity and to fuse racial harmony?

Aside from its historical importance, the Harlem Renaissance—as a literary movement—is rather difficult to define. There is, for example, no fixed or generally agreed upon date or event that serves as a point of origin for the movement. One might easily assign this date to the publication of McKay's poems *Harlem Shadows* (1922), Alaine Locke's anthology *The New Negro* (1925), or Cullen's anthology Caroling Dusk (1927). Likewise, the general description of the movement as a Harlem Renaissance is often questioned, since most of the major writers, with the notable exceptions of Hughes and Cullen, actually did not live and work in Harlem. Finally, many of the themes and literary conventions defy definition in terms of what was and what was not a New Negro poet. Nonetheless, there was a common ground of purpose and meaning in the works of the individual writers that permits a broad definition of the spirit and intent of the Harlem Renaissance. Indeed, the New Negro poets expressed a deep pride in being Black; they found reasons for this pride in ethnic identity and heritage; and they shared a common faith in the fine arts as a means of defining and reinforcing racial pride. But in the literal expression of these artistic impulses, the poets were either romantics or realists and, quite often within a single poem, both. The realistic impulse, as defined best in the poems of McKay's *Harlem Shadows*, was a sober reflection upon Blacks as second class citizens, segregated from the mainstream of American socioeconomic life, and largely unable to realize the wealth and opportunity that America promised. The romantic impulse, on the other hand, as defined in the poems of Sterling Browns's *Southern Road* (1932), often found these unrealized dreams in the collective strength and will of the folk masses. In comparing the poems in *A Street in Bronzeville* with various poems from the Renaissance, it becomes apparent that Brooks agrees, for the most part, with their prescriptions for the New Negro. Yet the unique contributions she brings to bear upon this tradition are extensive: 1) the biting ironies of intraracial discrimination, 2) the devaluation of love in heterosexual relationships between Blacks, and 3) the primacy of suffering in the lives of poor Black women.

III

The first clue that *A Street in Bronzeville* was, at the time of its publication, unlike any other book of poems by a Black American is its insistent emphasis on demystifying romantic love between Black men and women. The "old marrieds," the first couple encountered on the walking tour of Bronzeville, are nothing like the youthful archetype that the Renaissance poets often portrayed:

> But in the crowding darkness not a word did they say.
> Though the pretty-coated birds had piped so lightly all the day.
> And he had seen the lovers in the little side-streets.
> And she had heard the morning stories clogged with sweets.
> It was quite a time for loving. It was midnight. It was May.
> But in the crowding darkness not a word did they say.

In this short, introductory poem, Brooks, in a manner reminiscent of Eliot's alienated *Waste Land* characters, looks not toward a glorified African past or limitless future, but rather at a stifled present. Her old lovers ponder not an image of their racial past or some symbolized possibility of self-renewal, but rather the overwhelming question of what to do in the here-and-now. Moreover, their world, circumscribed by the incantatory line that opens and closes the poem, "But in the crowding darkness not a word did they say," is one that is distinctly at odds with their lives. They move timidly through the crowded darkness of their neighborhood largely ignorant of the season, "May," the lateness of the hour, "midnight," and a particular *raison d'être*, "a time for loving." Their attention, we infer, centers upon the implicit need to escape any peril that might consume what remains of their lives. The tempered optimism in the poem, as the title indicates, is the fact that they are "old-marrieds": a social designation that suggests the longevity of their lives and the solidity of their marital bond in what is, otherwise, an ephemeral world of change. Indeed, as the prefatory poem in *A Street in Bronzeville*, the "old marrieds," on the whole debunks one of the prevalent motifs of Harlem Renaissance poetry: its general optimism about the future.

As much as the Harlem Renaissance was noted for its optimism, an important corollary motif was that of ethnic or racial pride. This pride— often thought a reaction to the minstrel stereotypes in the Dunbar traditionusually focused with romantic idealization upon the Black woman. A casual streetwalker in Hughes's poem, "When Sue Wears Red," for example, is magically transformed into an Egyptian queen:

> When Susanna Jones wears red
> Her face is like an ancient cameo
> Turned brown by the ages.
> Come with a blast of trumpets,
>   Jesus!
>
> When Susanna Jones wears red
> A queen from some time-dead Egyptian night
> Walks once again.

Similarly, six of the first seven poems in Cullen's first published work, *Color* (1925), celebrate the romanticized virtues of Black women. The second poem in the volume, "A Song of Praise," is particularly noteworthy in its treatment of the theme:

> You have not heard my love's dark throat,
>   Slow-fluting like a reed,
> Release the perfect golden note
>   She caged there for my need.
> Her walk is like the replica
>   Of some barbaric dance
> Wherein the soul of Africa
>   Is winged with arrogance.

In the same manner, McKay's sonnet, "The Harlem Dancer," extolls the misunderstood virtue of a cabaret dancer:

> Applauding youths laughed with young prostitutes
> And watched her perfect, half-clothed body sway;
> Her voice was like the sound of blended flutes
> Blown by black players upon a picnic day.
> She sang and danced on gracefully and calm,
> The light gauze hanging loose about her form;
> To me she seemed a proudly-swaying palm
> Grown lovelier for passing through a storm.

In *A Street in Bronzeville*, this romantic impulse for idealizing the Black woman runs headlong into the biting ironies of intraracial discrimination. In poem after poem in *A Street in Bronzeville*, within the well-observed caste lines of skin color, the consequences of dark pigmentation are revealed in drastic terms. One of the more popular of these poems, "The Ballad of Chocolate Mabbie," explores the tragic ordeal of Mabbie, the Black female heroine, who is victimized by her dark skin and her "saucily bold" lover, Willie Boone:

> It was Mabbie without the grammar school gates.
> And Mabbie was all of seven.
> And Mabbie was cut from a chocolate bar.
> And Mabbie thought life was heaven.

Mabbie's life, of course, is one of unrelieved monotony; her social contacts are limited to those who, like her, are dark skinned, rather than "lemonhued" or light skinned. But as Brooks makes clear, the larger tragedy of Mabbie's life is the human potential that is squandered:

> Oh, warm is the waiting for joys, my dears!
> And it cannot be too long.
> O, pity the little poor chocolate lips
> That carry the bubble of song!

But if Mabbie is Brooks's parodic victim of romantic love, her counterpart in "Ballad of Pearl May Lee" realizes a measure of sweet revenge. In outline, Brooks's poem is reminiscent of Cullen's *The Ballad of the Brown Girl* (1927). There are, however, several important differences. The first is the poem's narrative structure: Pearl May Lee is betrayed in her love for a Black man who "couldn't abide dark meat," who subsequently makes love to a white girl and is lynched for his crime of passion, whereas Cullen's "Brown Girl" is betrayed in her love for a white man, Lord Thomas, who violates explicit social taboo by marrying her rather than Fair London, a white girl. Moreover, Cullen's poem, "a ballad retold," is traditional in its approach to the ballad form:

> Oh, this is the tale that grandams tell
> In the land where the grass is blue,
> And some there are who say 'tis false,
> And some that hold it true.

Brooks's ballad, on the other hand, dispenses with the rhetorical invocation of the traditional ballad and begins *in medias res:*

> Then off they took you, off to the jail,
> A hundred hooting after.
> An you should have heard me at my house.
> I cut my lungs with my laughter,
>   Laughter,
>   Laughter.
> I cut my lungs with my laughter.

This mocking tone is sustained throughout the poem, even as Sammy, Pearl May Lee's lover, is lynched:

> You paid for your dinner, Sammy boy,
> And you didn't pay with money.
> You paid with your hide and my heart, Sammy
> boy,
> For your taste of pink and white honey,
>   Honey,
>   Honey,
> For your taste of pink and white honey.

Here, one possible motif in the poem is the price that Pearl May Lee pays for her measure of sweet revenge: the diminution of her own capacity to express love and compassion for another—however ill-fated—human being. But the element of realism that Brooks injects into her ballad by showing Pearl May Lee's mocking detachment from her lover's fate is a conscious effort to devalue the romantic idealization of Black love. Furthermore, Pearl

May Lee's macabre humor undermines the racial pride and harmony that was an important tenet in the Renaissance prescription for the New Negro. And, lastly, Pearl May Lee's predicament belies the social myth of the Black woman as *objective correlative* of the Renaissance's romanticism.

In another poem that uses the Blues tradition as its thematic structure, Brooks takes the reader backstage, inside the dressing room of Mame, "The Queen of the Blues." As the central figure in the poem, Mame is similar to Sterling Brown's Ma Rainey, "Mother of the Blues":

> When Ma Rainey
> Comes to town,
> Folks from anyplace
> Miles aroun'
> From Cape Girardeau,
> Poplar Bluff,
> Flocks in to hear
> Ma do her stuff.

But where Ma Rainey is realized as a mythic goddess within Black folk culture, Mame is shown to be the double victim of sexual and racial exploitation. Her social role is that of a less-than-willing performer

> Mame was singing
> At the Midnight Club.
> And the place was red
> With blues.
> She could shake her body
> Across the floor.
> For what did she have
> To lose?

The question of loss in the poem becomes a chilling, moral refrain: "For what did she have / To lose?" This question is literally answered by the other losses in Mame's private life: her mother, father, relatives, and children. Indeed, unlike the celebrated public performances of Ma Rainey that transformed private griefs into public theatre:

> O Ma Rainey,
> Sing yo' song;
> Now you's back
> Whah you belong,

> Git way inside us,
> Keep us strong . . .

Mame sings primarily to exorcise herself of the frustrations of unrequited love and intraracial discrimination:

> I loved my daddy.
> But what did my daddy
> Do?
> I loved my daddy.
> But what did my daddy
> Do?
> Found him a brown-skin chicken
> What's gonna be
> Black and blue.

Nonetheless, Mame's problem, as the "Queen of the Blues," might well be her lack of conformity within the blues tradition. Her questioning rebuke of her profession suggests misplaced values: "But when has a man / Tipped his hat to me?" The most obvious answer, as more than one critic of the poem has suggested, is that the pinches and slaps Mame receives are part of the time-honored rituals of a blues performance. But as a Black woman whose frustrated life compares with Mabbie and Pearl May Lee, Mame is authentic. Her complaint is not about her demeaning social role as a nightclub performer who is paid to flesh-out the dreams and sexual aspirations of her largely male audience, but more substantially about her dignity as a human being. The real price Mame pays is the loss of her female identity. What she laments is the blurred distinction between her stagelife as a romantic prop and her real life as a Black woman.

IV

To be sure, the Harlem Renaissance poets were not solely romantic in their portrayal of Black women; there was, within their poetry, an equally strong impulse towards realism. In "Harlem Shadows," for example, McKay shows the seamier side of Harlem nightlife, wherein "little dark girls" prowl the streets as prostitutes:

> I hear the halting footsteps of a lass
>   In Negro Harlem when the night lets fall

>Its veil. I see the shapes of girls who pass
>   To bend and barter at desire's call.
>Ah, little dark girls who in slippered feet
>Go prowling through the night from street to street!

And Sterling Brown, although he is less dramatic than McKay in his poem "Bessie," nonetheless recognizes the realistic underside of urban life for Black women:

>Who will know Bessie now of these who loved her;
>   Who of her gawky pals could recognize
>Bess in this woman, gaunt of flesh and painted,
>   Despair deep bitten in her soft brown eyes?

>Would the lads who walked with her in dusk-cooled byways
>   Know Bessie now should they meet her again?
>Would knowing men of Fifth St. think that Bessie ever
>   Was happy-hearted, brave-eyed as she was then?

For Hughes, too, the Black woman in "Young Prostitute" is described not as an Egyptian cameo, but rather as a "withered flower":

>Her dark brown face
>Is like a withered flower
>On a broken stem.
>Those kind come cheap in Harlem
>So they say.

In each of the above poems, the impulse toward romantic idealism of Black women gives way to critical realism; the mythic disguises that mask the harsh realities of social and economic deprivations are stripped away, and poor Black women are revealed as the most likely victims of racism within American society.

For Brooks, unlike the Renaissance poets, the victimization of poor Black women becomes not simply a minor chord but a predominant theme of *A Street in Bronzeville*. Few, if any, of her female characters are able to free themselves from the web of poverty and racism that threatens to strangle their lives. The Black heroine in "obituary for a living lady" was "decently wild / As a child," but as a victim of society's hypocritical, puritan standards, she

fell in love with a man who didn't know
That even if she wouldn't let him touch her breasts she
was still worth his hours.

In another example of the complex life-choices confronting Brooks's women, the two sisters of "Sadie and Maude" must choose between death-in-life and life-in-death. Maude, who went to college, becomes a "thin brown mouse," presumably resigned to spinsterhood, "living all alone / In this old house," while Sadie who "scraped life / With a fine-tooth comb" bears two illegitimate children and dies, leaving as a heritage for her children her "fine-tooth comb." What is noticeable in the lives of these Black women is a mutual identity that is inextricably linked with race and poverty.

For Hattie Scott, Brooks's protagonist in a series of vignettes that chronicle the life of a Black domestic worker, the struggle to assert a female identity begins with the first poem, "the end of day." Hattie's life, measured by the sun's rising and setting, is described as a ceaseless cycle of menial tasks. The second poem in the series, "the date," details Hattie's attempt to free herself from the drudgery of domestic work:

> Whatcha mean talkin' about cleanin' silver?
> It's eight o'clock now, you fool.
> I'm leavin'. Got somethin' interestin' on my mind.
> Don't mean night school.

Hattie's "date" in the third poem, an appointment "at the hairdresser's" turns out to be a rather farcical attempt to have her hair done in an "upsweep" with "humpteen baby curls." Like Sadie's comb, Hattie's "upsweep" becomes symbolic of her persistent efforts to assert a positive identity. The reader senses, though, that her cosmetic changes, like her previous efforts with "Madam C. J. Walker" and "Poro Grower" (two hairdressers that promise instant beauty), will end in marginal success. Indeed, in the poem that follows, "when I die," Hattie imagines her funeral as a solitary affair attended by "one lone short man / Dressed all shabbily."

The final poem in the series, "the battle," ends not on a note of personal triumph for Hattie, but rather resignation and defeat. Hattie's neighbor and spiritual counterpart, Moe Belle Jackson, is routinely beaten by her husband:

> Moe Belle Jackson's husband
> Whipped her good last night.
> Her landlady told my ma they had
> A knock-down-drag-out fight.

Hattie's perception of the beating is charged with the anger and indignation of a *secret sharer* who, perhaps, realizes her own life in Moe Belle's predicament:

> I like to think
> Of how I'd of took a knife
> And slashed all the quickenin'
> Out of his lowly life.

Nonetheless, in what is surely one of the finest examples of macabre humor in Brooks's poetry, Hattie combines psychological insight and laconic understatement in her final musings about Moe Belle's fate:

> But if I know Moe Belle,
> Most like, she shed a tear,
> And this mornin' it was probably,
> "More grits, dear?"

Brooks's relationship with the Harlem Renaissance poets, as *A Street in Bronzeville* ably demonstrates, was hardly imitative. As one of the important links with the Black poetic tradition of the 1920s and 1930s, she enlarged the element of realism that was an important part of the Renaissance worldview. Although her poetry is often conditioned by the optimism that was also a legacy of the period, Brooks rejects outright their romantic prescriptions for the lives of Black women. And in this regard, she serves as a vital link with the Black Arts Movement of the 1960s that, while it witnessed the flowering of Black women as poets and social activists as well as the rise of Black feminist aesthetics in the 1970s, brought about a curious revival of romanticism in the Renaissance mode.

However, since the publication of *A Street in Bronzeville*, Brooks has not eschewed the traditional roles and values of Black women in American society; on the contrary, in her subsequent works, *Annie Allen* (1949), *The Bean Eaters* (1960), and *In the Mecca* (1968), she has been remarkably consistent in identifying the root cause of intraracial problems within the black community as white racism and its pervasive socioeconomic effects. Furthermore, as one of the chief voices of the Black Arts Movement, she has developed a social vision, in such works as *Riot* (1969), *Family Pictures* (1970), and *Beckonings* (1975), that describes Black women and men as equally integral parts of the struggle for social and economic justice.

PAUL A. LACEY

Denise Levertov:
A Poetry of Exploration

In her "Statement on Poetics" in 1959 Denise Levertov wrote:

> I believe poets are instruments on which the power of poetry
> plays. But they are also makers, craftsmen: It is given to the seer
> to see, but it is then his responsibility to communicate what he
> sees, that they who cannot see may see, since we are "members
> one of another."

A poem is a living thing, not merely by courtesy of metaphor, but
literally. And it is a mystery not to be solved but to be approached reverently,
meditated upon, and affirmed. Both her critical writing and her poetry insist
on such an approach to poetry and, behind it, to life. Poems should evidence
an "inner harmony" which is in "utter contrast to the chaos" of life, but not
a manufactured harmony or a fantasy compensation for the way things really
are. "For me, back of the idea of organic form is the concept that there is a
form in all things (and in our experience) which the poet can discover and
reveal." As the lines from "The Artist" put it, "The true artist: capable,
practicing skillful, / maintains dialogue with his heart, meets things with his
mind." The act of writing poetry is first an act of opening oneself to
experience in such a way that its *inscape* becomes revealed to us.

From *The Inner War: Forms and Themes in Recent American Poetry*, by Paul A. Lacey © 1972
Fortress Press. Used by permission of Augsburg Fortress.

As her critical writings testify, the language of mystery—though not mystification—most appropriately expresses how poems are "given" to and received by the poet. Sense experiences, memories, the unconscious, some image or word come together, constellate for the poet. In order to *have* or grasp and *interpret* this complex of experiences, the poet must discover some "expressive and unifying act," some form, "an inscape that relates the apparently unrelated." This he does through meditation and contemplation, opening up to or centering down upon this constellation of elements. Denise Levertov deliberately uses words from the religious vocabulary and acknowledges their source. "The act of art evokes a spirit, and in assuming the existence of a spirit, and the possibility of a transformation by means of that spirit, it is an act of prayer. It is a testimony of that *participation mystique*, that involvement of the individual in a life beyond himself, which is a basic element of religion in the broadest and deepest sense."

The poet "muses," which she defines literally as standing openmouthed, waiting for "inspiration." As things fall together into a pattern, a correspondence between those things and words occurs. The poet is "brought to speech." "Correspondence," "counterparts," "analogies," "resemblances," "natural allegories," are all words which Denise Levertov uses to speak of poetic forms in relation to reality. "Such a poetry is exploratory."

> All trivial parts of
> world-about-us speak in the forms
> of themselves and their counterparts!
>   ("A Straw Swan at Christmas")

General discussions of methods of poetic composition are notoriously unhelpful when used to gloss particular poems, and this would be especially true for Denise Levertov's poetry, for she is telling us neither "how-to-write-an-organic poem" nor even "how-I-write." Discourse cannot teach us how to intuit, but we may catch from her tone and attitude in her critical writings some ways in which our reading may be exploratory, as her poetry is. A good test case is her poem "Illustrious Ancestors," from *Overland to the Islands* (1958).

> The Rav
> of Northern White Russia declined,
> in his youth, to learn the
> language of birds, because
> the extraneous did not interest him; nevertheless
> when he grew old it was found

he understood them anyway, having
listened well, and as it is said, "prayed
                with the bench and the floor." He used
what was at hand—as did
Angel Jones of Mold, whose meditations
were sewn into coats and britches.
                Well, I would like to make,
thinking some line still taut between me and them,
poems direct as what the birds said,
hard as a floor, sound as a bench,
mysterious as the silence when the tailor
would pause with his needle in the air.

The poem opens with an artless telling of a family tale. If we are used to looking to the ends of lines for strong words or active verbs to carry the energy of the poem, we are disappointed: "the," "because," "nevertheless," do not drive us forward. The flat tone and matter-of-fact handling of details seem, in fact, to undercut the promise of the title. But the anecdote engages us deeply, for it resonates like a good Hasidic tale. The words and details invite meditation by their very simplicity and artlessness. For what strikes us first is that the miraculous itself is being treated matter-of-factly. And from that simple contrast others become clear: youth and age, ignorance and wisdom, the extraneous and what lies at hand. The Rav, caught up in one understanding of the spiritual life in his youth, declines to learn what is extraneous, the language of the birds. But in his old age, because he attended to the unmysterious and everyday disciplines of Hasidism, that other capacity has come as an additional gift. The implications of the tale are rich. On the one hand, there might be the danger of pride in the Rav's decision that the language of the birds was uninteresting and extraneous; but he may also have avoided a temptation to greater pride in the piling up of *power*. In refusing to study what is a secret to man, he skirts the temptations of the magical—often associated with the demonic in Martin Buber's *Tales of the Hasidim* and his historical chronicle *For the Sake of Heaven*. The Rav did not focus on achieving powers, but on "listening well" and "praying *with*" the tools and furniture of his workaday life, "He used what was at hand." Because he had ears, he heard, as Jesus' parable in the Gospel of Mark puts it; because he learned how to listen well, he discovered in the wisdom of old age that nothing is extraneous.

The Hasidic tale of the Rav could be complete in itself, but this poem concerns inheritance and keeping faith with one's gifts, so the poet tells about an ancestor from the other side of the family and another tradition. Angel

Jones also used what was at hand in such a way as to spiritualize its nature. We know of him only that he *sewed* his meditations into everyday garments, "Coats and britches." The matter-of-fact becomes a bearer of the miraculous without ceasing to preserve its original nature. Both ancestors were *makers*, and the poet affirms that some line is "still taut between me and them." She meditates on them, as they did on what was around them, and discovers what kind of poems she wants to make. Here she gathers up the threads which have run through the poem and weaves them together into the fabric she wants for her poems: concretion, precision, and through them the mysterious and the silent.

Such a reading of the poem seems to rest primarily on the idea-content, but what has made the ideas available to us, and filled them with their peculiar value, has much more to do with tone and rhythm, the movement along that taut line which connects the illustrious ancestors to the poet and the poet to the reader, than with the ideas themselves.

The poem does not call attention to itself; but its quiet stateliness leads us to those qualities of directness, hardness, and soundness, and finally to the suspension at the end of the poem, the slowing down which leaves us silent and still in the presence of mystery. The poem is like the ancestors, ordinary and yet illustrious, filled with light.

Both the subject matter and the treatment of "Illustrious Ancestors" lead a critic to ask what values of Hasidism have affected Denis Levertov's poetry. *The Jacob's Ladder* is introduced by one of the *Tales of the Hasidism: Later Masters* which throws light on both the form of that book and on all her poetry. Rabbi Moshe of Kobryn, meditating on the story of Jacob's ladder, sees Jacob as everyman. The ladder stands on the earth but reaches the heavens; man is one of countless shards of clay, but his soul reaches to heaven. "'And behold the angels of God ascending and descending on it'— even the ascent and descent of the angels depend on my deeds."

We may note, first of all, that the particular way Rabbi Moshe breaks open the story tells us a great deal. He speaks out of the tradition of exegesis found in the Talmud—text and commentary on it which combines the most profound respect for every word with the greatest freedom for the imagination to play on the text. The rabbi, like the artist, "maintains dialogue with his heart, meets things with his mind." Jacob and what befell him is history, but it is also allegory; it has meaning in itself and in the correspondences it reveals in all human lives. Behind this exegetical method is a specific anthropology, expressed by Denise Levertov in Saint Paul's words from the Epistle to the Romans, "we are members one of another." One finds in Hasidism a deep-rooted humanism and ethical concern. One also finds an equally deeprooted respect for the creation, this world, as an abode of holiness. Another tale of Rabbi Moshe of Kobryn, which immediately follows the one quoted in *The Jacob's Ladder*, in *Tales of the Hasidim: Later Masters*, brings all these elements together:

> The rabbi of Kobryn taught:
> God says to man, as he said to Moses: "Put off thy shoes from thy feet"—put off the habitual which encloses your foot, and you will know that the place on which you are now standing is holy ground. For there is no rung of human life on which we cannot find the holiness of God everywhere and at all times.

One *puts off* the habitual but does not repudiate it; when the habitual is seen afresh it testifies to the holy. Such a view worked out in the writing of poetry necessarily carries with it a distinct perception of the role of the poet. He can be neither the seer nor the maker as those two models have been understood by many poets since the Romantic movement; the poet is neither God who makes all things nor Adam who names all things. He is not the rebel or outcast defying God and making a contemptuous, magical fantasy world. If we do not become too enamored of the image, we might say that the poet is like Jacob in Rabbi Moshe's tale, who sees *in a dream*, the ladder between heaven and earth, who puts off the habitual and perceives the holy, and for whom seeing carries an imperative to act.

One would expect, from Denise Levertov's affinities for other poets and for her illustrious ancestors, that her poetry would be marked by delight in shapes and textures, strange, evocative words, clearly delineated scenes. She is always interested by *inwardness*, what gives meaning to shape, texture, and scene, but much of the music of her poetry comes from her delight in the details of things themselves.

The religious response to a mystery is celebration, not explanation. At her best, Denise Levertov communicates both the holiness in a scene and the "greeting of the spirit," in John Keats's phrase, which makes it real to man. "She has no superior in this clarification of a scene," says Robert Duncan, ". . . that crossing of the inner and the outer reality, where we have our wholeness of feeling in the universe."

If her poetry has its typical excellences, it has its typical weaknesses, as well. A number of the early poems fail to engage our deeper interest precisely because they assert what they do not persuade us of a meaningful correspondence between scene and an inner reality. One person's celebration can be another's dull party, after all; and though the capacity to celebrate is valuable, it does not necessarily lead to a broader range of experience or insight. Where the poems fail, they do so typically for one of two reasons: they inflate or sentimentalize an experience, or they grasp for counterparts too hastily and produce false analogies.

No method of meditation can guarantee success, and a poetry of exploration must be valued for the quality of its exploring, not merely for its success in finding, but there are inherent problems in Denise Levertov's poetic method. To wish poems to be a counterforce, to have an inner harmony "in utter contrast to the chaos in which they exist," can lead to filtering out too much of the chaos too soon. Musing, meditating, recollecting emotion in tranquility—which is a particular form of poetic meditation—can flatten out the highs and lows of a life and produce "'common speech'/ a dead level," in place of poetry. Those who have practiced the art of meditation testify how hard it is to break away from familiar ideas and stock responses; the tendency is to graft the new onto the familiar, rather than to launch forward into the threatening and the unexpected.

In "Notes of a Scale" Denise Levertov refers to one of the *Tales of the Hasidim: The Early Masters*, which might serve as a gloss on her poetry. Rabbi Elimelekh distinguishes between two kinds of wonders, those produced by magicians as illusions to surprise others, and those he calls wonders "from the true world" which God enables one to perform. The latter take the performer by surprise—they are given, not learned.

> A wonder
> from the true world,'
> he who accomplished it
> 'overwhelmed with the wonder
> which arises out of his doing,' . . .

Magic is a learned skill, which depends on drawing from one's stock with facility. The true wonders come when the learned response, the stereotypes, the methods of meditation are broken open. One may also distinguish two kinds of poems in the same way. The first rests almost entirely on the associative process taking place in the poet's mind.

The second kind of poem, the true wonder, must be difficult to describe or it would not be what it is. Some common characteristics may be suggested, however. The darker side of experience and the unconscious have more play. Things go more deeply into the poet. The poem proceeds both associatively and dialogically, in Buber's sense. Things are *themselves* first, with their own clarity and individuality; they do not lose their natures in a divine All or gain value because we perceive their symbolic meaning. Buber insists, when he speaks of the *I–Thou* relationship, that it be called *meeting* or *witnessing*. We are addressed and we answer. He speaks of the "complete relational event" which is knowing the *Thou*. ". . .No 'going beyond sense—experience' is necessary; for every experience, even the most spiritual, would yield us only an *It*. Nor is any recourse necessary to a world of ideas and values, for they cannot become presentness to us."

>From the shrivelling gray
silk of its cocoon
a creature slowly
    is pushing out
to stand clear—

                        not a butterfly,
                            petal that floats at will across
                            the summer breeze
                        not a furred
                        moth of the night
                            crusted with indecipherable
                            gold—

some primal-shaped, plain-winged, day-flying thing.

Nothing has to be said of the relational event; it requires no predicate. It need not suggest counterparts or archetypes to speak to us. This event, rightly called "The Disclosure," stands in its own radiance, and to attach qualities to it, even the quality of holiness, would lessen its value. We know someone observes what is happening, but the perceptions pursue the *via negativa* [negative way] "not a butterfly, . . . not a furred moth," until the "thing" stands clear as itself. It does not come for naming; in fact the poet never gains even that degree of power over it which comes with knowing something's name.

Louis Martz, speaking of the meditative poem in English, says that it records the creation of " . . . a self that is, ideally, one with itself, with other human beings, with created nature, and with the supernatural." The typical meditative poem begins with the fact of separation, at least the distinction of subject and object, and by processes of association, memory, imagination, and "conversation" between subject and object, it creates that self which is at one with itself and everything not-itself.

But there is another kind of meditation, found in the poetry of Robert Bly, James Wright, and Gary Snyder as well as in Denise Levertov, where the discovery or creation of the self is unimportant, and only *seeing* matters.

Zaddik, you showed me
the Stations of the Cross

and I saw
not what the almost abstract

tiles held—world upon world—
but at least

a shadow of what
might be seen there if mind and heart

gave themselves to meditation,
deeper

and deeper into Imagination's
holy forest. . . .

                    ("Letter to William Kintner")

The three books, *With Eyes at the Back of Our Heads*, *The Jacob's Ladder*, and *O Taste and See*, impress us with her serene delight in the world and pleasure in making poems which celebrate the world, "all that lives / to the imagination's tongue."

In the presence of so much which is good, one feels misanthropic to complain at what is lacking, but the poems are weakened from lack of a serious treatment of evil. The world in which "doubleness," suffering, and evil must be fought, if only to a draw, every day, is not taken very seriously in the poems.

Evil has no existence in itself but is only good "in abeyance," apparently. In "The Necessity" she takes the Hasidic image of the divine sparks encased in all things waiting for the *Teshuvah*, man's act of repentance which sets in motion God's redemption of His creation. But she uses this image to describe the making of poetry.

each part
of speech a spark
awaiting redemption, each
a virtue, a power

in abeyance unless we
give it care

> our need designs in us. Then
> all we have led away returns to us.

Even "During the Eichmann Trial," from *The Jacob's Ladder*, and "A March," from *O Taste and See*, two poems which take their subjects directly from contemporary social issues, both center on the appropriate inner response to the issue rather than on arguing a course of action.

Not until *The Sorrow Dance* (1967) and *Relearning the Alphabet* (1970) does she pursue the vision of evil any farther. With *The Sorrow Dance* she has broadened and deepened the range of her poetry to correspond to the degree of involvement she now has in social concerns. The dominant tone in the book is grief; not just in the larger occasions for grief, the death of the poet's older sister and the war in Vietnam, but even in the poems rejoicing in the natural world, where joy and the awareness of mortality support one another. In place of what Ralph Mills, Jr. called "poetry of the Immediate," we find poetry of the absent, of the hard-won insight or confirmation. The poetry is characterized by reassessment of the past and a reaching after new experiences in order to consolidate them within the self.

In grieving we prolong the pain of loss by *recollecting* both what gave us joy and what made us guilty in the relationship. The process is analogous to artistic creation in that memory and imagination work together to apprehend the significant form which makes available to us the ongoing meaning of a life or a cluster of events. Recollection leads on to incorporation of the other, forgiven and forgiving, into ourselves, and we take up life again, strengthened by the virtues and spirit of those we have lost. The whole dynamic is beautifully imaged in Denise Levertov's phrase, "The Sorrow Dance."

"The Wings" strikes the dominant note immediately. Something "heavy," "black," hangs hidden from view on the speaker's back. "I can't see it, can't move it." Is it "pure energy I store" or "black / inimical power, cold"? Is it to be identified with "terror, stupidity / of cold rage" or is it black only because it is pent up? The very simplest contrasts begin to bear complex implications. "Black" and its echo or rhyme words play off against "white" "flight," and "light." Similarly, "humped and heavy" plays off against a fountain of light," "the power of flight." But potency must always be ambiguous.

> could I go
> on one wing,
>
> the white one?

The poems abide in the ambiguity of potency. They trace its dark roots and speak of the testing which so often precedes the receiving of new power: emptiness, incapacity, frustration, and incoherence. The poet recognizes in "The Mutes" that the groans of lust a woman hears from men in the subway are "grief-language," "language stricken, sickened, cast down / in decrepitude." They are sounds of impotence but they translate into other languages—into a wordless tribute to her grace, into a changed pace, into understanding of life around her. She feels their truth on her pulse: the sounds of impotence become sounds of power as the subway train comes echoing through the tunnel to jar to a halt,

> while her understanding
>
> keeps on translating:
> 'life after life after life goes by
>
> without poetry,
> without seemliness,
> without love.'

In *O Taste and See* her metaphor for the artist was the All-Day Bird, "striving / in hope and / good faith to make his notes / ever more precise." Now it is the earthworm, "out of soil by passage / of himself /constructing / castles of metaphor!" Whereas the All-Day Bird sang full-heartedly of "Sun / light. / Light / light light light," the worm "throws off" his artifacts by contracting and expanding the "muscle of his being." The images speak of hard labor, being closed in, tilling oneself, but not for the purpose of making art. The artifacts are thrown off as a by-product of the real work, which is aerating "the ground of his living." The artist humbly makes his soul, brings vitality to the ground of living—which sounds so close to Tillich's "ground of being"—and becomes a completed self.

Descent and ascent, from the periphery to the center and out again, renewed—the patterns of the elegy shape "The Sorrow Dance." From generalized despair, the perception of formlessness and incoherence, we move to the particular cause of grief and guilt memorialized in the "Olga Poems," which are the heart of the book. Through grief, the opening up to sorrow, the return from emotional death, we reach a provisional affirmation, the beginnings of new strength. The poet recognizes the world of "The Mutes," where language is "stricken, sickened." In "The Whisper" is a world of terror "filling up fast with / unintelligible signs, . . . arhythmic." Only after the self has been reconstituted by internalizing or incorporating the object of grief within itself, confirming the worthiness of this grief, can the poet recognize that "The Closed World" was the inner world. She quotes from Blake, "If the Perceptive Organs close, their Objects seem to close also."

"Incorporation" or internalization requires facing the threatening *otherness*, the shadow side of one's existence represented by the characteristics of another person, particularly one with whom there has been an unhealed breach. In "A Lamentation" the poet translates all her sister's negative qualities into her own betrayals and denials. She has denied all grief, at the cost of the vitality of love: "Grief dismissed, / and Eros along with grief."

> That robe or tunic, black gauze
> over black and silver my sister wore
> to dance *Sorrow*, hung so long
> in my closet. I have never tried it on.
>   And my dance
> was *Summer*

To dance *Summer* betrayed her "autumn birthright" in order to please others. Sorrow always characterized Olga; denial of sorrow characterized herself, she now believes. She has betrayed not only her sister—the kind of betrayal the "easy" child feels for profiting by the sibling's difficulties—but she has betrayed her own nature as well.

She has lost definition, as has her world. "Pink sunstripes," "spaces of blue timidly steady" are her colors, not black and silver, the emblems and plumes of her sister. "There are hidden corners of sky / choked with the swept shreds, with pain and ashes." The poem achieves no resolution, but the process of opening up has begun. Blackness, darkness, shadow contend with pink and blue. Sentence fragments image the disconnectedness of her experience, the devaluing of the "I" which should be their subject.

The method of the "Olga Poems" is recollection, the calling back together of a person now "bones and tatters of flesh in earth." To recollect is also to comprehend—to grasp, to assemble in coherent form. Naturally enough, what we did not comprehend in the living person will engage us most in recollecting him. The "Olga Poems" explore the differences between the sisters, from the differences in age and physical maturation to the deep spiritual breaks between them. Olga is always the dark one, both physically and spiritually. At nine she was swept with rage and shame at seeing a slum; where her sister at the same age sees "pride in the whitened doorsteps." At an early age, *"Everything flows,"* the Heraclitean doctrine, strikes her consciousness as a counsel of despair. Her sister links the phrase to the hymn

"O God, Our Help in Ages Past," *"Time / like an everlasting stream / bears all its sons away."* She therefore puts it in the context of Christian hope.

The contrasts begin to stand clear. Olga never perceives order in her life or in the world, but she longs to impose it. She wants "to brow-beat / the poor into joy's / socialist republic," to label the disorder on her desk, base her verses on Keble's *Christian Year,* "To change, / to change the course of the river!"

> But dread
> was in her, a bloodbeat, it was against the rolling dark
> oncoming river she raised bulwarks, .

Energy and will characterize Olga, as her sister recalls her; she pits her strength *against* the flow. "What rage for order / disordered her pilgrimage." Olga is a pilgrim—a seeker after holiness—but also a "Black one, incubus," unable to be led along a peaceful path. The tension between these two makes her the cause of disaster to herself and others, "disasters bred of love."

The poet, the easy child, who trusted order and flow, must salvage from her sister's life some principle to give it meaning. She finds it in the "candle of compassion" which shone through the darkness.

> Black one, black one,
> there was a white
> candle in your heart.

"That kind candle" alone remains when the "comet's tail" of hatred, the disasters, even history had "burned down." A definition of Olga's life grows out of the images of natural force—the flame and the river—associated with her. They can represent meaningless flux—the disorder which Olga feared— but they can also image pattern, a cycle of fulfillment in which life and death have deeper meaning. Retracing her sister's life is more than an act of reconciliation, for Olga has not only been an *opposite* to come to terms with, she has also been a forerunner. Accordingly, she is example and warning. Since we must all trace some of the same steps through life to death, what must be learned is in what spirit to make the trip.

Only when we have internalized the values, or come to terms with the threats, which the loved one represented to us, can we pronounce a final benediction over him. So, in the "Olga Poems" Denise Levertov opens herself to the painful and fragmentary memories until they begin to cohere around a few images and impressions: the pilgrim, the river and the sea, the "everlasting arms," the candle, music. These she gathers up for a final re-creation of her sister's life and an affirmation of its continuing value for her. Finally, the poet remembers her sister's eyes, and the effect is as if she looks her fully in the face for the first time.

> Your eyes were the brown gold of pebbles under water.
> I never crossed the bridge over the Roding, dividing
> the open field of the present from the mysteries,
> the wraiths and shifts of time sense Wanstead Park held
>   suspended,
> without remembering your eyes. Even when we were estranged
> And my own eyes smarted with pain and anger at the thought of
>   you.
> And by other streams in other countries, anywhere where the
>   Light
> reaches down through shallows to gold gravel. Olga's
> brown eyes . . .

Here is no argument, but by the subtlest associations past and present, change and permanence, the specific and the universal come together—freighted with the most personal meaning and made available to us by that loving recollection, "Olga's brown eyes." In a fashion which recalls but does not imitate the "turn" of traditional elegy, the announcement that the loved one lives in a new form, Denise Levertov brings together those "other streams in other countries," the light reaching down to gold gravel, to create a mood of unity with the world and with her sister. In this context she can speak of their estrangement and face frankly the most terrible facts about her sister's life, not because they are now explained but because the mystery of this other life has been taken into her own, to enlarge and nourish it.

> Through the years of humiliation,
> of paranoia and blackmail and near starvation, losing
> the love of those you loved, one after another,
> parents, lovers, children, idolized friends, what kept
> compassion's candle alight in you, that lit you
> clear into another chapter (but the same book) 'a clearing
> in the selva oscura,
> a house whose door
> swings open, a hand beckons
> in welcome'?

>   I cross
> so many brooks in the world, there is so much light

> dancing on so many stones, so many questions my eyes
> smart to ask of your eyes, gold brown eyes,
> the lashes short but the lids
> arched as if carved out of olivewood, eyes with some vision
> of festive goodness in back of their hard, or veiled, or shining,
> unknowable gaze . . .

The final poem of "The Sorrow Dance" section, "To Speak," moves from lamentation to speech, from darkness to light, from the closed world to a new opening, from underground to the surface. Gathering up the themes and key words of the whole section, it confirms passage through a time of testing to a new endurance.

The disjunction of inner and outer life of which she speaks here she shows us, with authority, in these poems. She does not repudiate one of those worlds to live without tension in the other; she acknowledges the anguish of knowing both of them out of synchronization.

> I have seen
> not behind but within, within the
> dull grief, blown grit, hideous
> concrete facades, another grief, a gleam
> as of dew, an abode of mercy,
> have heard not behind but within noise
> a humming that drifted into a quiet smile.
>
> ("City Psalm")

The insight stands by itself, not to be doubted, not expected to transform the horror and grief of life. Everything becomes transparent, revealing "an otherness that was blessed, that was bliss. / *I saw Paradise in the dust of the street.*" The valuing of holiness and the capacity to abide with a mystery, qualities which marked Denise Levertov's earliest poetry, run much deeper as influences in the poetry of *The Sorrow Dance*. Emotions and words are tough and knotty; the poetry shows a distrust of aestheticizing raw emotions.

The images for the inner world in "Life at War" reveal some of the changes which the poet is undergoing in understanding the holy. One inner world is that of the "Didactic Poem," a world of dark, vampire-like spirits. Another represented by body fluids, "the mucous membrane of our dreams," "husky phlegm," struggles to throw off the corruption of the first. The war is the outward sign of this inner depravity, it is "the knowledge that jostles for space / in our bodies. . . ."

We have breathed the grits of it in, all our lives,
our lungs are pocked with it,
the mucous membrane of our dreams
coated with it, the imagination
filmed over with the grey filth of it: . . .

"Life at War" refers not only to what it feels like to be alive when a war is going on, in Denise Levertov's hands that experience broadens out to describe what it means when the self is at war *with* itself. The Closed World becomes an encysted world. She emphasizes the point in "Second Didactic Poem" by describing our task as making "the honey of the human." Again biological action symbolizes the activity of a healthy inner life. The honey of man is being " 'more ourselves' / in the making," a process of "selving," in Hopkins's fine word. Corruption, dirt, virulence, the extraneous can all be turned to "Nectar, / the makings of the incorruptible," if the creature itself is healthy.

                    enclosed and capped
with wax, the excretion
of bees' abdominal glands.
Beespittle, droppings, hairs
of beefur: all become honey.
Virulent micro-organisms cannot
survive in honey.
                    The taste,
the odor of honey:
each has no analogue but itself.

Our gathering, containing, working, "active in ourselves," creates that honey which has no analogues. In this extended metaphor, Denise Levertov has given us an image of individuation—the more powerful because it plays off against so many other images of life at war.

The decay of language and vision which operates as a major thematic thread in *The Sorrow Dance* finds expression both explicitly and in the montagelike, deliberately unfinished forms she employs in *Relearning the Alphabet*. Particularly in "An Interim" and "From a Notebook: October '68–May '69," two long poems which, with "Relearning the Alphabet," dominate the book, she borrows heavily from newspaper stories, letters, journal entries to give a documentary—and fragmentary—quality.

The titles tell a story: "Despair," "Tenebrae," "Wanting the Moon," "Not to Have," "A Defeat," "Craving," "Mad Song," "A Hunger." So do fragments and clipped sentences which make up stanzas and whole poems. "If I should find my poem is deathsongs. / If I should find it has ended, when I looked for the next step."

The vision of unity rests on a kind of innocence, but in these poems both innocence and knowledge are a kind of damnation. She pictures a Black boy grabbing armfuls of gladioli in the Detroit Riots of 1967, but her imagination can do nothing with the picture, so the boy stands there, like a daydream whose action we cannot control, "useless knowledge in my mind's eye." She repeats "Biafra, Biafra, Biafra," to enlarge the "small stock of compassion / grown in us by the imagination," "trying to make room for more knowledge in my bonemarrow," but again the imagination fails, for she can find nothing to do.

In place of the easy inspiration of her earlier poems, that assurance of the connectedness of things, the unity between life and poems, there is now hunger, "a longing silent at song's core." Useless knowledge is guilty knowledge, what the traditional phrase means by "knowledge of sin." It presents itself as burden, loss of motive, existential distrust, "useless long-ing." The organic relationship between language and reality—so important to Denise Levertov—can no longer be assumed.

> O language, mother of thought,
> are you rejecting us as we reject you?
>
> Language, coral island
> accrued from human comprehensions,
> human dreams,
>
> you are eroded as war erodes us.

In place of the old singleness of vision—which allowed "nakedness" of language and innocent inspiration—the poet sees with fractured vision, "multiple vision." "Advent 1966" speaks out of that multiple vision, contrasting Southwell's vision of the Burning Babe, "prefiguring / the Passion upon the Eve of Christmas," with our vision of the burned children of Vietnam, "as off a beltline, more, more senseless figures aflame." Christ's suffering redeems—"furnace in which souls are wrought into new life"—but the multiple, repeated suffering of the children damns.

> Because in Vietnam the vision of a Burning Babe
> is multiplied, multiplied,
>   the flesh on fire

not Christ's, as Southwell saw it, prefiguring
the passion upon the Eve of Christmas,

but wholly human and repeated, repeated,
infant after infant, their names forgotten,
their sex unknown in the ashes,
set alight, flaming but not vanishing,
not vanishing as his vision but lingering,

cinders upon the earth or living on
moaning and stinking in hosptals three abed;

because of this my strong sight,
my clear caressive sight, my poet's sight I was given
that it might stir me to song,
is blurred.

The suspended phrases, lingering over the gift of sight, fall to the harshness of "blurred." Nightmare images follow: a cataract filming over the inner eyes, a monstrous insect possessing one and looking out through the eye-sockets "with multiple vision." Sight remains strong and clear—"the insect / is not there, what I see is there"—but there is nothing for the sight to caress.

Her vision is still single, then, in that it perceives an inherent order in things, but it has enlarged to include a profound awareness of evil. In the seven-part poem, "An Interim," she contrasts the harmony of the natural world with the disorder of America and the tensions surrounding her husband's acts of resistance to the Vietnam War. "An Interim" is one exercise of several in the book probing the deepest psychological and moral problem of the radical dissenter—how to translate resistance to what he perceives as all-pervasive evil into a positive peace. Many things may support the dissenter—adherence to a clear moral code, companionship with like-minded people, outrage, but also paranoia and hatred. The poem evolves around two definitions of peace, peace represented by nature—"Peace as grandeur. Energy / serene and noble,"—and peace defined by the spiritual effect of its opposite—"The soul dwindles sometimes to an ant / rapid upon a cracked surface."

Inner peace cannot come to the resister unless he has first experienced that soul-dwindling. Like the poet, his work is to repossess the soul, but that can only be done by larger acts of restoration, including restoring virtue to language by making words accord with deeds. So the poet tests her way from one to another model of resistance, counterpointing passages praising the grandeur of ocean and sun with news accounts of a noncooperator's prison fast, reflections on the self-immolation of "the great savage saints of outrage" who burned themselves, diary entries and excerpts from the poet's letters concerning her husband's impending trial. She rejects none of the models, but affirms as her own, working "to make from outrage / islands of compassion others could build on." Of such resisters she says, "Their word if good, / language draws breath again in their *yes* and *no*, / true testimony of love and resistance."

The poem represents an attempt to regain organic form—in life more than in literary creation—not a successful discovery of form. Overcoming her "cramp of fury" leads her into diffuse and flat writing. Yet we feel behind what is more a sketch for a poem than a finished work the regaining of perspective, a renewed trust in the virtue of language and the virtue of men.

"From a Notebook: October '68–May '69" pursues the same impressionistic method, gathering up phrases of poetry, fragments from reading, distant and recent memories, intense experiences into a notebook-poem which explores the choice, "Revolution or death." This exploration proceeds on several levels—the political and social are the most obvious, but the deepest and most influential is the personal, signaled by the weaving of nineteenth-century poems about death into the fabric of her reflections. Moving into middle age has been an important theme in both *The Sorrow Dance* and *Relearning the Alphabet*; in "From a Notebook" the question of the old labor song, *"Which side are you on?"* refers not only to the choice indicated by "Revolution or death" but also by the contrast between the world of the young and that of the aging. At stake is learning how to live the second half of a life, how to grow as a poet.

The poem circles its subjects, exemplifying in its method what it "discovers" as its conclusion: that revolution just not be merely circular and life not merely linear, but that both must radiate from a center.

The rhythm of the opening section is set by the repeated phrase "Revolution or death," which acts on us as though the throb of train wheels repeated it. Working into that rhythm are those suggested by *"Which side are you on?"* and the biblical question "What makes this night different from all other nights?" Everything speaks of choice: choosing a side, being of the chosen people, choosing life with the young, because "Death is Mayor Daley," Death is also *"Unlived life / of which one can die."* Revolution is identified with "prismatic radiance pulsing from live tissue," and with resisters "blowing angel horns at the imagined corners," pronouncing a benediction over the world in an image borrowed from John Donne.

A counterstatement follows in the second section. Death is not only "the obscene sellout," it is also lovely and soothing. Over against this, the image of the pulsing brain:

                              The will to live
        pulses.   Radiant emanations
        of living tissue, visible only
        to some photo-eye we know
        sees true because mind's dream-eye,
        inward gage, confirms it.
                        Confirmation,
        a sacrament.

"How to live and the will to live," "revolution or death," objects, events, memories cluster around an unknown, shifting center which gives them "a character that throughout all transformations / reveals them connatural." Her life, seen as the tension of opposites, is also centered around something to which the opposites relate.

Enantiodromia, the being torn apart by opposites, which Jung speaks of as the problem of the mature person, aptly describes both the polarization one sees in American society and the conflicts within the self that Denise Levertov has explored since *The Sorrow Dance*; "Revolution or death" speaks simultaneously of the political and the psychic life.

Language again serves as a symbol for what is happening to the poet. Her roots are in the nineteenth century, so she is out of touch with those she most wants to know. Though she chooses revolution her words do not reach forward into it. "Language itself is my one home, my Jerusalem," but in this age of refugees she too has been uprooted.

        My diction marks me
        untrue to my time;
        change it, I'd be
        untrue to myself.

Part II is not "a going beyond" but a return and reexamination of themes. It is a meditation on revolution itself, which she describes as a new life, as like the secret uprising of the moon, as pervasive as "odor of snow, freshwater, / stink of dank / vegetation recomposing."

Her husband, an intransigent pacifist friend, A. J. Muste become human symbols of resistance, revolution, and peace-making, both because of their

own individual integrity and because the fullest human life is only a beginning.

What people can do together, as in the making of the People's Park in
Berkeley, also symbolizes the revolution. "The War / comes home to us . . ."
she says, when the People's Park is seized by the police. In the action of
clearing the land, however, she has seen "poets and dreamers studying / joy
together," finding in the cleared land a New World,

> each leaf of
> the new grass near us
> a new testament . . .

The revolution she finally affirms is like a force of nature: a tree rising
out of a flood, a sea full of swimmers, islands—like the islands of compassion
in "In the Interim"—"which step out of the waves on rock feet."

"Relearning the Alphabet" recapitulates the book, gathering up its
dominant themes, words, and images and making them the milestones of a
journey from anguish back to "the ah! of praise." The device which shapes
the poem, patterning it on the ABC books of childhood, allows many rich
influences to operate. The organization is, on the surface, simple and
arbitrary, since the sequence in which we learn the letters of the alphabet has
no significance in itself, yet it is as absolute as numeral order. This is a quest-
poem, however, and quests also move from point to point in what first
appears to be an arbitrary sequence but eventually stands out as a necessary
order where each test prepares us for the next. To relearn the alphabet
requires going back to first things, to childhood.

"Relearning the Alphabet" is a poem of exploration, retracing an inner
landscape which corresponds to the outward landscape—Vietnam, Biafra,
Boston, Milwaukee, Berkeley, Maine—over which the other poems have
ranged. What has been sought, or mourned, in those poems—joy, the moon,
inspiration—is sought here.

It is also a recapitulation of her poetic life, gathering phrases and
references from several of her own poems and from other poets, Hasidic
tales, and fairy tales. In form the poem is also a recapitulation; she has
relearned the alphabet by trying its sounds.

The poem begins in broken phrases, words displayed together
kaleidescopically, but they touch on the stages of the quest; joy to be found
in the extremes of anguish and ardor; to be relearned as unthinking knowledge; to be protected and fed with anguish and ashes.

> Joy—a beginning. Anguish, ardor.
> To relearn the ah! of knowing in unthinking

joy: the beloved stranger lives.
Sweep up anguish as with a wing-tip,
brushing the ashes back to the fire's core.

"The fire's core" runs through the poem as a signature for the contrarieties
of joy, changing and enlarging in meaning as the poet appropriates more of
her experiences and insights into the framework offered by alphabetical
order.

Hoping and wanting are important, but they make nothing happen.
Being open, following the leading, are all the questor has. She has guides on
her quest, but they lead by misdirection and by making her stumble. When
she is "called forth" by a question, she only knows what she was unable to
find:

> Lost in the alphabet
> I was looking for
> the word I can't now say
(love)

But the calling forth occurred through the love in a question, and
suddenly she finds herself home again, back from the false quests.

> I am trusted, I trust
> the real that transforms me.
>
> And relinquish
> in grief
> *the seeing that burns through, comes through*
> *to fire's core;* transformation, continuance,
> as acts of magic I would perform, are no longer
> articles of faith.

False quests are those we will ourselves to make—wanting the moon.
Being "called forth" depends on letting go, relinquishing what is most
precious to the will. The whole book has been concerned with holding onto
or recapturing vision and joy, or satisfying hunger and longing. It has been
marked by distrust of former innocence, near-repudiation of former
simplicity and easy inspiration. But always she has wanted confirmation of
her past, "transformation, continuance," and many of the poems have fought
through to magnificently enlarged vision, still rooted in "imagination's holy
forest" as she had known it. In "Relearning the Alphabet" the final
relinquishment occurs, the recognition that "acts of magic" and "articles of

faith" are "rules of the will—graceless / faithless," and that she must yield all desire, all yearning for vision or wisdom, before the treasure will disclose itself. And the treasure is a new trust, a recognition that holiness is, both in the world and in the self.

> Relearn the alphabet,
> relearn the world, the world
> understood anew only in doing, under-
> stood only as
> looked-up-into out of earth,
> the heart an eye looking,
> the heart a root
> planted in earth.
> Transmutation is not
> under the will's rule.

Everything the poet wanted has been given, but neither in the form nor with the meaning she had willed. Confirmation, joy, the fire's core—she has gained each through the making of poetry. *Relearning the Alphabet* represents a completion and a new beginning. In her "Statement on Poetics" in 1959, Denise Levertov had said, "Insofar as poetry has a social function it is to awaken sleepers by other means than shock." In her last two books we are aware of the terrible shocks she has sustained and the struggle she has passed through to regain or earn her eloquence.

> All utterance
> takes me step by hesitant step towards
> —yes, to continuance: into
> that life beyond the dead-end where
> . . . I was lost.

We find a new sophistication in her understanding of what it means to be "members one of another." It has consequences for political action, from making a people's park to conspiring against "illegitimate authority." That enlarged understanding has brought new subjects to her poetry and an enlarged practice in writing "organic" poetry. The inherent form behind things, the truth, has been sought through montage and documentary. The poetry which results sometimes seems extravagant, rough, or unfinished. But we trust it because we trust the life it comes out of and the sense of holiness which inspires Denise Levertov to write.

J. D. McCLATCHY

Anne Sexton: Somehow to Endure

Even the covers of an Anne Sexton book are contradictory. The poet posed demurely on their jackets: a sun-streaked porch, white wicker, the beads and pleated skirt, the casual cigarette. Their tame titles—literary or allusive: *To Bedlam and Part Way Back*, *All My Pretty Ones*, *Love Poems*, *Transformations*, *The Book of Folly*. And yet beyond, inside, are extraordinary revelations of pain and loss, an intensely private record of a life hungering for madness and stalked by great loves, the getting and spending of privileged moments and suffered years. The terrible urgency of the poems, in fact, seems to invite another sort of contradiction, the kind we feel only with strong poets: disappointments. Occasionally there are poems which frankly misfire for being awkward or repetitious, stilted or prosaic. [A. Alvarez] has caught it:

> So her work veers between good and terrible almost indiscriminately. It is not a question of her writing bad poems from time to time, like everybody else; she also prints them cheek by jowl with her purest work. The reason, I suppose, is that the bad poems are bad in much the same way as her good ones are good: in their head-on intimacy and their persistence in exploring whatever is most painful to the author.

From *Anne Sexton: The Artist and Her Critics.* © 1978 by J. D. McClatchy. Indiana University Press, 1978.

91

The influences on her poetry—ranging from Rilke, Lawrence, Rimbaud and Smart, to Jarrell, Roethke, Lowell, Plath, and C. K. Williams—were easily acquired, obviously displayed, and often quickly discarded, while a few deeper influences—like that of Neruda—were absorbed and recast. She described herself as "a primitive," yet was master of intricate formal techniques. Her voice steadily evolved and varied and, at times, sought to escape speaking of the self, but her strongest poems consistently return to her narrow thematic range and the open voice of familiar feelings. *Do I contradict myself? Very well then I contradict myself.* For the source of her first fame continued as the focus of her work: she was the most persistent and daring of the confessionalists. Her peers have their covers: Lowell's allusiveness, Snodgrass's lyricism, Berryman's dazzle, Plath's expressionism. More than the others, Sexton resisted the temptations to dodge or distort, and the continuity and strength of her achievement remain the primary witness to the ability of confessional art to render a life into poems with all the intimacy and complexity of feeling and response with which that fife has been endured.

Endurance was always her concern: why must we? how can we? why we must, how we do: "to endure,/somehow to endure." It is a theme which reenacts not only the sustained source of her poetry but its original impulse as well. At the age of twenty-eight, while recovering from a psychotic break-down and suicide attempt, she began writing poems on the advice of her psychiatrist: "In the beginning, the doctor said, 'Write down your feelings because someday they might mean something to somebody. No matter how despairing you are, there are other people going through this who can't express it, and if they should read it they would feel less alone.' And so he gave me my little reason to go on; it shifted around, but that was always a driving, driving force." . . .

Surprisingly little has been written with any authority on the subject of confessionalism, which has become, under the rubric of "sincerity," an impulse behind many of the significant social movements and styles since 1960.

One of the few studies available is Theodor Reik's *The Compulsion to Confess*, a work which, while hardly exhaustive, at least opens up a few theoretical approaches toward an understanding of the "compulsion" and its results. Broadly, Reik defines a confession as "a statement about impulses or drives which are felt or recognized as forbidden," and their expression involves both the repressed tendency and the repressing forces. If this secular interpretation seems to exclude the usual religious (and even legal) sense of the term as narrowed to facts and intentions, they can easily be added to Reik's definition without any loss to the force of his point.

To some extent, then, the poetry is therapeutic; or as D. H. Lawrence said, "One sheds one's sicknesses in books—repeats and presents again one's emotions, to be master of them." Eric Erikson underscores this aspect of the situation by reminding that "the individual's mastery over his neurosis begins where he is put in a position to accept the historical necessity which made him what he is." Acceptance becomes survival. Anne Sexton: "writing, and especially having written, is evidence of survival—the books accumulate ego-strength." And so confessional poets are driven back to their losses, to that alienation—from self and others, from sanity and love—which is the thematic center of their vision and work. The betrayals in childhood, the family romance, the divorces and madnesses, the suicide attempts, the self-defeat and longing—the poets pursue them in their most intimate and painful detail. . . .

We learn what we are by relearning what we have become. But what is important to note now is the essentially narrative structure of the process, of one's experiences recounted in this time as remembered in their own past time. And narrative is likewise the most distinctive structural device in confessional poetry. The importance and integrity of chronology affect both the way in which individual poems are composed and the way they are collected into sequences and volumes, and these arrangements, in turn, are of thematic importance as facts or memories, shifting desires or needs or anxieties or gratifications change the landscape of personality. Sexton's poem "The Double Image," for instance, is a closely written and carefully parted account of her hospitalization and her necessary separation from her mother's shame and her daughter's innocence. The poem opens with the specificity of the achieved present—"I am thirty this November. . . . We stand watching the yellow leaves go queer"—and then drifts back through three years of madness and bitter history, to Bedlam and part way back, its larger thematic concerns held in precise details—dates, objects, places, names—among which are studded still smaller stories that memory associates with the main narrative. The destructions that survival implies in the poem are given their haunting force and authenticity by the history which the narrative leads the reader through so that he himself experiences the dramatic life of events and feelings. . . .

The rhetorical importance of confessional subject matter—especially insofar as it involves a characteristically Freudian epistemology—leads, in turn, to another consideration. In his most important gloss on the mediation of art, Freud wrote: "The essential *ars poetica* lies in the technique of overcoming the feeling of repulsion in us which is undoubtedly connected with the barriers that rise between each single ego and the others." Or between the single ego and its history, he might have added. And among the barriers the self constructs are the familiar defense mechanisms: repression, displacement, suppression, screen memories, condensation, projection, and so on. Such psychological techniques, in turn, have their rhetorical analogues, not surprisingly those most favored by modernist poets and their New Critics: paradox, ambiguity, ellipsis, allusion, wit, and the other "tensions" that correspond to the neurotic symptoms by which the self is obscured. And in order to write with greater directness and honesty about their own experiences, Sexton and the other confessional poets have tended to avoid the poetic strategies of modernism—to de-repress poetry, so to speak—and have sought to achieve their effects by other means. Sexton's turn toward open forms, as though in trust, is an example. In general, it can be said of Sexton's poems, as of other confessional poems, that the patterns they assume and by which they manage their meanings are those which more closely follow the actual experiences they are recreating—forms that can include and reflect direct, personal experience; a human, rather than a disembodied voice; the dramatic presentation of the flux of time and personality; and the drive toward sincerity. By this last concept is meant not an ethical imperative, but the willed and willing openness of the poet to her experience and to the character of the language by which her discoveries are revealed and shared. Not that the structures of sincerity abandon every measure of artifice. While she may have associated the imagination so strongly with memory, Sexton realized as well that the self's past experiences are neither provisional nor final, that even as they shape the art that describes them, so too they are modified by that very art. The flux of experience, rather than its absolute truth, determines which concerns or wounds are returned to in poem after poem, either because they have not yet been understood or because the understanding of them has changed. And Sexton is sharply aware, in her work, of the difference between factual truth and poetic truth— of the need to "edit" out, while trying not to distort, redundant or inessential "facts" in the service of cleaner, sharper poems. In a crucial sense, confessional art is a means of *realizing* the poet.

As the poet realizes himself, inevitably he catches up the way we live now: especially the personal life, since our marriages are more difficult than our wars, our private nightmares more terrifying than our public horrors. In addition, then, to our sense of the confessional poet as a survivor, he or she functions as a kind of witness. What may have begun as a strictly private need is transformed, once it is published, into a more inclusive focus—and here one recalls Whitman's "attempt, from first to last, to put a *Person*, a human being (myself, in the latter half of the Nineteenth Century, in America) freely, fully, and truly on record." The more naked and directly emotional nature of confessional poems heightens the integrity and force of their witness to the inner lives of both poets and readers; or, as Sexton has remarked, "poems of the inner life can reach the inner lives of readers in a way that anti-war poems can never stop a war." The final privatism of poetry itself, in other words, affords the confessional poet a certain confidence in using the details of intimate experience in ways that earlier would have been considered either arrogant or obscure. And the ends to which those details are put are not merely self-indulgent or self-therapeutic—or, in Robert Lowell's phrase, "a brave heart drowned on monologue." Of her own work, Anne Sexton once reminisced: "I began to think that if one life, somehow made into art, were recorded—not all of it, but like the testimony on an old tombstone—wouldn't that be worth something? Just one life—a poor middle-class life, nothing extraordinary (except maybe madness, but that's so common nowadays)—that seems worth putting down. It's the thing I have to do, the thing I want to do—I'm not sure why." And she went on to describe a reader's response to this "testimony": "I think, I hope, a reader's response is: 'My God, this has happened. And in some real sense it has happened to me too.' This has been my reaction to other poems, and my readers have responded to my poems in just this way."

Perhaps the most telling evidence of this sort of response are the countless letters that anonymous readers sent to Sexton, explaining how her poetry revealed their own troubled lives to them and often making impossible demands on the poet, so strong was the readers' sense of the real, suffering person in the poetry. It is no wonder that, with bitter wit, Sexton once described herself in a poem as "mother of the insane." But at a deeper level, there is some dark part in any one of us which her work illuminated, often distressingly. Like Wordsworth, who wished to allow his audience "new compositions of feeling," Sexton's response to her own experience becomes a model for a reader's response to his or her own. The poems function as instruments of discovery for the reader as well as for the poet, and the process of discovery—ongoing through poems and collections, as through life—is as important as the products, the poems which the poet has drawn directly out of her experience, often as isolated stays against confusion. The immediacy of impact and response, and the mutual intimacy between poet and reader, correspond with an observation by Ernst Kris on aesthetic distance: "When psychic distance is maximal, the response is philistine or intellectualistic. At best, the experience is one of passive receptivity rather than active participation of the self. . . . [But] when distance is minimal the reaction to works of art is pragmatic rather than aesthetic." To emphasize the "pragmatic" response of readers to this poetry—even though the term describes the response of most poets to their experience, however the subsequent poem may inform it—may be viewed as an effort to minimize the "art" of the poems. I hope my subsequent remarks will describe that art sufficiently, or at least with more attention to real questions than most critics have so far paid Sexton.

Despite the authority and abundance in *To Bedlam and Part Way Back*, Sexton was careful, perhaps compelled, to include an apologia, a poem called "For John, Who Begs Me Not to Enquire Further"—addressed to her discouraging teacher John Holmes, and so finally to the critic in herself. The poem's title echoes the book's epigraph, from a letter of Schopenhauer to Goethe concerning the courage necessary for a philosopher: "He must be like Sophocles's Oedipus, who, seeking enlightenment concerning his terrible fate, pursues his indefatigable enquiry, even when he divines that appalling horror awaits him in the answer. But most of us carry in our heart the Jocasta who begs Oedipus for God's sake not to inquire further. . . ." The sympathy she can afford for Homes—"although your fear is anyone's fear,/like an invisible veil between us all"—recalls Freud's sense of the repulsion with the self and others which art overcomes. Her cautious justification is modeled on her psychiatrist's plea: "that the worst of anyone/can be, finally,/an accident of hope." And the standard she sets herself is simply making sense:

> Not that it was beautiful,
> but that, in the end, there
> was a certain sense of order there;
> something worth learning
> in that narrow diary of my mind,
> in the commonplaces of the asylum
> where the cracked mirror
> or my own selfish death
> outstared me.

Part of that order is substantive and thematic, the urge to recover and understand the past: "I have this great need somehow to keep that time of my life, that feeling. I want to imprison it in a poem, to keep it. It's almost in a way like keeping a scrapbook to make life mean something as it goes by, to rescue it from chaos—to make 'now' last." But if the ability to extend the past and present into each other further depends upon the orders of art, that art cannot succeed without a prior commitment to honesty—or, to use Sexton's peculiar term, as a confessional poet she must start with a wise passivity, with being "still." That word occurs in her poem about the tradition, "Portrait of an Old Woman on the College Tavern Wall," where the poets sit "singing and lying/around their round table/and around me still." "Why do these poets lie?" the poem goes on to question, and leaves them with mortal irony "singing/around their round table/until they are still." Whether death or silence, this "stillness" is the view of experience, both prior to and beyond language, from which her ordering proceeds. The difficulty, as she knows in another poem, "Said The Poet to The Analyst," is that "My business is words":

> I must always forget how one word is able to pick
> out another, to manner another, until I have got
> something I might have said . . .
> but did not.

The business of the Analyst—again, an internal figure, a sort of artistic conscience—is "watching my words," guarding against the Jocasta who would settle for "something I might have said" instead of what must be revealed.

Sexton's business with words—the ordering of statement and instinct—is the adjustment of their demands to her experience: in her figure, to make a tree out of used furniture. Though her attitudes toward form evolved, from the beginning there was an uneasy ambivalence: the poet insisting on control, the person pleading, "Take out rules and leave the instant," as she said in one interview. Her solution was to use the metaphor of deceit, but to reverse it into a very personally inflected version of form:

> I think all form is a trick to get at the truth. Sometimes in my hardest poems, the ones that are difficult to write, I might make an impossible scheme, a syllabic count that is so involved, that it then allows me to be truthful. It works as a kind of super-ego. It says, "You may now face it, because it will be impossible ever to get out" . . . But you see how I say this not to deceive you, but to deceive me. I deceive myself, saying to myself you can't do it, and then if I can get it, then I have deceived myself, then I can change it and do what I want. I can even change and rearrange it so no one can see my trick. It won't change what's real. It's there on paper.

Though her early work occasionally forces itself with inversions and stolid High Style, her concern for the precisions of voice and pace reveal her care in indulging a lyric impulse only to heighten the dramatic. What Richard Howard has said of her use of rhyme is indicative of her larger sense of form: "invariably it is Sexton's practice to use rhyme to bind the poem, irregularly invoked, abandoned when inconvenient, psychologically convincing." The truth—getting tricks, in other words, serve as a method of conviction for both poet and reader. For the poet, form functions to articulate the details and thrust of her actual experience, while for the reader it guides his dramatic involvement in the re-creation: both convictions converging on authenticity, on realization. And so the voice is kept conversational, understated by plain-speech slang or homely detail—its imagery drawn from the same sources it counterpoints, its force centered in the pressure of events it contours, the states of mind it maps. This is clearly the case with the poems of madness in the first section of *To Bedlam and Part Way Back.*

M. L. Rosenthal has seen in these poems "the self reduced to almost infantile regression," but more often the voice is that of an older child, which implies a consciousness that can experience the arbitrariness of authority and the sufferings of loss without understanding either chance or cause. The inferno of insanity opens, appropriately, with the poet lost in the dark wood of her "night mind":

> And opening my eyes, I am afraid of course
> to look—this inward look that society scorns—
> Still I search in these woods and find nothing worse
> than myself, caught between the grapes and the thorns.
> ("Kind Sir: These Woods")

The disorientation necessitates the search: here, the descent into her own underworld, as later she will ascend part way back. Likewise, the figure of the child—so important in Part Two, where it subsumes both the poet and her daughter—introduces the themes of growth and discovery, of the growth into self by discovering its extremes, as in the poem addressed to her psychiatrist:

> And we are magic talking to itself,
> noisy and alone. I am queen of all my sins
>   forgotten. Am I still lost?
>   Once I was beautiful. Now I am myself,
> counting this row and that row of moccasins
>   waiting on the silent shelf.
> ("You, Dr. Martin")

The struggle to find "which way is home" involves the dissociation and resumption of different personalities ("Her Kind," "The Expatriates," "What's That"), the limits of paranoia and mania ("Noon Walk on the

Asylum Lawn," "Lullaby"), and the dilemma of memory that drives pain toward exorcism ("You, Dr. Martin," "Music Swims Back to Me," "The Bells," "Said the Poet to the Analyst").

Though, as she says, there is finally "no word for time," the need to restore it is the essential aspect of the ordering process:

> Today is made of yesterday, each time I steal
> toward rites I do not know, waiting for the lost
> ingredient, as if salt or money or even lust
> would keep us calm and prove us whole at last.
>
> ("The Lost Ingredient")

What has been lost, along with sanity, is the meaning of those who made her, and this first book introduces us to the cast she will reassemble and rehearse in all her subsequent work, even through "Talking to Sheep" and "Divorce, Thy Name is Woman" in *45 Mercy Street:* the hapless boozy father, the helpless cancer-swollen bitch of a mother, the daughters as both victims and purifiers, the shadowy presence of her husband, the analyst as dark daddy and muse, the clutching company of doomed poets—and most touchingly, the great-aunt whom she calls Nana. Sexton's obsession with her Nana—the "Nana-hex" she calls it later—results from both sympathy and guilt. "She was, during the years she lived with us, my best friend, my teacher, my confidante and my comforter. I never thought of her as being young. She was an extension of myself and was my world." For this very reason, when her great-aunt, after a sudden deafness, had a nervous breakdown from which she never recovered, the poet could find her both an emblem of her own suffering and a source of guilt for fear she had somehow caused it. Nana is brought on tenderly in the lyrical elegy "Elizabeth Gone," but in the next poem, "Some Foreign Letters," her life is used as the focus of the poet's own anxieties as she sits reading the letters her great-aunt had sent to her family as a young woman on her Victorian Grand Tour. The poem proceeds by verse and refrain—Nana's letters of her youth, the poet's images of the same woman different—to point up the disjunction between memories: Nana's diaried ones, which have trapped her youth in an irretrievable past, and the poet's own memories of Nana trapped in age and lost to death:

> Tonight your letters reduce
> history to a guess. The Count had a wife.
> You were the old maid aunt who lived with us.
> Tonight I read how the winter howled around
> the towers of Schloss Schwöbber, how the tedious

language grew in your jaw, how you loved the sound
of the music of the rats tapping on the stone
floors. When you were mine you wore an earphone.

The "guilty love" with which the poem ends is the poet's own ambivalent response to her inability to have rescued her Nana—even as she realizes she will not be able to save herself—from the facts that are fate, a fife that cannot be unlived or chosen. The last stanza's pathos derives from its prediction of what has already occurred, the proof that guilt is suffered again and again:

Tonight I will learn to love you twice;
learn your first days, your mid-Victorian face.
Tonight I will speak up and interrupt
your letters, warning you that wars are coming,
that the Count will die, that you will accept
your America back to live like a prim thing
on a farm in Maine. I tell you, you will come
here, to the suburbs of Boston, to see the blue-nose
world go drunk each night, to see the handsome
children jitterbug, to feel your left ear close
one Friday at Symphony. And I tell you,
you will tip your boot feet out of that hall,
rocking from its sour sound, out onto
the crowded street, letting your spectacles fall
and your hair net tangle as you stop passers-by
to mumble your guilty love while your ears die.

The poet speaks her warning here not as a suspicious Jocasta but as a knowing Tiresias, helpless before time, that most visible scar of mortality. And the family to which she resigns Nana is, of course, her own as well, and the self-recovery which the volume's arrangement of poems plots necessarily moves to recover her parents, as so much of her later work too will do.

The book's second section is The Part Way Back, in the sense of both return and history. The painful realizations of adjustment, the lessons of loss and recovery weight the book's two anchor poems—"The Double Image" and "The Division of Parts." They are long poems, explorations lengthened to accommodate their discoveries and unresolved dilemmas, and extended by subtle modulations of voice and structure to dramatize their privacies. "The Double Image," the book's strongest and most ambitious poem, is actually a sequence of seven poems tracing the terms of Sexton's dispossession—similar to Snodgrass's "Heart's Needle," which was its model. The other poem, which clearly echoes Snodgrass's voice as well, is an independent summary of her losses, and makes the subsequent poems seem to have insisted themselves on her later. If that was the case, there is reason for it, since the jagged lines of the first poem reflect the uncertain hesitancy in naming the guilt that had caused her self-hatred and her suicide attempts and breakdown. It is addressed, in retrospect, to the daughter whose infant illness released the long-held guilt:

> a fever rattled
> in your throat and I moved like a pantomime
> above your head. Ugly angels spoke to me. The blame,
> I heard them say, was mine. They tattled
> like green witches in my head, letting doom
> leak like a broken faucet;
> as if doom had flooded my belly and filled your bassinet,
> an old debt I must assume.

She tries to solve her life with death—"I let the witches take away my guilty soul"—but is forced back from the "time I did not love/myself" to face the new life she has made in her child and the old life she had made for herself. She assumes the old debts in the following narrative of her recovery. If the first poem turned on her commitment and the loss of her daughter, the second turns on her release and the loss of her mother, to whom she returns as "an angry guest," "an outgrown child." The poet had grown "well enough to tolerate/myself," but her mother cannot forgive the suicide attempt and so cannot accept her daughter: she "had my portrait/done instead," a line that refrains the tedium and repressed menace that punches out each stanza. The tension of presence begins to sort the past; the church is another Bedlam, her parents her keepers:

> There was a church where I grew up
> with its white cupboards where they locked us up,
> row by row, like puritans or shipmates
> singing together. My father passed the plate.
> Too late to be forgiven now, the witches said.
> I wasn't exactly forgiven. They had my portrait
> done instead.

The third poem opens up the deaths in and of relationships. Sexton's distance from her own daughter gains its double reference: "as if it were

normal/to be a mother and be gone." As the poet gathers her strength, her
mother sickens, and madness, love-loss, and death are drawn into a single
figure which points again at guilt. Her mother's cancer—"as if my dying had
eaten inside of her"—accuses Sexton with questions that "still I couldn't
answer." The fourth poem is centered as an interlude of partial return and
acceptance: Sexton back from Bedlam, her mother from the hospital, her
daughter from the exile of innocence. The fact of survival converts its
sterility into patience: the blank, facing portraits mirror the reversal of
concern:

> During the sea blizzards
> she had her
> own portrait painted.
> A cave of a mirror
> placed on the south wall;
> matching smile, matching contour.
> And you resembled me; unacquainted
> with my face, you wore it. But you were mine
> after all.

The fifth poem begins to draw the women together into a chorus, their roles
merging into a new knowledge:

> And I had to learn
> why I would rather
> die than love, how your innocence
> would hurt and how I gather
> guilt like a young intern
> his symptoms, his certain evidence.
>
> We drove past the hatchery,
> the hut that sells bait,
> past Pigeon Cove, past the Yacht Club, past Squall's
> Hill, to the house that waits
> still, on the top of the sea,
> and two portraits hang on opposite walls.

The sixth is a self-study, the poet finding herself in the distanced image of
her mother, as in the next poem she discovers how selfish are the maternal
motives of love. But in this poem, it is the process of life that learns from *la
nature morte*:

> And this was the cave of the mirror,
> that double woman who stares
> at herself, as if she were petrified
> in time—two ladies sitting in umber chairs.
> You kissed your grandmother
> and she cried.

The final poem, again addressed to the poet's daughter, summarizes her learning:

> You learn my name,
> wobbling up the sidewalk, calling and crying.
> You call me *mother* and I remember my mother again,
> somewhere in greater Boston, dying.

But the last stanza unwinds into a tentative resumption of guilt—its last line speaking, with an odd irony, the voice of Jocasta: "And this was my worst guilt; you could not cure/ nor soothe it. I made you to find me."

In "The Division of Parts," Sexton carries the account past her mother's death, which has left her, on Good Friday, with "gifts I did not choose." The last hospital days are retold, and the numbness with which they stun her implies the larger truth of the poem:

> But you turned old,
> all your fifty-eight years sliding
> like masks from your skull;
> and at the end I packed your nightgowns in suitcases,
> paid the nurses, came riding
> home as if I'd been told
> I could pretend
> people live in places.

But people live not in space or places, but in time and in others, and their demands puzzle the poet's guilt: "Time, that rearranger/ of estates, equips/me with your garments, but not with grief." Her inheritance steals on her "like a debt," and she cannot expiate her loss: "I planned to suffer/and I cannot." Unlike "Jesus, *my stranger,*" who assumed "old debts" and knew how and why to suffer, Sexton is emptied of belief by need:

> Fool! I fumble my lost childhood
> for a mother and lounge in sad stuff
> with love to catch and catch as catch can.

> And Christ still waits. I have tried
> to exorcise the memory of each event
> and remain still, a mixed child,
> heavy with cloths of you.
> Sweet witch, you are my worried guide.

In this book Sexton realizes the motive of her subsequent books: "For all the way I've come/I'll have to go again." Only ever part way back, she tries her art against her mind—"I would still curse/ you in my rhyming words/ and bring you flapping back, old love"—but her litany of incantatory adjectives cannot lose loss, and if she cannot love it, she has learned to live it.

The religious note introduced at the end of *To Bedlam and Part Way Back*, evoked by the death which aligns it with other needs and losses, is even more apparent in her next book, *All My Pretty Ones* (1962). Two of its best-known poems—"For God While Sleeping" and "In the Deep Museum"—are really part of a much larger group that threads through all her collections, on through "The Jesus Papers" in *The Book of Folly* and into "Jesus Walking" in *The Death Notebooks* and the major poems in *The Awful Rowing Toward God*, whose title best describes the project. Though she herself referred to these poems as "mystical," they are more obviously religious since their concerns are always the human intricacies of need and belief, and their context is Sexton's need for belief and her inability to believe as that dilemma interacts with her relationships to herself and others, the dead and dying. This explains too why her religious poetry centers almost exclusively on the person of Jesus, the central figure of belief who himself despaired at the end, who brought love and found none, who gave life and was nailed to a tree. But her relationship to Jesus, as it develops through the books, is an ambivalent one. On the one hand, he serves as a sympathetic emblem of her own experience: "That ragged Christ, that sufferer, performed the greatest act of confession, and I mean with his body. And I try to do that with words." This is the force of the poems in *All My Pretty Ones*. To touch a crucifix—"I touch its tender hips, its dark jawed face,/ its solid neck, its brown sleep"—is to remind herself of poetry's work for salvation:

> My friend, my friend, I was born
> doing reference work in sin, and born
> confessing it. This is what poems are:
> with mercy
> for the greedy,
> they are the tongue's wrangle,
> the world's pottage, the rat's star.
>   ("With Mercy for the Greedy")

The Christ who is "somebody's fault," like the poet, is "hooked to your own weight,/jolting toward death under your nameplate" ("For God While Sleeping"). But at the same time, Sexton is fascinated by another Jesus: "Perhaps it's because he can forgive sins." Like her psychiatrist, Jesus is a man who can take on her guilt, a man who suffers with her and for her. This is the Jesus "In the Deep Museum," where gnawing rats are the "hairy angels who take my gift," as he blesses "this other death": "Far below The Cross, I correct its flaws. Her purest statement of this sense of Christ comes in *The Death Notebooks*, in "Jesus Walking": "To pray, Jesus knew,/is to be a man carrying a man." It is the simplicity of such strength which takes the measure of weaker men in her life, especially her father, whose death brings him into the poetry of *All My Pretty Ones. . . .*

[But her] decisive book, *Live or Die* (1966), announces [important changes.] With its longer poems in open forms which more subtly accommodate a greater range of experience, and with a voice pitched higher to intensify that experience, *Live or Die* represents not a departure from her earlier strengths but the breakthrough into her distinctive style. Perhaps the most immediate aspect of that style is its more extravagant use of imagery:

> I sat all day
> stuffing my heart into a shoe box,
> avoiding the precious window
> as if it were an ugly eye
> through which birds coughed,
> chained to the heaving trees;
> avoiding the wallpaper of the room
> where tongues bloomed over and over,
> bursting from lips like sea flowers. . . .
>
> ("Those Times . . .")

This is the sort of imagery that will be even more exploited in later books where "like" becomes the most frequently encountered word. It is a technique that risks arbitrary excesses and embarrassing crudities, that at its best can seem but a slangy American equivalent of Apollinaire's surrealism: *Les nuages coulaient cornme un flux menstruel.* But it is crucial to remember, with Gaston Bachelard, that "we live images synthetically in their initial complexity, often giving them our unreasoned allegiance." And Sexton's use of images is primarily psychotropic—used less for literary effect than as a means to pry deeper into her psychic history, to float her findings and model her experience. As she said, "The poetry is often more advanced, in terms of my unconscious, than I am. Poetry, after all, milks the unconscious. . . .

"Images are the heart of poetry. And this is not tricks. Images come from the unconscious. Imagination and the unconscious are one and the same. . . ." And if Rimbaud was right to demand of such associative poetry a *"dérèglement de tous les sens,"* it can be seen as Sexton's necessary road of excess through her experiences of madness and the disorientation of her past, so that her metaphors are a method not to display similarities but to discover identities.

Although *Live or Die* shows, for this reason, the influence of her readings in Roethke and Neruda, a more important factor was the new analyst she began seeing while at work on this book. He was more interested in dreams than her earlier doctors had been, and Sexton found herself dealing more directly with her unconscious: "You taught me/to believe in dreams) thus I was the dredger" ("Flee on Your Donkey"). Several poems in *Live or Die* are direct dream-songs—"Three Green Windows," "Imitations of Drowning," "Consorting with Angels," "In the Beach House," and "To Lose the Earth." The latent content in these poems—such as the primal scene of "the royal strapping" in "In the Beach House"—is expressive but abandoned to its own independence, unlike more conscious fantasies such as "Menstruation at Forty," in which themes of death and incest are projected onto the imagined birth of a son. The insistence of the unconscious also draws up the poems of her childhood—"Love Song," "Protestant Easter," and especially "Those Times . . .," one of the book's triumphs. Robert Boyers has described *Live or Die* as "a poetry of victimization, in which she is at once victim and tormentor," and "Those Times . . ." torments the poet with her earliest memories of victimization: "being the unwanted, the mistake/that Mother used to keep Father/from his divorce." Her suffering was as silent as her envy of a doll's perfection:

> I did not question the bedtime ritual
> where, on the cold bathroom tiles,
> I was spread out daily
> and examined for flaws.

But her felt exclusion was assumed and rehearsed in a closet's dark escape, where she sat with her hurts and dreams, as later she would sit in madness and poetry:

> I did not know that my life, in the end,
> would run over my mother's like a truck
> and all that would remain
> from the year I was six
> was a small hole in my heart, a deaf spot,
> so that I might hear
> the unsaid more clearly.

   The other crucial influence on *Live or Die is* the play she wrote at the time—first titled *Tell Me Your Answer True* and eventually produced in 1969 as *Mercy Street*—sections of which were carried over as poems into *Live or Die* and lend the book its character of psychodrama. Sexton's description of herself during a poetry reading could apply to her presence in this book as well: "I am an actress in my own autobiographical play." The vitality, even the violence, of the book's drama of adaptation recall Emily Dickinson's sly lines:

> Men die—externally—
> It is a truth—of Blood—
> But we—are dying in Drama—
> And Drama—is never dead.

To match the expansive forms and intense imagery of these poems, the voice that speaks them grows more various in its effects, matching a strident aggression or hovering tenderness with the mood and matter evoked. Above all, there is energy, whether of mania or nostalgia. And it is more expressly vocative here, as her cast is introduced separately and her relationship to each is reworked: her father ("And One for My Dame"), mother ("Christmas Eve"), daughters ("Little Girl, My Stringbean, My Lovely Woman," "A Little Uncomplicated Hymn," "Pain for a Daughter"), husband ("And One for My Dame," "Man and Wife," "Your Face on the Dog's Neck"), and Nana ("Crossing the Atlantic," "Walking in Paris"). There is a very conscious sense about these poems of the times since her first book that she has spent with her living and her dead. "A Little Uncomplicated Hymn," for instance, alludes directly to "The Double Image" to catch at a perspective for the interval; the new poem, according to Sexton, was the "attempt to master that experience in light of the new experience of her life and how it might have affected her and how it affects me still; she wasn't just an emblem for me any longer. Every book, every poem, is an attempt to master things that aren't ever quite mastered." And so one watches her recircling her experiences to define and refine her understanding of them. Her parents are written of more sharply, and her regret is less for what she has lost than for what she never had. Her great-aunt's account of her youth in Europe, which structures "Some Foreign Letters," was the motive for Sexton's attempt to retrace in person Nana's Journey—"I'd peel your life back to its stare"—both to solve the riddle of Other People ("I come back to your youth, my Nana,/ as if I might clean off/ the mad woman you became,/ withered and constipated,/ howling into your own earphone"), and so to solve her own origins ("You are my history (that stealer of children)/ and I have entered you"). But the attempt is not only abandoned, it is impossible, she cannot walk off her history, the past cannot be toured, only endured: where I am is hell. . . .

The demand for release into life, as the title *Live or Die* balances her options, is the counterweight to the measure of death in the book, scaled from suicide attempts ("Wanting to Die," "The Addict") to the deaths of past figures who were part of her—John Holmes ("Somewhere in Africa") and Sylvia Plath ("Sylvia's Death"). "Flee on Your Donkey" struggles with the ambiguous impatience, introducing it first as weariness with "allowing myself the wasted life": "I have come back/ but disorder is not what it was./ I have lost the trick of it!/ the innocence of it!" Her desire for communion—"In this place everyone talks to his own mouth"—reverses her earlier escape inward: "Anne, Anne,/ flee on your donkey,/ flee this sad hotel." And by the time she can write the simple title "Live" over the book's last poem, the "mutilation" that previous poems had struck off is renounced. The evidence of survival is enough: "Even so,/ I kept right on going,/ a sort of human statement" that says finally: "I am not what I expected." If her guilt has not been solved, it has at least been soothed by her acceptance of and by her "dearest three"— her husband and daughters. And if the resolution of "Live" sounds unconvinced, unconvincing, it is because of Sexton's dependence on others, lulling the self into a passive tense.

The survival achieved, the rebirth delivered, is then praised in *Love Poems* (1969), in many ways her weakest collection. . . . The masks she wears in *Love Poems* don't hide Sexton's confessional impulse, they avoid it. Her motive may well have been to search out new voices. Certainly this is the case with her next work, *Transformations* (1971). She began these versions of Grimms' tales on the advice of her daughter after an extended dry spell in her work, and when, five poems later, she had written "Snow White and the Seven Dwarfs," she felt she should continue the experiment into a book which would release a more playful aspect of her personality that her earlier books had neglected. . . .

The book's Ovidian title points to Sexton's first fascination with Grimm—one which Randall Jarrell spoke of in his poem "The Märchen":

> Had you not learned—have we not learned, from tales
> Neither of beasts nor kingdoms nor their Lord,
> But of our own hearts, the realm of death—
> Neither to rule nor die? to change, to change!

The power of fairy tales has always resided in their "changed" dream-landscapes, and Freud discussed them as "screen memories," survivals of persistent human conflicts and desires, narratives whose characters and situations are symbolic of the unconscious dramas in any individual's psyche. With this in mind, the psychoanalytical uses of the word "transformations" bear on Sexton's work. It can refer both to the variations of the same thematic material represented in a patient's dreams of experience and to the process by which unconscious material is brought to consciousness. So too Sexton's poems are variations on themes familiar from her earlier work—at one point she says, "My guilts are what/ we catalogue"—transformed into fantasies or dreams discovered in the Grimm tales, which are anyone's first "literature" and become bound up with the child's psyche. The introductions that precede each story—replacing the analogous moral pointing in the fairy tale—usually isolate her more private concern in each, and the tales which elaborate them include subjects ranging from adultery ("The Little Peasant") to despair ("Rumpelstiltskin") to deception ("Red Riding Hood") to parents' devouring their children ("Hansel and Gretel") . . . .

The fabular impulse behind *Transformations* is resumed in *The Book of Folly* (1972), both in the three short stories included among the poems and in "The Jesus Papers" sequence, which is a taunting, Black-mass transformation of the salvation story. The entire book, in fact, has a summary quality to it. The forged stylization of *Love Poems* returns in "Angels of the Love Affair," six sonnets on love's seasons. The angel in each is the "gull that grows out of my back in the dreams I prefer," and those dreams are hushed, flamboyant, touching memories of certain sheets, bits of dried blood, lemony woodwork, a peace march—all the abstracted details of moments that are warm only in her darknesses. But what is more important is her return to the fully confessional mode: "I struck out memory with an X/ but it came back./ I tied down time with a rope/ but it came back" ("Killing the Spring"). On the simplest level, the detritus of time has clustered new collisions or crises: the death of her sister—"her slim neck/ snapped like a piece of celery" in a car crash—or the national disasters ("The Firebombers," "The Assassin"). Generally, the subjects she recircles are familiar, but her angle of attack and attitude is new: more self-conscious, often more strident and defiant, more searching. . . .

It is the sense of what still remains to be lost that occasions a tonal shift. In contrast with "You, Dr. Martin" or "Cripples and Other Stories," a new poem to her psychiatrist, "The Doctor of the Heart," is scornfully reductive, resentful of the soothing instead of solving, challenging the doctor with her history and her art:

> But take away my mother's carcinoma
> for I have only one cup of fetus tears.

> Take away my father's cerebral hemorrhage
> for I have only a jigger of blood in my hand.
>
> Take away my sister's broken neck
> for I have only my schoolroom ruler for a cure.
>
> Is there such a device for my heart?
> I have only a gimmick called magic fingers.

Whether the mind is too strong or not strong enough to adjust to the violent changes that death forces on us no longer seems to matter to the poem's manic finale:

> I am at the ship's prow.
> I am no longer the suicide
>
> with her raft and paddle.
> Herr Doktor! I'll no longer die
>
> to spite you, you wallowing
> seasick grounded man.

This defiance of death demands, first of all, that the tyranny of her own impulse toward suicide be fully evoked: she must "lie down/ with them and lift my madness/ off like a wig," since "Death is here. There is no/ other settlement" ("Oh"). And for this reason she returns, in "The Other," to what has always terrified her poetry: the alien self she cannot escape, who insanely possesses her and can keep her from the self that makes poems and love and children:

> When the child is soothed and resting on the breast
> it is my other who swallows Lysol.
> When someone kisses someone or flushes the toilet
> it is my other who sits in a ball and cries.
> My other beats a tin drum in my heart.
> My other hangs up laundry as I try to sleep.
> My other cries and cries and cries
> when I put on a cocktail dress.
> It cries when I prick a potato.
> It cries when I kiss someone hello.
> It cries and cries and cries

until I put on a painted mask
and leer at Jesus in His passion.

As in *Live or Die*, these are the dreams that confront endurance. Reformulated, death and madness, which had once seemed her only innocence, come to the silence she is writing against:

The silence is death.
It comes each day with its shock
to sit on my shoulder, a white bird,
and peck at the black eyes
and the vibrating muscle
of my mouth.

("The Silence")

The *Book of Folly's* remembrance of things past is likewise more direct when it turns to her family. "Anna Who Was Mad"—Anna, the anagram for the Nana whose namesake Sexton is—alternates interrogative and imperative lines to force the guilt of cause and effect: "Am I some sort of infection?/ Did I make you go insane?" . . .

The book's centering six-poem sequence, "The Death of the Fathers" is surely one of Sexton's triumphs, daring in its explorations and revelations, its verse superbly controlled as the voice of each poem is modulated to its experience, now shifting to the declaratives of a child, now heightening to involved regrets and prayers. While watching Sexton trace memories of her father mixed with sexual fantasies, one must recall Freud's sense of the origin of childhood memories:

Quite unlike conscious memories from the time of maturity, they are not fixed at the moment of being experienced and afterwards repeated, but are only elicited at a later age when childhood is already past; in the process they are altered and falsified, and are put into the service of later trends, so that generally speaking they cannot be sharply distinguished from phantasies.

Similarly, since fantasies become memories, it becomes impossible and useless beyond a certain point to distinguish between "events" that happened and fears or desires imagined so strongly that they might as well have happened. And further, Freud writes that the "screen memories" made of childhood traumas "relate to impressions of a sexual and aggressive nature, and no doubt also to early injuries to the ego (narcissistic mortifications). In this connection it should be remarked that such young children make no sharp distinction between sexual and aggressive acts, as they do later."

Sexton's sequence divides naturally into two parts of three poems each, the first set in childhood to evoke her father, and the second set in the present to focus his double death and the "later trends" that have occasioned the fantasies in the first. The opening poem, "Oysters," is her initiation, at once a fantasy of self-begetting and a memory of desire that, once conscious, defeats innocence. She is Daddy's Girl having lunch with her father at a restaurant, and fearfully eats her oysters—"this father-food," his semen. "It was a soft medicine/ that came from the sea into my mouth) moist and plump./ I swallowed." Then they laugh through this "death of childhood" the child was defeated./ The woman won." The second poem, "How We Danced," continues the fantasy in an Oedipal round:

> The champagne breathed like a skin diver
> and the glasses were crystal and the bride
> and groom gripped each other in sleep
> like nineteen-thirty marathon dancers.
> Mother was a belle and danced with twenty men.
> You danced with me never saying a word.
> Instead the serpent spoke as you held me close.
> The serpent, that mocker, woke up and pressed against me
> like a great god and we bent together
> like two lonely swans.

And the third poem, "The Boat," though it reverts to an earlier time, is a kind of coital coda to her subconscious victory. This time Leda's swan is her godlike captain, out in the same sea from which the oysters came, "out past Cuckold's Light," where "the three of us" ride through a storm that her father masters, but at its height there is the moment which both resolves her fantasies and predicts their destruction, in a memory of violence both sexual and aggressive:

> Now the waves are higher;
> they are round buildings.
> We start to go through them
> and the boat shudders.
> Father is going faster.
> I am wet.
> I am tumbling on my seat
> like a loose kumquat.

> Suddenly
> a wave that we go under.
> Under. Under. Under.
> We are daring the sea.
> We have parted it.
> We are scissors.
> Here in the green room
> the dead are very close.

The second part narrates the death of the fathers. In "Santa," the child's mythic sense of her father is killed: "Father,/ the Santa Claus suit/ you bought from Wolff Fording Theatrical Supplies,/ back before I was born,/ is dead." After describing how her father dressed up her childhood—when "Mother would kiss you/ for she was that tall"—she comes to liquor's reality principle: "The year I ceased to believe in you/ is the year you were drunk." And by the time her father, in turn, dressed up for her own children, the emptiness of having replaced her mother is apparent: "We were conspirators,/ secret actors) and I kissed you/ because I was tall enough./ But that is over." "Friends" details another death, as her father is distanced by doubt. The Stranger in her childhood could have been any of the men who would come to steal her from her father, but this family friend is more ominous:

> He was bald as a hump.
> His ears stuck out like teacups
> and his tongue, my God, his tongue,
> like a red worm and when he kissed
> it crawled right in.
>
> Oh Father, Father,
> who was that stranger
> who knew Mother too well?

The question this poem ends on—"Oh God,/ he was a stranger,/ was he not?"—is answered brutally in the last poem, "Begat," a kind of family romance in reverse:

> Today someone else lurks in the wings
> with your dear lines in his mouth
> and your crown on his head.
> Oh Father, Father-sorrow,
> where has time brought us?

Today someone called.
"Merry Christmas," said the stranger.
"I am your real father."
That was a knife.
That was a grave.

The father she had called hers dies again—the stranger takes "the you out of
the *me*"—and the poems end with a pathetic elegy on the distance she has
come since childhood and the first poem of this sequence, since the
understood desire. The end rises to a last regret with the simple details of
intimacy's allowances and sadnesses, and the memory of her father dressed as
Santa turns as raw as the blood they no longer share, the "two lonely swans"
who danced in fantasy are now fired by betrayal and loss:

Those times I smelled the Vitalis on his pajamas.
Those times I mussed his curly black hair
and touched his ten tar-fingers
and swallowed down his whiskey breath.
Red. Red. Father, you are blood red.
Father,
we are two birds on fire.

The blend of memory and fantasy in "The Death of the Fathers," each
sharpening and supporting the effect of the other, is the culmination of
Sexton's confessional style. Her next book, *The Death Notebooks* (1974),
develops this technique still further. . . .

Clearly the most significant and successful poem in *The Death Notebooks*
is "Hurry Up Please It's Time," a sort of long, hallucinatory diary-entry:
"Today is November 14th, 1972./ I live in Weston, Mass., Middlesex
County,/ U.S.A., and it rains steadily/ in the pond like white puppy eyes."
The style is pure pastiche, mixing dialect and dialogue, nursery rhymes and
New Testament, references ranging from Goethe to Thurber, attitudes
veering between arrogance and abasement. At times she is "Anne," at times
"Ms. Dog"—becoming her own mock-God. She can sneer at herself
("Middle-class lady,/ you make me smile"), or shiver at what "my heart, that
witness" remembers. The recaptured spots of time—say, a quiet summer
interlude with her husband and friends—are run into projected blotches
spread toward the death to come. And though its expansive free form dilutes
all but its cumulative force, the poem is an advance on the way "The Death
of the Fathers" had whispered its confessions.

Sexton's two posthumously published collections—*The Awful Rowing Toward God* (1975) and *45 Mercy Street* (1976)—are largely disappointing and anticlimactic, except when isolated poems in either book echo earlier successes.... Still, they remain as flawed evidence of Sexton's steady boldness, her readiness to risk new experiments in verse to record renewed perceptions of her experience in life, in the manner Emerson claimed that art is the effort to indemnify ourselves for the wrongs of our condition. There is, as one critic has said of her, "something awesome, even sublime in a woman who is not afraid to sound crude or shrill so long as she is honest, who in her best work sounds neither shrill nor crude precisely because she is honest." Her courage in coming true not only made Sexton one of the most distinctive voices in this generation's literature, and a figure of permanent importance to the development of American poetry, but has revealed in its art and its honesty a life in which we can discover our own.

MARGARET HOMANS

Adrienne Rich:
A Feminine Tradition

Association with nature and exclusion from speaking subjectivity amount to two different ways of placing the woman in dualistic culture on the side of the other and the object. Although the configurations of Mother Nature and Romantic egotism create problems specific to the nineteenth century, and although society and literature have undergone enormous changes since then, our language is still what it was and it continues to create for the woman poet many of the same impediments encountered by nineteenth-century women, if in different forms. Returning these specifically nineteenth-century problems to their context in a general and continuing tradition of the objectification of women, I should like to suggest in this chapter that poetry by women is still and is likely to remain conditioned by its response to various manifestations of masculine authority, and that women poets today might learn from the nineteenth century's range of failed and successful strategies for writing within the same tradition. The women poets then and now must distinguish the advantageous from the detrimental in their inheritance from Eve. Eve as she is read by masculine culture is interchangeable with Mother Nature: the object of men's conversation, beautiful but amoral, the "mother of all living" (Genesis 3:20), and best kept under control and silent. Eve as Dickinson reads her and as she might be read by others is the first human speaker to learn a non-literal language, and

From Homans, Margaret: *Women Writers and Poetic Identity: Dorothy Wordsworth, Emily Bronte, and Emily Dickinson*. © 1980 by Princeton University Press. Reprinted by permission of Princeton University Press.

therefore the most suitable prototype for poetic subjectivity. Dorothy Wordsworth is a docile daughter of nature, hoping that her docility will make up for the fall; Brontë is like a guilty Eve, repeating over and over a violation of male authority for which she believes the punishment is death; Dickinson celebrates Eve's duplicity, her invention of the art of concealment. To become poets, women must shift from agreeing to see themselves as daughters of nature and as parts of the world of objects to seeing themselves as daughters of an Eve reclaimed for their poetry.

With the aim of countering the traditional illusions about femininity, the prevailing feminist opinion is that poetry by women must report on the poet's experience as a woman, and that it must be true. Although it is appropriate that readers learn to expand their notions of what constitutes acceptable poetic subject matter—motherhood is as universal and as potentially imaginative an experience as, say, romantic love—this emphasis on truth implies a mistaken, or at least naïve, belief about language's capacity not just for precise mimesis but for literal duplication of experience. Elsewhere, I cited the use of Muriel Rukeyser's phrase "No more masks!" to call for a feminist poetry that would resolve women's difficult position within a dualistic culture simply be declaring an end to dualism; another anthology's title, *The World Split Open*, refers to the consequence of "one woman's" telling "the truth about her life" in Rukeyser's "Kathë Kollwitz." Whether or not these borrowings represent Rukeyser fairly, they assume that telling the truth without any sort of mask is both possible and desirable. Patriarchal culture may have particularly misused language in its perceptions of women, as feminist arguments maintain, but language is inherently fictive and creates masks whether or not the speaker or writer wishes it. The hope that language can gradually be released from a heritage of untruths about women may not be entirely deluded, but when those lies reinforce and are reinforced by the inherently fictive structure of language, it is chasing phantoms to expect that language will suddenly work for the expression of women's truth. This aim is fundamentally antithetical to the aims of poetry, and doom itself by denying itself the power that poetry genuinely offers.

Dickinson's discovery that to depart from dualistic language is to risk becoming either silent or incomprehensible was prompted by conditions that still prevail. Since her day writers and readers have become even more aware of the way dualism pervades language, in part through semiology, which has made a science of the necessary discrepancy between a word and its referent. Though Dickinson made a private and relatively early revolution in challenging herself and her future readers to imagine alternatives to dualistic thinking, no self-conscious writer today can believe in the goal of a unitary language such as Dickinson's contemporaries could still have imagined. The call for a women's language that, on the model of a single-sex society, would be free of masculine fictions about women is just such an anachronistic dream. A close reading of Dickinson demonstrates that the best course is to embrace and exploit language's inherent fictiveness, rather than to fight against it. Almost nothing would remain after the excision from language of undesirable fictions and the hierarchical structures that support them. Luce Irigaray arrives by way of, psychoanalysis at a position quite close to Dickinson's poetic sense of language's limits, a hundred years later, when she says that there may well be woman's language, but that it sounds like babbling; free from dualism, it does not make any of even the rudimentary distinctions upon which ordinary comprehensibility rests. Because the very notion of a sign is based on dualism, the words of this language bear indeterminate and non-repeating relations to their referents, and its syntax, lacking the ordinary relationship between subject and object, excludes logic and any possibility of linear reading. Impracticable as it may be, this projected non-dualistic language is at least more genuinely revolutionary and poetically suggestive than the goal of a feminist literal language in which words and their referents would be exactly determinate—language, furthermore, whose original is Adam's speech.

The naïve wish for a literal language and the belief in poetry's capacity for the duplication of experience foster a conception of the feminine self in poetry that is, paradoxically, even more egotistical than some of the masculine paradigms from which it intends to free itself. In the poetics of "female experience," the poet's own female "I" must be unabashedly present in the poem, in order for the poem to be true. The poet must not hide behind a mask of convention or let her modesty exclude her from the poem altogether. This emphasis on self sounds at first like the answer to Dorothy's evasions of self, or to Brontë's uncertainty about the external sources of her power, as if these impediments to poetry had been removed by twentieth-century women's increasing self-confidence. But when Rich says ". . . I am Adrienne alone" or when Alta names herself in a poem ("my name is Alta. / I am a woman."), that particular, personal "I" differs greatly from the sense of self that underlies much of Romantic poetry. Wordsworth, egotist though he is, does not name himself Wordsworth; "creative soul" and "Poet" are names that enlarge the self, where explicit naming would diminish it. Claiming one's own subjectivity seems, from the example of the nineteenth-century poets, a necessary precondition of writing poetry, but the unmasked and reductive "I" is only a further function of that belief in the literal, that it can be expressed and have literal effects. The new "I" has nothing to do with creative power; its purpose is to make poetry approximate as closely as possible a personal, spoken communication. It will not do simply to perform a poor imitation of the masculine "I" for the sake of asserting equality, because true equality is inconceivable within the conceptual framework of dualism. Dickinson's poems in which the self is composed of two identical, self-regarding parts point to a sense of self that undermines dualism far more effectively than the self-centered, single "I" of feminist poetry.

To place an exclusive valuation on the literal, especially to identify the self as literal, is simply to ratify women's age-old and disadvantageous position as the other and the object. Contemporary poetry by women that takes up this self-defeating strategy risks encounters with death that are destructive both poetically and actually. The current belief in a literal "I" present in poetry is responsible for the popular superstition that Sylvia Plath's death was the purposeful completion of her poetry's project, the assumption being that if the speaker is precisely the same as the biographical Plath, the poetry's self-destructive violence is directed toward Plath herself, not toward an imagined speaker. This reading of Plath is unfair to the woman and, by calling it merely unmediated self-expression, obscures her poetry's real power. In poem after poem depicting or wishing for physical violence, the imagery of violence is part of a symmetrical figurative system, and death is figured as a way of achieving rebirth or some other transcendence. Plath's project may not thus be very different from that of Dickinson, who speaks quite often from beyond the grave, reimagining and repossessing death as her own in order to dispel the terrors of literal death. However, within that figurative system the poet embraces a self-destructive program that must soon have been poetically terminal, even if it did not bring about the actual death. . . .

A mask, however despised by those who call for an end to them in women's poetry, provides for any poet a necessary separation between the self and the poem, just as the knowledge of language's fictiveness, the origin of masks, can mediate between a woman poet and the cultural dictate that women are objects. To embrace a belief in the literal means to embrace death, not death transformed but actual death. Rich's poem "Diving into the Wreck" became for many readers in the early 1970s a manifesto of feminist poetry, because of its androgynous collectivity and because of its polemic about discarding our old myths about the sexes in order to see "the wreck and not the story of the wreck / the thing itself and not the myth." And yet even here, the diver depends on the mask that permits her to see these things under water and that in fact stands between her and death: "my mask is powerful / it pumps my blood with power." The poem thus qualifies its own wish for total revelation, knowing that such qualification is not an evasion but a necessity if the poet is to go on writing. The poem, further, makes its point about discarding myths in the highly figurative framework of a miniature allegory, demonstrating as part of its polemic that the mask that figuration provides is not incompatible with feminist rhetoric. A belief in figuration is life-giving.

The dangerous acceptance of literalization appears also in poems bearing on the idea of the mother, making a point of contact between the nineteenth-century poets and their recent inheritors. None of the nineteenth-century poets were themselves mothers, but all the modern poets mentioned here were or are mothers. The nineteenth-century poets could consider motherhood from the removed viewpoints of tradition and of their remembered daughterhoods; even so, the subject was troubling. Whatever difficulties they experienced in relation to the concept of motherhood are multiplied for the women for whom it is not a concept but a consuming reality. Motherhood is literal creativity. It must be difficult for a woman to choose as her vocation poetry or figurative creativity, perhaps to the detriment of the maternal vocation with which she is expected to be contented, because the values associated with motherhood and with poetry are so very different. It may be that developing a poetics of literal truth, however impossible an aim, is the most logical response to this situation, the only poetics that might be expected to compete with motherhood on motherhood's untranslatable terms. When Rich turns her attention to motherhood, she writes in non-fiction prose rather than in verse, explaining, analyzing, and arguing rather than inventing. The term "non-fiction" helps to account for the switch: the subject of motherhood calls forth a desire to avoid fictions and to approximate the truth. Motherhood resists incorporation into the traditional values of poetry.

The entrance of psychoanalytic insights into common language has made it possible for a woman's identity with her mother to be openly accepted and for her struggles with this relationship to become appropriate topics for poetry. Relative to the covert mentions of the mother in works by Dorothy and Brontë, the mother's inhibiting influence is all on the surface in Sexton's poetry, perhaps fulfilling Irigaray's aim to have women reclaim their maternal origins. Yet because motherhood still represents the same group of values and qualities that it represented in the nineteenth century, this greater certainty about identity between mother and daughter does nothing to relieve what was threatening about the suggestions of that identity for Dorothy and Brontë, but instead intensifies it enormously. "I see around me tombstones grey" presents an extreme case of earth as the devouring mother identified with death; the speaker cannot allow herself to imagine transcendence for herself after death, in spite of her dislike for the idea of a final mortality, because of her closing non-ironic acknowledgment that she is identified with that maternal earth. The figure of the mother in Dorothy's "Irregular Verses" ("To Julia Marshall—A Fragment") and the implicit figure of Mother Nature in other poems block her efforts and even her desire to become a poet. These maternal figures seem ominous enough; but compared with Sexton's and Plath's the nineteenth-century image permits at least an illusion of freedom. There is now no possibility of plausibly imagining an alternative transcendence.

Plath's late poem on the mother, "Medusa," uses with even greater intensity the same counterproductive or suicidal strategy that informs the poems about the father: the poem implicates the speaker herself in the attack on the mother, not because she must die in order to get rid of her, as in the case of the father, but because the two women are too much alike. The mother's love is expressed as a grotesque sucking (she is pictured as having tentacles that grasp with suckers) that causes mother and child to exchange places. What the speaker is trying to deny is an identification with her mother that is mediated by the Christian myth of transubstantiation:

> Who do you think you are?
> A communion wafer? Blubbery Mary?
> I shall take no bite of your body.

The refusal to identify with the mother also means a refusal of nourishment, past and present, so that to deny the mother is also to deny the self. The mother is identified with physical properties of motherhood that are seen here horrifically: "Fat and red, a placenta / Paralyzing the kicking lovers," "Bottle in which I live, / Ghastly Vatican"; and although these belong to the mother, the poem's concern with identity between daughter and mother implies the speaker's fear that they are hers too. The final line is ambiguous: "There is nothing between us" suggests both that the "Old barnacled umbilicus" has been severed and that there is nothing separating them.

Two of Sexton's farewells to her mother, written after her mother's death, endeavor to free themselves of the mother's presence, but both poems are weighted with the tug of origins back to death. The memory of the mother is at least restrictive, often fatal. In "The Division of Parts" the poet as daughter is loaded with guilt at her mother's death, so much so that she cannot "shed my daughterhood," and is haunted in sleep by her mother's image. She is able to shift this burden somewhat, from herself as daughter to the more neutral position of "inheritor" (the occasion of the poem is the division of the mother's property between three sisters) by reducing the mother to an aspect of language. A torrent of words descriptively naming the mother closes with "my Lady of my first words," so that the inheritance is of language; this gift alone can be accepted without guilt. In "The Double Image" the portraits of mother and daughter hang opposite each other, so similar that they seem instead one portrait and its reflection in a mirror. The poet's closing guilty address to her own daughter, "I made you to find me," echoes the implied words of the poet's mother earlier in the poem, "I made you to kill me":

> She turned from me, as if death were catching,
> as if death transferred,
> as if my dying had eaten inside of her.
> . . . .
> On the first of September she looked at me
> and said I gave her cancer.
> They carved her sweet hills out
> and still I couldn't answer.

In Plath's "Edge" one of the ways of figuring death is that the "perfected" woman has reincorporated her dead children back into her body. Sexton, making an even more explicit relation between death and maternity, makes pregancy grotesquely the metaphor for her mother's death from cancer:

> That was the winter
> that my mother died,
> half mad on morphine,
> blown up, at last,
> like a pregnant pig.

Later in the same poem she puns on the word "deliver," having it refer both to childbirth and to deliverance from suffering. If her mother gives birth to death, then the poet herself is death's twin. In "The Death Baby" the poet imagines her own babyhood as "an ice baby"; then, exactly repeating her mother, she pictures her death—assumed her to be a voluntary act—as the taking up of the death baby, "my stone child/with still eyes like marbles." When she holds the death baby, death itself "will be / that final rocking," where rocking also means turning into rock.

"That final rocking:" Adrienne Rich ends *The Dream of a Common Language*, so far her most didactically feminist book, in a highly affirmative mood, with a woman who turns into a rock. "Transcendental Etude" (1977), the book's closing poem, bewilderingly celebrates a number of male visions of femininity that have always restricted women, both humanly and poetically, and yet this celebration is made in the name of a revolutionary feminism. To overturn Freud's views on femininity is the twentieth-century woman's equivalent for the nineteenth century's objections to patriarchal religion, and a poem of a year earlier, "Sibling Mysteries," introduces the grounds for anti-Freudian sentiment with textbook clarity:

> The daughters never were
> true brides of the father
>
> the daughters were to begin with
> brides of the mother
>
> then brides of each other
> under a different law

"Transcendental Etude" enlarges experiential Lesbianism into an aesthetic project, at the same time enacting a program for recovering lost maternal origins. "A whole new poetry" will spring from the identity of self, lover, and mother, through the enlarging and consoling of the self:

> Birth stripped our birthright from us,
> tore us from a woman, from women, from ourselves
> so early on
> and the whole chorus throbbing at our ears
> like midges, told us nothing, nothing
> of origins, . . .
>
> Only: that it is unnatural,
> the homesickness for a woman, for ourselves,
> for that acute joy at the shadow her head and arms
> cast on a wall, her heavy or slender
> thighs on which we lay, flesh against flesh,
> . . . .
> *This is what she was to me, and*
> *this is how I can love myself—*
> *as only a woman can love me.*

The reader scarcely has a chance to consider whether this love that obliterates difference can be productive poetically, because before going on the poem enacts the promised return to the mother, in a final passage that is ostentatiously old-fashioned both in its imagery and in its import for poetry.

> Vision begins to happen in such a life
> as if a woman quietly walked away
> from the argument and jargon in a room
> and sitting down in the kitchen, began turning in her lap
> bits of yarn, calico and velvet scraps,
> laying them out absently on the scrubbed boards
> in the lamplight, . . .

More little objects, domestic and natural, all with traditional feminine associations, are described for ten further lines. It is implied that the woman is arranging them, but we see only the objects, while she has faded from view. This description is followed by a polemic against the traditional values of art:

> Such a composition has nothing to do with eternity,
> the striving for greatness, brilliance—
> only with the musing of a mind
> one with her body, . . .

The poems in *The Dream of a Common Language* are presumably something more than this and it is misleading for the poet to celebrate such absent musings as a paradigm for poetry, even though the poem keeps on being seductively lovely. The woman is passive and stereotypically lacking in an identity of her own:

> with no mere will to mastery,
> only care for the many-lived, unending
> forms in which she finds herself, . . .

She becomes both a dangerous object and the cure for the wound it inflicts (the traditional types for the woman as whore and as saint), becoming at last (but not finally, the poem suggests)

> the stone foundation, rockshelf further
> forming underneath everything that grows.

This ending may not be literally suicidal, as identity with the mother is for Sexton, but it is poetically terminal. Instead of "a whole new poetry beginning here," as promised, both poem and book end here with a return to the mother, to mothers of the past. Earlier the poem seemed to be proposing to take a detour into the past in order to reincorporate the past into the present, but the return never takes place. What happens in this poem is uncannily like the process of Dorothy's "A Winter's Ramble in Grasmere Vale," even to the point of the similarity of the closing images. Rich's "rockshelf" if uncomfortably close to the beautiful rock Dorothy encounters on a walk originally undertaken, as Rich's poem is, in a spirit of searching for newness; the rock is the emissary from Mother Nature that prevents her from continuing both her search and her poem. (Plath's mother in "Medusa" too may turn her into stone.) Rich's rock is an image of mother as nature, the chthonic feminine object whose existence as the valorized image of womanhood has impeded and continues to impede the ability of women to choose, among many other things, the vocation of poet. The great difference between Dorothy and Rich is that Rich is fully conscious of all the cultural implications of her exhortation, and willfully propounds this image when she could have chosen any other, whereas Dorothy can scarcely see around the impressive bulk of her brother's views. Dorothy has no polemical purpose; Rich knows her language is lovely enough to persuade us that she embraces inarticulateness, and that we should, too. Rich's lovely woman in the lamplight, turning her back on "argument and jargon," is as much a threat to the life of the female mind as Dickinson's Mother Nature, who "Wills Silence—Everywhere—." The poem exhorts a twin impossibility; the literal in a poem, and this sort of woman as poet.

Two earlier poems in the same volume take a different position relative to the literal, and although Rich does not grant them the polemical force of standing last and of announcing themselves as models for a new poetry, they do suggest possibilities for poetry somewhere between total acquiescence to male paradigms of femininity and an unimaginable revolution in language. Like "Transcendental Etude" they look back at tradition, but not only do they avoid the trap of feminist literalism that that poem endorses, they also endeavor to find positive value in tradition. "To a Poet" (1974) is at once a critique of the poetics of the literal and a positive revision of Romantic egotism. Quoting, with significant changes, the first two lines of Keats' sonnet "When I have fears," Rich invites Keats to leave the solitude produced by his fear of mortality ("—then on the shore / Of the wide world I stand alone") and join a collectivity of poets. Gently correcting Keats' sorrowing inwardness, she carries Keats' special capacity for generous sympathy into this poem and beyond the point where Keats took it himself, to an actual address to other poets who might share Keats' own anxieties. Here are Keats' lines:

> When I have fears that I may cease to be
>   Before my pen has gleaned my teeming brain

and here is Rich's version:

> *and I have fears that you will cease to be*
> *before your pen has glean'd your teeming brain*

In addition to having Keats turn from addressing himself to addressing someone else, the poet fuses her "I" with his in an even subtler sympathy. The lines come in the middle of an address to a woman poet who is "dragged down" by the confining vocation of impoverished motherhood but for whom poetry is still somehow just possible:

> Language floats at the vanishing-point
> *incarnate*   breathes the fluorescent bulb
> *primary*   states the scarred grain of the floor
> and on the ceiling in torn plaster laughs   *imago*

The grand and abstract poetic language that his woman finds (in the traditional location of the sublime, "the vanishing-point") transcends her circumstances. The speaker then describes a different woman who lives

> where language floats and spins
> *abortion*   in
> the bowl

At the opposite pole from the first woman's chance at a saving transcendence, for this woman word and object are one in a way that fully realizes the worst connotations of the closing of "Transcendental Etude." In a literalization of Keats' metaphor of the fertility of the mind, which he fears to lose, this woman must forgo her literal fertility and, because of this, any mental fertility she might have. This word that literally floats and then vanishes literalizes the transcendent language that figuratively floats at the vanishing-point for the first woman. Could this second woman write at all, she would be able only to repeat in a language close to literal a horrifying "female experience." While the poem corrects Keats in order to direct his and the poet's sympathy toward the suffering woman, it also endorses Keats as a way of correcting the idea of a reductive poetry of female literalism. Keats has already started the imaginative process he seeks when he chooses the word "gleaning" as a figure for writing poetry: layering Keats' poem with her own, Rich reminds us of the powerful transport figuration offers.

"To a Poet" makes its peace with tradition through a high degree of selectivity: Keats' sympathy and relative lack of self-centeredness are exceptional among the Romantics. "Phantasia for Elvira Shatayev" (1974) takes on, in order to revise, a much larger and more difficult portion of tradition. The poem admits and inserts itself into a dualistic system and makes its mark not by undermining it—as in Dickinson's more radical project—but by claiming to meet its challenge—to cross the various boundaries it sets upthrough a feminist rhetoric. At the same time, the poem undermines the same literalism that "To a Poet" decries. It at once accepts and stretches beyond its limits the notion of a poetry of female experience: although the poem's pretext is an actual event, the deaths of the members of a women's mountain-climbing team, the experience is utterly unlike what is usually meant by "female experience," and the poem is in any case about transcending experience. The poem escapes the likelihood of its readers confusing its "I" with the author by having an overtly fictive persona, Elvira Shateyev imagined as speaking from beyond her death, but as when the poet fuses her own "I" with Keats' in "To a Poet," titling the poem "Phantasia for . . ." makes it clear that the poet is speaking here too. This layered persona is, furthermore, ready to take up other personae:

> If in this sleep I speak
> it's with a voice no longer personal
> (I want to say   *with voices*)

This collectivizing of the self is central to the poem's revision of Romantic egotism, and to its effort to find an explicitly feminist transcendence. Instead of a poet-hero solitary in his self-consciousness, the poem presents a group, heroic in its mutuality: "*I have never seen / my own forces so taken up and shared / and given back.*" The poem solves for itself the nineteenth-century women's fear that poetic power may be located only outside the self: poetic voice and power are here in an everywhere that is not other.

The poem asserts that transcendence need not belong exclusively to the masculine imagination. The poem's setting crowds it with memories of Romantic poetry's strivings after sublimity and of its assertions of imaginative power-Wordsworth's mountain visions in Books VI and XIV of *The Prelude*, Shelley's "Mont Blanc" and Promethean scenarios in Shelley and Byron—and of the Miltonic and Biblical mountains of vision that precede these. But having joined this company, the speaker and her companions, women of power and vision of their own, pass into the universal in a way that is overtly feminist. The poem harmoniously pairs what might be viewed as a traditionally masculine form of transcendence with a new and self-consciously feminist one:

Every cell's core of heat   pulsed out of us
into the thin air   of the universe
the armature of rock beneath these snows
this mountain   which has taken   the imprint of our
minds
through changes elemental and minute
as those we underwent
to bring each other here
choosing ourselves   each other   and this life
whose every breath   and grasp   and further foothold
is somewhere   still enacted   and continuing

The first two lines of this passage represent a literal or physical transcendence of the body in death, which shifts imperceptibly into the major Romantic project of having the mind transcend its boundaries to imprint nature with its power. The last two lines reach another Romantic goal, to transcend the limits of death and find beyond it power and sublimity. Between these two Romantic projects and linking them syntactically is a transcendence of the individual self that identifies itself here and elsewhere as explicitly feminist. Not content simply to find for this feminist transcendence a place alongside them, the poem's extraordinary claim is that these Romantic projects are fulfilled only through it. It holds that the transcendence the Romantics sought was impossible under the conditions of Romantic egotism and is only possible through collectivity. The subordinate clauses that begin in the transitions between the pivotal lines, "changes elemental and minute / as those we underwent" and "this life / whose every breath . . .," cause the first of the Romantic projects to be measured by and the second to be dependent upon the feminist project's achievement; only by first crediting the power of collectivity can the reader then enter into the feeling that neither the mountain nor death create insuperable barriers to consciousness. The passage makes these transcendences occur, and it makes them a totality.

The speaker's grieving husband is portrayed at first as finite and other, somewhat stereotypically and unfairly as women often are portrayed where the self is male. Climbing the mountain to bury her, his boots leave "their geometric bite / colossally embossed" on the snow; compared to the limitless women, he is enclosed in selfhood:

You come (I know this)   with your love   your loss
strapped to your body   with your tape-recorder   camera
ice-pick

He will bury them "in the snow   and in your mind / While my body lies out here." The poem enters into the nineteenth-century problem of the woman dying into nature, but here it is the universe—"the possible," not chthonic nature—of which she has become a part, and death generates speech rather than curtailing it. The husband is put in the position of the male poet who gains his central speaking self from the silent otherness of the women he buries, but unlike Lucy and Margaret, these women cannot be buried in nature, nor can they be silenced:

> When you have buried us   told your story
> ours does not end   we stream
> into the unfinished   the unbegun
> the possible

But this man is engaged in a generous and loving action that atones for the speaker's memory of having "trailed" him on previous climbs when the old relations between the sexes still obtained. Through him, the poet forgives the male poets their limitations and accepts with grace what they have to offer; the poem is beyond anger.

Where "Transcendental Etude" foils its own feminist program by uncritically accepting what amounts to the male paradigm of the woman who merges with nature, "Phantasia" makes stronger claims for its feminism by revising and incorporating another traditional paradigm. Rather than the woman's becoming a rock, "the armature of rock" of the snow-covered mountain takes "the imprint of our minds." To imprint a rock is to re-engage a strategy like Dickinson's, to ask language's difference to reopen an apparent closure. By so beautifully having the dead climber speak, "Phantasia" performs (as do many of Dickinson's poems) one of the highest and most traditional imaginative functions: it calls the dead back to life. Having made outrageous claims for its fiction-making power, the poem closes with a final, powerful act of figuration:

> *What does love mean*
> *what does it mean   "to survive"*
> *A cable of blue fire ropes our bodies*
> *burning together in the snow   We will not live*
> *to settle for less   We have dreamed of this*
> *all of our lives*

Like Dickinson's "long, big shining fibre," this cable of blue fire is both infinitely suggestive, and irreducible and untranslatable. It joins the bodies together simultaneously as it joins them to sublime regions; and it makes the necessity for figuration inseparable from the necessity for collectivity and for transcendence.

"Phantasia for Elvira Shatayev" makes figuration necessary; "Transcendental Etude" ends by trying to make an end to figuration. The woman who becomes a rock begins her figurative life quite neutrally, as a metaphor for the manner in which vision takes place in the new life of women loving women: "Vision begins to happen in such a life / as if a woman quietly walked away. . . ." In other words, the poet can now write poetry that does not engage in abstract preludes to action, but that instead takes action itself. The woman is a figure for vision, or for poetry. But what begins to happen in such a poem is that the figure for vision becomes the vision itself; not only is this how vision occurs, but also this is the sort of vision that occurs. To prove that exhortations are over and that practice has begun, the poem stops using abstract terms like "spirit" and "poetry," and does something very practical: it gives us a concrete image. The image is at once tenor and vehicle, both a figure for vision and the vision itself. This collapse of the usual structure of rhetoric is repeated at the close of the passage, where it is said that the woman becomes the broken glass and the soothing leaf and the rockshelf, rather than, conventionally, that she is like these things. This is an undoing of rhetoric that can never be an undoing of language, in the manner of Dickinson's very different kind of undoing, because what it points toward is an impossible conflation of word and referent, or signifier and signified. This conflation is also the aim of that other tenet of contemporary women's poetry, to speak literally and to be true. A woman, fortunately, can be a rock only in a poem; language's difference saves this poetics from itself.

BARBARA HARDY

Sylvia Plath:
Enlargement or Derangement?

I

Passions of hate and horror prevail in the poetry of Sylvia Plath, running strongly counter to the affirmative and life-enhancing quality of most great English poetry, even in this century. We cannot reconcile her despairing and painful protest with the usual ideological demands of Christian, Marxist, and humanist writers, whether nobly and sympathetically eloquent, like Wordsworth, breezily simplified, like Dylan Thomas, or cunning in ethical and psychological argument, like W. H. Auden or F. R. Leavis. Her poetry rejects instead of accepting, despairs instead of glorying, turns its face with steady consistency towards death, not life. But these hating and horrified passions are rooted in love, are rational as well as irrational, lucid as well as bewildered, so humane and honourable that they are constantly enlarged and expanded. We are never enclosed in a private sickness here, and if derangement is a feature of the poetry, it works to enlarge and generalise, not to create an enclosure. Moreover, its enlargment works through passionate reasoning, argument and wit. Its judgment is equal to its genius.

The personal presence in the poetry, though dynamic and shifting, makes itself felt in a full and large sense, in feeling, thinking and language. In view of certain tendencies to admire or reject her so-called derangement as a revelatory or an enclosed self-exploration, I want to stress this breadth

From *The Advantage of Lyric: Essays on Feeling in Poetry*. © 1977 by Indiana University Press.

and completeness. The poetry constantly breaks beyond its own personal cries of pain and horror, in ways more sane than mad, enlarging and generalising the particulars, attaching its maladies to a profoundly moved and moving sense of human ills. Working through a number of individual poems, I should like to describe this poetry as a poetry of enlargement, not derangement. In much of the poetry the derangement is scarcely present, but where it is, it is out-turned, working though reason and love.

I want to disagree with David Holbrook's view that hers is a schizophrenic poetry which "involves us in false solutions and even the *huis clos* circuits of death," while indeed agreeing with much that he has to say about the cult of schizophrenia in his essay "The 200-inch distorting mirror" (*New Society*, 11 July 1968).

> Sylvia Plath's poetry demands a selfless mirror-role from us; we feel that it would be worse than inhuman of us not to give it. If this involves us in entering into her own distorted view of existence, never mind. We will bravely become the schizoid's 200-inch astronomical reflector.

An excessive love for the cult of pain and dying, in such tributes as those of Anne Sexton and Robert Lowell, seems to divert our attention from the breadth and rationality of Sylvia Plath's art. Lowell is strongly drawn to that very quality which David Holbrook finds repulsive or pathetic, the invitation to a deadly closure:

> There is a peculiar, haunting challenge to these poems. Probably many, after reading *Ariel*, will recoil from their first over-awed shock, and painfully wonder why so much of it leaves them feeling empty, evasive and inarticulate. In her lines, I often hear the serpent whisper, 'Come, if only you had the courage, you too could have my rightness, audacity and ease of inspiration.' But most of us will turn back. These poems are playing Russian roulette with six cartridges in the cylinder, a game of 'chicken', the wheels of both cars locked and unable to swerve.

It seems worth recording a different reaction.

I want to begin by looking at a poem from *Ariel* which shows how dangerous it is to talk, as Holbrook clearly does, and as Lowell seems to, about the "typical" Sylvia Plath poem, or even the "typical" late poem. I must make it clear that I do not want to rest my case on the occasional presence of life-enhancing poems, but to use one to explain what I mean by imaginative enlargement. "Nick and the Candlestick" (from *Ariel*, 1965; written October/November 1962) is not only a remarkable poem of love, but that much rarer thing—are there any others?—a fine poem of maternal love. It is a poem which moves towards two high points of feeling, strongly personal and particular, deeply eloquent of maternal feeling, and lucidly open to a Christian mythical enlargement. The first peak comes in the tenth stanza, and can perhaps be identified at its highest point in one word, the endearment "ruby," which is novel, surprising, resonant, and beautiful:

> Remembering, even in sleep,
> Your crossed position.
> The blood blooms clean
>
> In you, ruby.
> The pain
> You wake to is not yours.

The second peak comes at the end, in a strongly transforming conclusion, a climax in the very last line. It comes right out of all that has been happening in the poem but transforms what has gone before, carrying a great weight and responsibility, powerfully charged and completing a process, like an explosion or a blossoming:

> You are the one
> Solid the spaces lean on, envious.
> You are the baby in the barn.

The final enlargement is daring, both in the shock of expansion and in the actual claim it makes. She dares to call her baby Christ and in doing so makes the utmost claim of her personal love, but so that the enlargement does not take us away from this mother, this child, this feeling. This most personally present mother-love moves from the customary hyperbole of endearment in "ruby" to the vast claim. When we look back, when we read again, the whole poem is pushing towards that last line, "You are the baby in the barn." The symbol holds good, though at first invisibly, for the cold, the exposure, the dark, the child, the mother, the protection, and the redemption from a share of pain. Each sensuous and emotional step holds for the mother in the poem and for Mary: this is the warmth of the mother nursing her child in the cold night; this is a proud claim for the child's beauty and the mother's tenderness; this is love and praise qualified by pain. Any mother loving her child in a full awareness of the world's horror—especially seeing it and feeling it vulnerable and momentarily safe in sleep—is re-enacting the feeling in the Nativity, has a right to call the child the baby in the barn.

"Ruby" is a flash of strong feeling. It treasures, values, praises, admires, measures, contemplates, compares, rewards. Its full stretch of passion is only apparent when the whole poem is read, but even on first encounter it makes a powerful moment, and strikes us as thoroughly formed and justified at that stage. Like every part of the poem, even the less urgent-sounding ones, it refers back and forwards, and has also continuity not only within the poem but with larger traditions of amorous and religious language, in medieval poetry (especially *The Pearl*), in the Bible, in Hopkins. The fusion of the new and the old is moving. This baby has to be newly named, like every baby, and has its christening in a poem, which bestows a unique name, in creative energy, as ordinary christenings cannot, but with something too of the ritual sense of an old and common feeling. Sylvia Plath is a master of timing and placing, and the naming endearment comes after the physically live sense of the sleeping child, in the cold air, in the candlelight, in its healthy colour. The mildly touched Christian reference in "crossed position" prepares for the poem's future. Its gentleness contrasts strongly, by the way, with the violence of very similar puns in Dylan Thomas, and confirms my general feeling that Sylvia Plath is one of the very few poets to assimilate Thomas without injury, in an entirely benign influence. Her sensuous precision is miles away from Thomas: "ruby" is established by the observation, "The blood blooms clean/In you," and the comparison works absolutely, within the poem, though it has an especially poignant interest when we think of the usual aggressiveness and disturbance of redness in her other poems, where the blooming red of tulips or poppies are exhausting life-demands, associated with the pain of red wounds, or the heavy urgency of a surviving beating heart. Here it is a beloved colour, because it is the child's, so in fact there is a constancy of symbolism, if we are interested. "Clean," like "crossed" and "ruby" has the same perfectly balanced attachment to the particularity of the situation—this mother, this baby—and to the Christian extension. "The pain/You wake to is not yours" works in the same way, pointing out and in, though the words "out" and "in" do less than justice to the fusion here.

The perfected fusion is the more remarkable for being worked out in a complex tone, which includes joking. Like the medieval church, or the Nativity play, it can be irreverent, can make jokes about what it holds sacred, is sufficiently inclusive and sufficiently certain. So we are carried from the fanciful rueful joke about "A piranha/Religion, drinking/Its first communion out of my live toes" to the final awe. Or from the casual profane protest, "Christ! they are panes of ice" to the crossed position, the pain not his, the baby in the barn. An ancient and audacious range.

If this is a love-poem, it is one which exists in the context of the other *Ariel* poems, keeping a sense of terrors as well as glories, in imagery which is vast and vague: the stars "plummet to their dark address"; and topically precise and scientific: "the mercuric/Atoms that cripple drip/Into the terrible well." It is a poisoned world that nourishes and threatens that clean blood. Perhaps only a child can present an image of the uncontaminated body, as well as soul, and there is also present the sense of a mother's fear of physical contamination. The mercuric atoms are presumably a reference to the organo-mercury compounds used in agriculture, and the well seems to be a real well. There may also, I suppose, be a reference to radioactive fall-out. Ted Hughes has a note about the poet's horror of "the chemical poisonings of nature, the pileup of atomic waste," in his article "The Chronological Order of Sylvia Plath's Poems" (*Triquarterly*, no. 7, Fall 1966).

The poet loves and praises, but in no innocent or ideal glorying. This is a cold air in which the candle burns blue before yellow, nearly goes out, reminds us of the radiance in so many paintings of Mother and Child, but also of a real cold night, and of the miner's cold, his dark, his cave, his nightwork, his poisoned breathing. The intimacies and protections and colours are particular too: "roses," "the last of Victoriana," "soft rugs." The expansion moves firmly into and out of a twentieth-century world, a medieval poetry, ritual, and painting, and the earliest Christ-story, and this holds for its pains and its loving. It moves from light to dark, from love to fear. It moves beyond the images of mother-love, indeed begins outside in the first line's serious wit, "I am a miner." It uses—or, better, feels for—the myth of Redemption not in order to idealise the particulars but rather to revise and qualify the myth, to transplant it again cheerfully, to praise only after a long hard look at the worst. The love and faith and praise are there, wrung out and achieved against the grain, against the odds. David Holbrook is sorry that Sylvia Plath, judged from *The Bell Jar*, shows no experience of togetherness. This poem seems to embarrass his case, and it strikes me as being beyond the reach of such diagnosis or compassion. She said of the poem, in a BBC broadcast quoted by Lois Ames: "a mother nurses her baby son by candlelight and finds in him a beauty which, while it may not ward off the world's ill, does redeem her share of it."

True, it is not typical. There are two other very loving poems of maternal feeling, "Metaphors" and "You're," happy peals of conceits, but nothing else moves so, between these two extremities of love and pain, striking spark from such poles. "Nick and the Candlestick" is not proffered as an instance of togetherness, but as a lucid model of the enlargement I want to discuss.

At the heart of her poetry lies the comment that she herself made about this enlargement:

I think my poems come immediately out of the sensuous and emotional experiences I have, but I must say I cannot sympathize with these cries from the heart that are informed by nothing except a needle or a knife or whatever it is. I believe that one should be able to control and manipulate experiences, even the most terrifying—like madness, being tortured, this kind of experience—and one should be able to manipulate these experiences with an informed and intelligent mind. I think that personal experience shouldn't be a kind of shut box and mirror-looking narcissistic experience. I believe it should be generally relevant, to such things as Hiroshima and Dachau, and so on. (Triquarterly, no. 7, Fall 1966, p. 71)

It is interesting that Sylvia Plath uses the image of the mirror which David Holbrook also uses in that *New Society* article, called "The 200-inch distorting mirror," in order to reject the kind of poetry he also rejects (to my mind, rightly) and which he finds (to my mind, wrongly) in Sylvia Plath.

A mere explicit statement that the poet believes personal experience of pain should not be a mirror or a shut box but should be relevant to Hiroshima and Dachau, is plainly not an answer to Holbrook. Nor would a mere listing of such references do much: the intelligent poet can after all attempt but fail to break open the shut box, may impose intellectually schematic associations with the larger world. Resnais in *Hiroshima Mon Amour* seems to be open to the charge of using the larger pain of atomic war to illuminate his personal centre, so that the movement is not that of enlargement but of diminution. Something similar seems to happen in a good many Victorian attempts to enlarge the personal problem, to combine the personal and social pain, and we may well object that the endings of *Bleak House* and *Crime and Punishment* are unsuccessful attempts to solve the large pain by the smaller reconciliation. I have spent what may seem an excessive time on "Nick and the Candlestick" in order to establish not so much a typical feeling, but a form: the particularity and the generalisation run together in equal balance, asking questions of each other, eroding each other, unifying in true imaginative modification. I want to suggest that this is the mode of Sylvia Plath's major poetry, and that it succeeds exactly where Resnais failed. But it should be said, perhaps, that this problem of combination or enlargement works in a special way, involving artists working from experience of personal pain, depression, despair. The optimist, like Dickens and Dostoevsky, may well find it easy to join his larger pain and his smaller triumph. For the tragic artist like Sylvia Plath it is more the problem of competitive pains: how to dwell in and on the knives and needles of the personal life without shutting off the knives and needles in Biafra, Vietnam, Dachau, and Hiroshima. It is almost a problem of competing sensibilities, and the tragic artist's temptation in our time is probably to combine indecorously, like Resnais, to make the Hiroshima a metaphor for an adultery, to move from outer to inner and confirm an especially terrible shut box.

II

Before I move from "Nick and the Candlestick" to the more terrible fusions elsewhere in *Ariel*, I want to look at some of the earlier attempts in *The Colossus* (1960). Many of the poems here show a fairly familiar and conventional tension and control. In some poems there is a narrow sensuous or social image of something painful, something dying: the dryness, unpleasant fruition, hard and yellow starlight, and difficult "borning" of "The Manor Garden" have nothing to say for nature; the inhuman boom and monotony of "Night Shift" show men reduced to tend the machine; "Hardcastle Crags" defeat the walker's energy by massive indifference and hard labour. Such poems accumulate the sense of unreward, ugliness, labour, repulsion, hostility, but each makes only its individual assertion, proffering no generalisation.

In another group of poems in this volume, there is an attempt to break up such hardness, though scarcely to redeem or transform. Such poems as "Two Views of a Cadaver Room," "Watercolour of Grantchester Meadows," "The Eye-Mote" or "Black Rook in Rainy Weather" show a darkening, rather than a darkened, vision. Affirmation is there, is valued, but is unstable. The destructive eye-mote is there for good, enlarged and confirmed as more than temporary by the move towards Oedipus, so we know that the sight cannot return, that the "Horses fluent in the wind" are gone. In "Black Rook in Rainy Weather" the poem sets out a belief in meaningful experience, but the belief rocks unsteadily, the experience is erratic and unguaranteed, can only bring "A brief respite from fear/Of total neutrality." The vigour of the meaningful moment is certainly there, "hauling up eyelids," but in most of these poems that weigh gain against loss, there is less vigour, or a final movement towards the loss. "Black Rook" ends with the naming of the spasmodic trick, the random rare descent, but "The Eye-Mote" moves more characteristically away from the balance between easy fluid harmony, and the pained, blurred distorted vision, to tip the scales. We move over into blindness, guilt, loss of more than a small beauty. "Watercolour of Grantchester Meadows" has a dark landscape, uses the spring idyll ambiguously and sharpens one point to drive it hard against our senses and sense. It creates a swimmy swoony dream of spring, water, love, in the impressionist blurring and the little nursery plate brightness, to build a bridge from the world of (superficial) sweetness to destructiveness. In "Two Views of a Cadaver Room" the movement from death to love is deceptive: the poem allows only a tiny ambiguous space for "the little country" where the lovers can be "blind to the carrion army." No redeeming corner, this, because "foolish, Delicate" and "not for long," stalled only "in paint," and responding in true Brueghel disproportionateness to the earlier apparent redemption, in the first half of the poem, where after the dissection, "He hands her the cut-out heart like a cracked heirloom." All these poems, with the possible exception of "Black Rook," fall out of love with the world of love, yearn for it but know what they are up against. They share a certain static quality: the pastoral term, for instance, in the Grantchester Poem, is decorously but very carefully planning its own erosion, right from the start, and the poet's stance seems to be well outside the poem. Even in "The Eye-Mote," where there is an expansion into the Oedipus myth, it is told rather than enacted: "I dream that I am Oedipus." Though "the brooch-pin and the salve" effectively revise the splinter and the eye-bath, they do so by a movement of literary reference, very different from the total resonance in "Nick" where the poem is plainly gathering its strengths and meanings, like all the best art, from conscious and unconscious assembling. The brilliant stroke of wit in "Before the brooch-pin and the salve/Fixed me in this parenthesis" is perhaps a limited one: the pun is dazzling in the light of the Oedipal situation, and plainly relates to all those other poems about parent-relationships. But after a little reflection one begins to wonder if *parenthesis* is quite the best word, after all, for either the Oedipal blindness or a loss of innocence. A spurt of wit remains on the superficial level. As a pun, it is not quite up to Mercutio's or Lady Macbeth's.

Ted Hughes tells us, in his *Triquarterly* piece, that the personality of Oedipus and others were important *personae* in her life, but he is right to say that in this poem, and elsewhere, they may seem literary. It is not a matter of artificiality but of a certain thinness of feeling: the enlargement does not quite come off. Similarly, in the Grantchester poem, which strikes me perhaps as a subdued answer to Dylan Thomas's "Sir John's Hill" (just as "Nick" seems like a subdued answer to Hopkins's "The Starlight Night") the movement from the human situation to the animal world seems relaxed, cool, insufficiently felt—or rather, felt to be felt in the poem. Her feelings for Greek tragedy and animal life were evidently far from thinly literary, but in some of these poems they were not yet getting sufficiently incorporated and expressed.

There are a number of poems in *Colossus*, however, where a different stance and structure achieves something much more imaginatively substantial: "Lorelei," "All the Dead Dears," "Suicide Off Egg Rock," "Full Fathom Five," "Medallion," "The Burnt-Out Spa" and "Mussel Hunter at Rock Harbor" are most impressive poems of a dying fall. Each moves slowly and lucidly into a death or a longing for a death or a blessing of death. They are, if you like, perverse love-poems. Instead of working by the usual kind of enlargement, from the personal to the larger world, they attempt an empathetic drama, where a kind of death is explored, imagined, justified. If I list the last lines, a common quality in the conclusions can be my starting-point:

> Stone, stone, ferry me down there.
> ("Lorelei")

> Deadlocked with them, taking root as cradles rock.
> ("All the Dead Dears")

> The forgetful surf creaming on those ledges.
> ("Suicide Off Egg Rock")

> I would breathe water.
> ("Full Fathom Five")

> The yardman's/Flung brick perfected his laugh.
> ("Medallion")

> The stream that hustles us
> Neither nourishes nor heals.
> ("The Burnt-out Spa")

> this relic saved/Face, to face the bald-faced sun.
> ("Mussel Hunter at Rock Harbor")

Each poem is dramatised, individualised. Each constructs a different feeling for death. These conclusions, which all settle for death, are earned in separate and solidly substantial ways, emotionally intense and rationally argued, each working through a distinct human experience which ends by wanting death.

In "Lorelei" it is the peace of death that lures, which is why the sirens' song and their silence are both maddening. The sense of "maddening" is both superficial and profound, for the listener knows that what the sirens offer is illusion, cannot be a solicitation except in nightmare or when "deranged by harmony." The images are fully responsive: "descant from borders/Of hebetude, from the ledge/Also of high windows" and "Drunkenness of the great depths" and "your ice-hearted calling." It is the earlier "Sisters, your song/Bears a burden too weighty/For the whorled ear's listening" that earns the sense of inevitability in the final weight of "Stone, stone."

The same can be said of all the other poems in this group. Each makes its individual movement to death; each is a dying. In "All the Dead Dears" death is repulsive, but none the less urgent for that. The dead pull us, willy-nilly, into our graves and the three skeletons in the Archaeological Museum are suitably and grotesquely "unmasked" and "dry" witnesses to life's (death's?) eating-game. The poem moves step by step from the first instance, from the stranger-in-blood to the sense of ancestral pull, to the father's death, through the family feasts, into a coffin as inevitable as a cradle. The whole poem takes colour from the first grotesque image, so that her father's death (of course a recurring image) is seen in the right bizarre fashion: "Where the daft father went down/With orange duckfeet winnowing his hair," and the right, though typically very mild (it strengthens terribly once we see through it, though, this mildness) sense of the animal and human, and the live and dead, overlapping. The final Gulliver image completes the grotesque line and the imagery of a trap.

The image of clarity and cleanness at the end of "Suicide Off Egg Rock" finishes off the man who walks away from the debris of the beach and the muck of living—"that landscape/Of imperfections his bowels were part of." Each poem is a separate dying, thoroughly imagined. The apparently stoical image of the crab's face at the end of that very fine poem "Mussel Hunter at Rock Harbor" may look like an emblem proffered to the human world by the animals, but must take on the colour of all that goes before. It is only a crab face saved, a crab death, a scrupulous rejection of symbol made at the end of a poem that has slowly forced the human being to feel itself reduced in and by the seabeast world. The terrible "Full Fathom Five" creates an oceanic image with human features, and the real drowned father colours the terror and makes possible a childlike plea for water rather than thick and murderous air. "The Burnt-Out Spa" establishes, rather like "Suicide Off Egg Rock," a rubbishy land in contrast to a pure water, and this is reinforced in the final yearning for the purified human reflection: "It is not I, it is not I," whose sad wail is explained by all that has gone before.

These are individuated dramas of dying. The obsession is evident: the poetic flexibility, the inventive enlargements, and the self-explanatory structures show the control and the unenclosed sensibility. The actual mythological or literary symbols are part of such enlargement: the Lorelei, the drowned father in Ariel's song, the museum skeletons, Gulliver, the oriental crabface are all part of a dense formation of feeling, not tenuous-seeming annexes, like the Oedipus of "The Eye-Mote." It is such density that may take them to the verge of allegory, but keeps them substantially on its right side. Like much good poetry, it is tempted to be allegory, but refuses.

III

Moving to *Ariel*, the later volume, is to recognise that such inventiveness has become more powerful, and sometimes less lucid. In a poem of pain and delirium, "Fever 103°," the wildness and fast movement of the conceits are excused by the feverishness they dramatise. They cover a wide range. They jerk from Isadora's scarves to Hiroshima ash to lemon water and chicken water; from the bizarre conceit to the simple groping, "whatever these pink things are"; glimpses of horrors to lucidity, self-description, affectionateness, childishness: the range and the confusion establish the state of sickness. There are the other well-known poems of sickness, "Tulips," "In Plaster" and "Paralytic" which dramatise individual, and different, sick states, all of them appropriately formed, in process and style. Each of these four poems is personal (which is not to say that the *persona* is not imaginary: in "in Plaster" and "Paralytic" it seems to be so, judging from external and internal evidence) but each is a complete and controlled drama of sick mind and body. Because it is sickness that is overtly dramatised there is no sense of an improperly won competition with the world's ills. They are brought in, by a species of decorous hallucinations. But the plainness of the act of hallucination, the lucid proffering of a febrile, convalescent, enclosed or paralysed state, allows the larger world to make its presence properly felt. The burning in "Fever 103°" reminds us of atomic ash, while keeping the separation clear. The plaster cast in "in Plaster" reminds us of the other imprisonments and near-successful relationships: "I used to think we might make a go of it together/After all, it was a kind of marriage, being so close." I think Alun Jones is wrong to see this as an allegory about marriage: these poems of sickness allow her to suggest a whole number of identifications which move towards and back from allegory. David Holbrook seems to make a different though related error in his discussion of "Tulips": this is not a sick poem but a poem about being sick. Quite different. Of course it is a sick person who is drawn to poems about sickness, but the physical sickness makes up actual chunks of her existence, and sometimes the poems are about chilblains, cuts, influenza and appendicitis. She is drawn to sickness, mutilation, attacks, and dying, but each poem is a controlled and dynamic image with windows, not a lining of mirrors. In "Fever" and "In Plaster" the dramatised act of hallucination holds the personal and the social in stable and substantial mutual relationships, neither absorbing the other.

In "Tulips" there is a slow, reluctant acceptance of the tulips, which means a slow, reluctant acceptance of a return to life. The poem dramatises a sick state, making it clear that it is sickness. The flowers are hateful, as emblems of cruel spring, as presents from the healthy world that wants her back, as suspect, like all presents. They are also emblems of irrational fear: science is brilliantly misused (as it can be in feeble and deranged states of many kinds) and phototropism and photosynthesis are used to argue the fear: the flowers really do move towards the light, do open out, do take up oxygen. The tulips are also inhabitants of the bizarre world of private irrational fantasy, even beyond the bridge of distorted science: they contrast with the whiteness of nullity and death, are like a baby, an African cat, are like her wound (a real red physical wound, stitched so as to heal, not to gape like opened tulips) and, finally, like her heart. David Holbrook's analysis of this poem seems to stop short of the transforming end, which opens up the poem. The poem, like the tulips, has really been opening from the beginning, but all is not plain until the end, as in "Nick." Holbrook says, "The tulips, as emissaries of love, seem to threaten her with emptying of the identity: "the vivid tulips eat my oxygen"," but the tulips win, and that is the point. It is a painful victory for life. We move from the verge of hallucination, which can hear them as noisy, or see them as like dangerous animals, to a proper rationality, which accepts recovery. The poem hinges on this paradox: while most scientific, it is most deranged; while most surreal, it is most healthy:

> And I am aware. of my heart: it opens and closes
> its bowl of red blooms out of sheer love of me.
> The water I taste is warm and salt, like the sea,
> And comes from a country far away as health.

It is the country she has to return to, reluctant though she is: the identification of the breathing, opened, red, springlike tulips with her heart makes this plain. She wanted death, certainly, as one may want it in illness or, moving back from the poem to the other poems and to her real death, as she wanted it in life. But the poem enacts the movement from the peace and purity of anaesthesia and feebleness to the calls of life. Once more, the controlled conceits and the movement from one state to another create expansion. The poem opens out to our experience of sickness and health, to the overwhelming demands of love, which we sometimes have to meet. The symbolism of present-giving and spring-flowers makes a bridge from a personal death-longing to common experience: something very similar can be found in the short poem "Poppies in October" which uses a similar symbolism and situation for a different conclusion and feeling; and in the magnificent Bee poems, where the solid facts and documentations of beekeeping act as a symbolic base for irrational and frightening fantasy *and* as a bridge into the everyday and ordinary explanations and existences.

The concept of explicit hallucination seems useful. In the Bee poems we move away from the poetry of sickness to another kind of rejected allegory.

These poems stress technical mysteries. The craft and ritual of bee-keeping are described with a Kafkaesque suggestiveness, and can take off into a larger terror and come back after all into the common and solid world. In "The Bee Meeting," her lack of protective clothing, her feeling of being an outsider, then an initiate, the account of the disguised villagers and the final removal of disguise, the queenbee, the spiky gorse, the box—all are literal facts which suggest paranoic images but remain literal facts. The poem constantly moves between the two poles of actuality and symbolic dimension, right up to and including the end. A related poem, "The Arrival of the Bee Box," works in the same way, but instead of suggesting paranoiac fear and victimisation, puts the beekeeper into an unstable allegorical God-position. The casual slangy "but my god" unobtrusively works towards the religious enlargement:

> I am no source of honey
> So why should they turn on me?
> Tomorrow I will be sweet God, I will set them free.
>
> The box is only temporary.

After the suggestiveness comes the last line, belonging more to the literal beekeeping facts, but pulled at least briefly into the symbolic orbit. These are poems of fear, a fear which seems mysterious, too large for its occasion. They allow for a sinister question to raise itself, between the interpretation and the substance. The enlargement which is inseparable from this derangement is morally vital and viable: these poems are about power and fear, killing and living, and the ordinariness and the factual detail work both to reassure us and to establish that most sinister of fears, the fear of the familiar world. Perhaps the most powerful Bee poem comes in the New York edition of *Ariel*, "The Swarm" (also printed in *Winter Trees*). Here the enlargement is total and constant, for the poem equates the destruction of the swarm with a Napoleonic attack, and presents a familiar argument for offensive action: "They would have killed *me*." It presents two objective correlatives, the bees and Napoleon, in an unfailing grim humour

> Stings big as drawing pins!
> It seems bees have a notion of honour,
> A black, intractable mind.
> Napoleon is pleased, he is pleased with everything.
> O Europe! O ton of honey!

The humour comes out of the very act of derangement: imagine comparing this with that, just imagine. It depends on the same kind of rationally alert intelligence that controls "Fever 103°."

It is present in the great *Ariel* poems: "Lady Lazarus," "Daddy," "Death
& Co.," "A Birthday Present" and "The Applicant," which are very outgoing,
very deranged, very enlarged. In "Lady Lazarus" the *persona* is split, and
deranged. The split allows the poem to peel off the personal, to impersonate
suicidal feeling and generalise it. It is a skill, it is a show, something to look
at. The poem seems to be admitting the exhibitionism of suicide (and death-
poetry?) as well as the voyeurism of spectators (and readers?). It is also a foul
resurrection, stinking of death. This image allows her to horrify us, to
complain of being revived, to attack God and confuse him with a doctor, any
doctor (bringing round a suicide) and a Doktor in a concentration camp,
experimenting in life and death. It moves from Herr Doktor to Herr Enemy
and to miraclemakers, scientists, the torturer who may be a scientist, to
Christ, Herr God, and Herr Lucifer (the last two after all collaborated in
experiments on Adam, Eve, and Job). They poke and nose around in the
ashes, and this is the last indignity, forcing the final threat: "I eat men like
air." It is a threat that can intelligibly be made by martyred victims (she has,
red hair, is Jewish), by phoenixes, by fire, by women. The fusion and
dispersal, once more rational and irrational, makes the pattern of controlled
derangement, creating not one mirror but a hall of mirrors, all differently
distorting, and revealing many horrors. Such complexity of reference, such
enactment of desperation, hysteria and hate, permits at times the utterly bare
cry like the endearment in "Nick": "I turn and burn." Again, the range of
tone is considerable. There is the dry irony, only capable of life in such
surroundings of hysteria: "Do not think I underestimate your great
concern," and the slangy humour, "I guess you could say I've a call," which,
like the communion tablet in "Tulips" is an anti-religious joke, not a solemn
allusion, though you do not see the joke unless you feel the solemnity. There
is the sensuous particularity, extremely unpleasant. It is tactual, visual and
olfactory: "Pick the worms off me like sticky pearls," "full set of teeth" and
"sour breath." The sheer active hostility of the poem works through the
constant shift from one mode to another, one tone to another, one persona
to another. It races violently and spasmodically towards the climax.

This kind of structural derangement of structure, which allows for
collision, a complex expansion, and a turn in several directions, sometimes
becomes very surrealist in dislocation. It fragments into opaque parts, as in
that most baffling poem, "The Couriers," and in "The Applicant." We might
be tempted to see the enlargement in "The Applicant" as an allegory of
marriage, relationship, dependence, were if not for the violent twist with
which the poem shuffles off such suggestions:

First, are you our sort of a person?
Do you wear
A glass eye, false teeth or a crutch,
A brace or a hook,
Rubber breasts or a rubber crotch,

Stitches to show something's missing? No, no? Then
How can we give you a thing?
Stop crying.
Open your hand.
Empty? Empty. Here is a hand

To fill it and willing
To bring teacups and roll away headaches
And do whatever you tell it.
Will you marry it?
It is guaranteed

To thumb shut your eyes at the end
And dissolve of sorrow.
We make new stock from the salt.
I notice you are stark naked.
How about this suit—

Black and stiff, but not a bad fit.
Will you marry it?
It is waterproof, shatterproof, proof
Against fire and bombs through the roof.
Believe me, they'll bury you in it.

The hand to fill the empty hand and shut the eyes, or (later) the naked doll that can sew, cook, talk, move towards this allegory, but the black stiff suit "waterproof, shatterproof" in which "they'll bury you" moves away towards any kind of panacea or protection. What holds the poem together, controlling such opacities of derangement, is the violent statement of deficiency hurled out in the first stanza, and the whole violent imitation of the language of salesmanship, the brisk patter of question, observation, suggestion and recommendation. The enlargement works not just through the ill-assembled fragments—hand, suit, and in the later stanzas, doll—but through the satirised speech, which relates needs, deficiencies, dependence and stupid panaceas to the larger world. Life (or love) speaks in the cheap-jack voice, as well it may, considering what it may seem to have to offer. This is an applicant not just for relationship, for marriage, for love, for healing, but for life and death.

This brilliant linguistic impersonation works more generally in these poems, as a source of black humour, as satiric enlargement, as a link with ordinariness, as unselfpitying speech. It is present in small doses but with large effect in the massive, rushing, terrible poem, "Getting There." Here the death train is also the painful dying, the dragging life, also wars, machines, labour. The poem questions, and the questions stagger: "How far is it?/ How far is it now?" It dwells painfully and slowly in the present tense: "I am dragging my body," "And now detonations," "The train is dragging itself." Its derangements present animals and machines in a mangling confusion: the interior of the wheels is "a gorilla interior," the wheels eat, the machines are brains and muzzles, the train breathes, has teeth, drags and screams like an animal. There is a painful sense of the body's involvement in the machine, the body made to be a wheel. The image creates an entanglement, involves what Sartre calls the "dilapidation" of surrealism. There is the horror of a hybrid monster, a surrealist crossing of animal with machine. The rational arguments and logical connections are frightening in their precision. The wheel and the gorilla's face can be confused into one image, big, round, dark, powerful. Krupp's "brains" is almost literally correct. The train noise can sound like a human scream, the front of a train can look like a face.

The method of combination as well as the content, as in all good poetry, generates the passions. The sense of strain, of hallucination, of doing violence to the human imagery is a consequence of the derangements. The rational excuses simply play into the hands of such sense of strain, by making it work visually, bringing it close, giving it substance and connection with the real European world. The movement is a double one, it creates a trope and a form for unbearable pain, and intolerable need for release. It enlarges the personal horror and suggests a social context and interpretation, in Krupp, in the train, in Russia, in the marvellously true and fatigued "some war or other," in the nurses, men, hospital, in Adam's side and the woman's body "Mourned by religious figures, by garlanded children." And finally, in Lethe. Its end and climax is as good as that in "Nick":

> And I, stepping from this skin
> Of old bandages, boredoms, old faces
>
> Step to you from the black car of Lethe,
> Pure as a baby.

There is the naked appearance of the myth new-made, the feeling that Lethe has had to wait till now to be truly explained, as the Nativity had to wait for "Nick." After such pain of living and dying, after so many bewildered identifications, after such pressure and grotesque confusion, we must step right out of the skin. And when we do, the action reflects back, and the body seems to have been the train. This adds another extension of the derangement of human, animal, and mechanical. After this, only Lethe. The poem then begins to look like a nightmare of dying, the beginning of forgetting, the lurching derangements working as they do in dreams.

Once more, the expansion permits the naked cry. This happens more quietly and sadly in "The Moon and the Yew Tree" where the movement outward is against the Christian myth, but works so as to generalise, to show the active seeking mind in the exercise of knowledge and comparison. This movement explains, permits, and holds up the bare dreadful admission, "I simply cannot see where there is to get to." The feeling throughout is one of deep and tried depression. The moon is no light, no door:

> It is a face in its own right,
> White as a knuckle and terribly upset.

The oddity and childishness of the funny little analogy, and the simple bare statement, "terribly upset" all contribute to the tiredness. So does the science of "drags the sea after it like a dark crime" and the conceit "the O-gape of complete despair," which have a slight archness and flickering humour, like someone very tired and wretched who tries a smile. Nature is all too simply interpreted, coloured by "the light of the mind," is cold, planetary, black, blue. The moon is quite separate from the consolations of religion, though there are echoes of other myths which emphasise this, of Hecate and witchcraft, as in "The Disquieting Muses." Such sinister suggestions, like the remote and decorative images of the saints, "all blue,/Floating on their delicate feet over the cold pews,/Their hands and faces stiff with holiness" are made in a matter-of-fact, slightly arch way. These are Stanley Spencer-like visions, made in a childish, tired voice: "The moon is my mother. She is not sweet like Mary./Her blue garments unloose small bats and owls." The very quietness, compared with her more violent poems of fear, has its own stamp of acceptance. The several bald statements in the poem belong to the quiet tired prevailing tone: "How I would like to believe in tenderness" and "the message of the yew tree is blackness—blackness and silence."

This poem of deep depression still enlarges, still knows about the larger world, still tries a tired but personal humour:

Eight great tongues affirming the Resurrection.
At the end, they soberly bong out their names.

The poem's empathy is powerful, but it is perhaps most powerful when it is dropped. The end returns to the explicit act of interpretation—what do the moon and the yew tree mean?—of the beginning. The poem moves heavily into the meditation, then out of it. There has been an attempt at enlargement, but the colours here are the colours of the mind, and the attempts at mythical explanation or extension all fail. It seems like a poem about making the effort to write out of depression, where the act of enlargement is difficult, the distance that can be covered is short.

In "A Birthday Present" the same process shapes a different passion. The enlargement in this poem is again a movement towards Christian myth, this time a perverted annunciation. The poem longs for release, like so many others, but in its individual mood. This time she pleads and reasons carefully, patiently, with humility, is willing to take a long time over it. The pace of her poems varies tremendously, and while "Daddy," "Lady Lazarus" and "Getting There" move with sickening speed, "A Birthday Present" is appallingly slow. Its slowness is right for its patience and its feeling of painful burden. It is created by the pleas, "Let it not . . . Let it not," and the repetitions which here put the brakes on, though in other poems they can act as accelerators. Its questioning slows up, and so does its vagueness, and its unwillingness to argue endlessly—or almost endlessly. The humilities are piteously dramatised: "I would not mind . . . I do not want much of a present . . . Can you not . . . if you only knew . . . only you can give it to me . . . Let it not." There is the childishness, horrifying in the solemn pleasure of "there would be a birthday." From time to time there is the full, adult, knowing, reasoning voice, that can diagnose, "I know why you will not"; reassure, "Do not be afraid"; and be ironic, "O adding machine/Is it impossible for you to let something go and have it whole?/Must you stamp each piece in purple. . ."

It is not surprising that Sylvia Plath felt constrained to speak these late poems: they are dramatised, voiced, often opaque but always personalised. Their enlargements are made within the personal voice: groping for the resemblance to some war, some annunciation, some relationship, some institution, some Gothic shape, some prayer, some faith. Even where there is a movement towards the larger world, as in "The Moon and the Yew Tree" or "A Birthday Present," it has a self-consciousness, a deployment of know-ledge, a reasoning, a sense of human justice, that keeps it from being sick or private. The woman who measures the flour and cuts off the surplus, ad-hering "to rules, to rules, to rules," and the mind that sees the shortcomings of adding-machines is a *persona* resisting narcissism and closure, right to the death.

Ronald Laing is involved in that cult of schizophrenia which has encouraged both an excessive admiration and an excessive rejection of a clinically limited poetry of derangement. I believe that Sylvia Plath's poetry is not so limited, but I should nevertheless like to remember Laing's comment that few books in our time are forgiveable, and to suggest that *The Colossus* and *Ariel* are amongst those few.

R. B. STEPTO

Audre Lorde:
The Severed Daughter

Throughout the years, Afro-American poets and the New York publishing houses have had a both peculiar and predictable relationship. The "peculiar" aspect has been much the same as that which has branded so many other social and business relations as "peculiar": the dominance of race ritual in matters where "pure" human contact should prevail. What has been "predictable" is that the publishing of these poets, when it has occurred, has been in rushes or spates and usually in response to some kind of sociocultural movement or outburst—a "Negro renaissance" in the 1920s, a "Black revolution" in the 1960s—which to no small degree soon becomes, in the world of letters, as much a publisher's hype as a genuine aesthetic upheaval. All this demonstrates (as if we needed further demonstration) that, as institutions, the trade houses are as undeniably American as, say, a department store, an automobile corporation, or the U.S. Army; and that, as American businesses, they are no different from the rest when it comes to the art of making a buck.

But somehow we continue to expect the publishing houses to operate on a plane above that of race ritual and money-making because they are, to an astonishing degree, the discoverers of talent, arbiters of taste, and guardians of the written word. To be sure, many non-Afro-American poets fall into the trough, as it were, either because they are overlooked or because

From *Parnassus: Poetry in Review 8*, no. I (Fall/Winter 1979). © 1980 by Poetry in Review Foundation.

they couldn't or wouldn't ride the crest of a wave. But rarely have they been subjected to the kind of immorality and illiteracy that lies behind the stories too many good Afro-American poets often tell—stories which almost always seem to begin, "they rejected my poems because they weren't 'political,'" or worse, "they wouldn't take my manuscript because it wasn't 'black.'" These "readings" (of a market, perhaps, but not of poetry) from outwardly intelligent people linger and assault the poet and the poet's reviewer alike. While the poet is prompted to ask, "Shall I try again?" the reviewer cannot help wondering if a given book has been published because it has merit or because it has been construed to be part of yet another sociocultural "event." These latter queries are especially pertinent when the poet in question is offering his or her first book, but they pertain as well to the conditions of authorship concocted for or imposed upon the seasoned writer. The publication of a new book of poems, Audre Lorde's *The Black Unicorn* allows us to pursue these questions in several interesting ways, and to observe in particular how major publishing houses, perhaps with some assistance from an author, market a "black book" of poems in what is ostensibly a pause between "renaissances" or "revolutions." . . .

Audre Lorde's seventh volume of poems, *The Black Unicorn, is* a big, rich book of some sixty-seven poems. While *The Black Unicorn is* "packaged" (the prominent half-column of authenticating commentary from Adrienne Rich constitutes much of the wrapping), it really does not need this promoting and protecting shell. Perhaps a full dozen—an incredibly high percentage of these poems are searingly strong and unforgettable. Those readers who recall the clear light and promise of early Lorde poems such as "The Woman Thing" and "Bloodbirth," and recall as well the great shape and energy of certain mid-1970s poems including "To My Daughter the Junkie on a Train," "Cables to Rage," and "Blackstudies," will find in *The Black Unicorn* new poems which reconfirm Lorde's talent while reseeding gardens and fields traversed before. There are other poems which do not so much reseed as repeople, and these new persons, names, ghosts, lovers, voices—these new I's, we's, real and imagined kin—give us something fresh, beyond the cycle of Lorde's previously recorded seasons and solstices.

While *The Black Unicorn* is unquestionably a personal triumph for Lorde in terms of the development of her canon, it is also an event in contemporary letters. This is a bold claim but one worth making precisely because, as we see in the first nine poems, Lorde appears to be the only North American poet other than Jay Wright who is sufficiently immersed in West African religion, culture, and art (and blessed with poetic talent!) to reach beyond a kind of middling poem that merely quantifies "blackness" through offhand reference to African gods and traditions. What Lorde and

Wright share, beyond their abilities to create a fresh, New World out of ancient Old World lore, is a voice or an *idea* of a voice that is essentially African in that it is communal, historiographical, archival, and prophetic *as well as* personal in ways that we commonly associate with the African *griot*, *dyjli*, and tellers of *nganos:* and other oral tales. However, while Wright's voice may be said to embody what is masculine in various West African cultures and cosmologies, Lorde's voice is decidedly and magnificently feminine. The goal of *The Black Unicorn* is then to present this fresh and powerful voice, and to explore the modulations within that voice between feminine and feminist timbres. As the volume unfolds, this exploration charts history and geography as well as voice, and with the confluence of these patterns the volume takes shape and Lorde's particular envisioning of a black transatlantic tradition is accessible.

All this begins, as suggested before, in the first nine poems in which we encounter the legendary women and goddesses—the sisters and especially the mothers—who inaugurate Lorde's genealogy of timbres and visages. In poems such as "From the House of Yemanjá," "Dahomey," and "125th Street and Abomey," mothers including Yemanjá (goddess of oceans, mother of the other Orisha or Yoruba goddesses and gods) and Seboulisa ("The goddess of Abomey—'The Mother of us all'") appear, often in new renderings of the legends that surround them:

> My mother has two faces and a frying pot
> where she cooked up her daughters
> into girls
> before she fixed our dinner.
> My mother has two faces and a broken pot
> where she hid out a perfect daughter
> who was not me
> I am the sun and moon and forever hungry
> for her eyes

Much of this would be little more than mere reference of the sort alluded to before were the poems not galvanized and bound by the persona's unrelenting quest for freedom, voice, and women kin. At the beginning of the quest, the persona is a black unicorn, a protean figure who, in one manifestation, is a Dahomean woman with attached phallus dancing the part of Eshu-Elegba (Yemanjá's messenger son of many tongues) in religious ritual. At the end, she is a "severed daughter"—"severed" in that she is in a new but tethered geography ("125th Street and Abomey") and has cut away an imposed ritual tongue—who has found a voice of her own that can utter

"Whatever Ianguage is needed" (a skill allowed before only to Yemanjá's son)
and can even laugh.

> Half earth and time splits us apart
> like struck rock,
> A piece lives elegant stories
> too simply put
> while a dream on the edge of summer
> of brown rain in nim trees
> snail shells from the dooryard
> of King Toffah
> bring me where my blood moves
> Seboulisa mother goddess with one breast
> eaten away by worms of sorrow and loss
> see me now
> your severed daughter
> laughing our name into echo
> all the world shall remember.

As we move from the first set of poems about black mothers, daughters,
and sisters—women who can "wear flesh like war," conjoin "dying cloth,"
and "mock Eshu's iron quiver"—to those which come in the remaining three
sections, there is a subtle shift in poetic form that appears to signal, in turn,
a shift in focus from acquisition of voice to that of art. In the first set, in
stanzas such as

> The black unicorn is restless
> the black unicorn is unrelenting
> the black unicorn is not
> free.

and

> Mother I need
> mother I need
> mother I need your blackness now
> as the august earth needs rain.

Lorde makes effective use of the principle of repetition that is at the heart of
oral composition in all "pre-literate" cultures, and at the heart as well of such
conspicuous Afro-American art forms as the blues. (Indeed, each of the

stanzas just presented may be said to be a modified but identifiable blues verse.) In the remaining sections of the volume, repetition and other devices which are, in this context, referents in written art to oral forms, are largely forsaken in favor of the kind of taut free verse Lorde usually employs. What is fascinating about this, as suggested before, is that while the declarative voice forged in the first group of poems remains, that voice speaks less of discovering language and of moving, perhaps, from speech to laughter, and more of poems—of written art readily assuming the posture of a healing force.

This is true even of the poems about social unrest and injustice. In "Chain," for example, a poem prompted by a news item describing two teenage girls who had borne children by their natural fathers, there is the cry,

> Oh write me a poem mother
> here, over my flesh
> get your words upon me
> as he got his child upon me

Similarly, in "Eulogy for Alvin Frost" we find,

> I am tired of writing memorials to black men
> whom I was on the brink of knowing
>
> Dear Danny who does not know me
> I am
> writing to you for your father
> whom I barely knew
> except at meetings where he was
> distinguished
> by his genuine laughter
> and his kind bright words

In the final section, "Power" begins with yet another suggested distinction between poetry and speech,

> The difference between poetry and rhetoric
> is being
> ready to kill
> yourself
> instead of your children.

and ends with a very particular statement of confession and self-instruction,

> I have not been able to touch the destruction within me.
> But unless I learn to use
> the difference between poetry and rhetoric
> my power too will run corrupt as poisonous mold
> or lie limp and useless as an unconnected wire

As the latent sexuality in the final line suggests, the shift in *The Black Unicorn* in poetic concern from acquisition of voice to that of art concerns as well the articulation of a homosexual love that was only barely alluded to before in the many figurations of tongue as women-warriors' sword and speech. Indeed, the pulsing love poems, in which tongue finally becomes most explicitly an erotic tool and goal

> I am tempted
> to take you apart
> and reconstruct your orifices
> your tongue your truths your fleshy altars
> into my own forgotten image
>
>   ("Fog Report")

—and in which sex and art most explicitly meet—

> I do not even know
> who looks like you
> of all the sisters who come to me
> at nightfall
> we touch each other in secret places
> draw old signs and stories
> upon each other's back and proofread
> each other's ancient copy.

—consummate the volume in a rich if not altogether unexpected manner.

Whether or not the subject at hand is love, children under assault, people in prison, childhood "wars," or the quest for a certain rare literacy, the poet in *The Black Unicorn* steadily pursues (and defines in that pursuit) a viable heroic posture and voice for womankind. The success of the volume may be seen in the fact that when the poet declares in the final poem,

> I will eat the last signs of my weakness
> remove the scars of old childhood wars
> and dare to enter the forest whistling

we believe her. In this period between renaissance and/or revolutions, Lorde's verse may need promotion in order to sell, but that doesn't mean that the verse is thin or insignificant. *The Black Unicorn* offers contemporary poetry of a high order, and in doing so may be a smoldering renaissance and revolution unto itself.

RICHARD HOWARD

Amy Clampitt:
"The Hazardous Definition
of Structures"

Of [the] 50 poems [in Amy Clampitt's *The Kingfisher*], 14 have appeared in *The New Yorker*, consecrated there by the most fastidious editorial taste now (and for the last 25 years) operative in the world of commercial periodicals; in her own high middle ages, Amy Clampitt has had her first book published ninth in the Knopf Poetry Series, consecrated there by the most fastidious editorial taste now (and for the last four years) operative in the world of commercial publishing; embellished with commendations from Richard Wilbur and Helen Vendler, who has since reviewed the book at length in *The New York Review of Books* ("to enter a Clampitt poem is to enter a distinguished mind that then goes on an unpredictable journey of memory, association, musing, description, judgment, pining, correction and imagining"), this poetry is doomed to success.

Of course, success is perhaps the showiest way we have of ignoring our poets—thrusting them into the neglectful limelight where they can writhe— as if the sound were turned off on a brilliant screen—until someone rescues them from the pillory of acclaim. "A century from now," Vendler prophecies, "someone" will read Clampitt to find out "what, in the twentieth century, made up the stuff of culture." Pathetically, I can only add to this syndrome of camouflaging celebrity, for I too enjoy and admire these poems at just that pitch of enthusiasm which sets them beyond the pale—or the murk—where

From *Parnassus: Poetry in Review 11*, no. 1 (Spring/Summer 1983). © 1984 by Poetry in Review Foundation.

poems usually *take*. It seems to me that *The Kingfisher* has given me more
delight (what Roland Barthes calls *jouissance*, not *plaisir)* than any .first book
of poems since the first book of poems I read by A. R. Ammons. Amy
Clampitt does things in her own way, but of course unless we can say what
that way is, it is not perhaps really doing them. I shall try.

It has to do with some readily identifiable devices. Syntax, for one thing
("in Clampitt, one thing is sure to lead to another"—Vendler): the poem is
wreathed around its grammar, often being one very long sentence,
submissive to the voice, observant of the local inflections, but governing the
weight of the lines on the page, down the page, so that we know throughout
that we are within a governance, the thrall of grammar, which is the same
word, if you trace it far enough "back," as glamour. When the man
protesting against witches in the *Malleus Malleficarum* claims he knows he has
been ensorceled because "she cast a glamor about my member," we may
pre-empt his phrase and apply it to the elements of a Clampitt poem in its
articulation: she casts a glamour about its members which are not, here,
phallic but fraternal, participating agencies of subordination, because she
wields a pertinent grammar upon and within them. In this she brings to mind
not her immediate lineage (that matriarchal mass we begin to perceive:
Moore, Swenson—who also commends Clampitt's "keen mind" on the
jacket—Bishop, Van Duyn; we shall end by perceiving the connection these
poets have with certain lyric prose-writers: Paley, Ozick, most recently
Marilyn Robinson), but the incremental redundancies of Robert Browning,
whose music is syntactical, not a matter of chiming. Consider these parallel
stanzas:

Wheeling, the careening	All I believed is true!
winds arrive with lariats	I am able yet
and tambourines of rain.	All I want, to get
Torn-to-pieces, mud-dark	By a method as strange as new:
flounces of Caribbean	Dare I trust the same to you?
cumulus keep passing,	If at night, when doors are shut,
keep passing. By afternoon	And the wood-worm picks,
rinsed transparencies begin	And the death-watch ticks
to open overhead, Mediterranean	And the bar has a flag of smut,
windowpanes of clearness	And a cat's in the water-butt—
crossed by young gusts'	And the socket floats and flares,
vaporous fripperies, liquid	And the house-beams groan,
footprints flying, lacewing	And a foot unknown

leaf-shade brightening	I surmised on the garret-stairs,
and fading. Sibling	And the locks slip unawares
gales stand up on point	And the spider, to serve his ends,
in twirling fouettés	By a sudden thread,
of debris. The day ends	Arms and legs outspread,
bright-cloud-wardrobe	On the table's midst descends,
packed away. Nightfall	Comes to find, God knows what friends!
hangs up a single moon	If since eve drew in, I say,
bleached white as laundry,	I have sat and brought
serving notice yet again how	(so to speak) my thought
levity can also trample,	To bear on the woman away,
drench, wring and mangle.	Till I felt my hair turn gray . . .

There is a parallel confidence as well in the thread of syntax—except, of course, that Browning's sentence (on the right) will go on for eleven more stanzas: he is the more difficult poet, determinedly so. But as my little exhibition makes plain, Clampitt's other main device, or at least one you can collect for yourself by merely glancing at her page, is her science of enjambment (replacing rhyme by unwonted suspensions). This is probably the most arduous weapon in the armory of the regiment of women poets I have invoked—and on their discoveries we are still, as it were, banking. Clampitt ends her lines—breaks them open—in such a way as to show meanings not otherwise evident. The sense strikes against the ends of lines and their beginnings like a river defining itself by its entertainment now of one bank, now of the other, and this axiological enclosure becomes her signature, Clampitt's way of ensuring the meaning of every method that comes to hand.

The book's title, we may note, comes from Hopkins's famous sonnet: "As kingfishers catch fire, dragonflies draw flame"—something to do with the analogies, across realms of being, of comparable, exchangeable energies. In Hopkins as in Clampitt, any object, by fulfilling its distinctive nature, gives glory back to the energy which brought it into being—the energy which Hopkins calls God. For him (and for Him), the object cries: *what I do is me, for that I came*; for her, the glory is less clamorous: *"there being no past to speak of / other than setbacks."*

In Clampitt, we discover that the objects are likely to be broken, discarded, or ruined ones—a leak in the brickwork beside a stairway in the Times Square Subway: "as though we watched the hairline fracture/ of the quotidian widen to a geomorphic fissure"; and again the residue of junk on the littoral, "Beach Glass":

I keep a lookout for beach glass—
amber of Budweiser, chrysoprase
of Almadén and Gallo, lapis
by way of (no getting around it,
I'm afraid) Phillips'
Milk of Magnesia, with now and then a rare
translucent turquoise or blurred amethyst
of no known origin.

                              The process
goes on forever: they came from sand,
they go back to gravel,
along with the treasuries
of Murano, the buttressed
astonishments of Chartres,
which even now are readying
for being turned over and over as gravely
and gradually as an intellect
engaged in the hazardous
redefinition of structures
no one has yet looked at.

This transformation of discard into value is what we can listen for first in the poems of Amy Clampitt. In a poem like "Salvage" she will reach as far back as she writes forward,

      re-establishing
      with each arcane
      trash-basket dig
      the pleasures of the ruined.

In a culture like ours, near to drowning in its own garbage, she functions with a certain ecological security: waste not, want not, especially when it is out of others' waste that you can make up your own wants. Not surprisingly, there are fifteen pages of notes—not teasing, as in Eliot or Empson; not merely identifying, as in Moore; but midwifely: "the scheme may be clearer if this poem is thought of as a meditation in the form of a travelogue." One advantage about publishing your poems when you are so evidently a grownup (which means, of course: uncertain, as no adolescent can afford to be, about what being a grown-up means) is that you don't have to be nervous about being hard, obscure, or even just complicated. You just go ahead and tell how to get on with it. These poems are enormously allusive (nor does she reveal that we need to remember "milk of Magnesia" is a classical reference as willingly as she explains her Catholic ones: "clean as a crucifix—a thrift . . . that looks like waste"), and they are expansive too—from Iowa to Greece by way of Italy, France, and England, with flying visits to Africa and Tenochtitlán. I suppose that is one way of saying (not claiming) that the poet is "major," "strong," "relevant"—whatever the current cant for the poet who shoulders others out of the way: Clampitt expects you to be prepared to deal with *anything* in her poems, and if you are not, she will help you. What she calls the "hazardous redefinition of structures/ no one has yet looked at" is what we can listen for, look to initially, in her poems. They will reward us as only the new poet can, by making us re-order the old poets, and adding herself to what it is we can do to the world ("everything that is the case") by perceiving it. I shall praise *The Kingfisher* best by saying that its poet jeopardizes her second book extravagantly: I have never waited for *the next installment* with greater qualms, yet with greater confidence.

JOHN HOLLANDER

Tremors of Exactitude:
Vicki Hearne's Nervous Horses

V icki Hearne's first collection of poems is the work of a writer who trains
horses and reads Wittgenstein. [This book will not] satisfy easy expectations.
Hearne's *Nervous Horses* are both sinewy and agitated, as they are both actual
and figurative—the horses of modernity. Her poems, largely in supple and
controlled syllabic verse, are meditative but taut. In "Genuine and
Poignant," she shows she has learned Wallace Stevens's first lessons in poetic
dressage:

> Just that once, not to grieve, and the hill
> To stand suddenly bare and pure
> Confidently shaking its dust
> Through the warm window.

But she moves in other poems to the more animated subject of her horses
and her dogs. Aware of the philosophical problem of other minds, of how
(and even what) we know of others' thoughts and feelings, she treats the
otherness of animals as intimate and terrifying. The consciousness of those
animals, a beautifully hypothetical entity which keeps flickering in and out of
interest, the more we know and are with them, is among the things this book
so beautifully explores. The poems form a kind of romance in which our

From *Times Literary Supplement*, no. 4061 (January 30, 1981). © 1981 by John Hollander.

theories about how we ought sensibly to talk, and what the skilled experience of training animals leads one to say, are engaged in a dialectical sparring-match.

But she writes neither mock training-manuals, nor the journal notes of a self-conscious rider. Her poems often puzzle and are puzzled themselves; she is particularly concerned to avoid the way in which so much contemporary verse sets up and relates crude concepts of subject and object, experience and image, in an unacknowledged and unexplored realm of thought. The book's final, splendid "The Metaphysical Horse" is a poem about coming to terms with one's own metaphors—in this case, conceptions which are like mirror-images but which, having been lived with, allow her to end as follows:

> Circling elegantly we
> Glimpse the always receding
> True proposal in the glass
> And join the horses, who dance,
> Tremors of exactitude
> Flaring, still fresh on their limbs.

Hearne's practical experience of horses is at one with her interest in their mythologies. Plato's fable of horse and rider, Renaissance training manuals, the folklore of handlers, fall like shadows over her actual animals. She herself has what she calls in the title of one poem "The fastidiousness of the Musician"; exercises, lessons, set problems and puzzles are her typical occasions. The longest poem here, the penultimate "St. George and the Dragon" has a quasi-narrative line, but records the quest not of the mounted knight, but rather for him, in the fragmentations of a picture-puzzle. The problem of piecing together an imaginative construction that will hold harks back to James Merrill's jigsaw puzzle of memory in "Lost in Translation." Hearne's poem modulates this into an amusingly domesticated metaphor in which friends and teachers help the poet cope with the epistemological puzzles, trials and errors which occupy the whole of this distinguished first book.

NORTHROP FRYE

Jay Macpherson: Poetry in Canada, 1957

This is an unusually thin year: one good book, two promising ones, and a miscellaneous assortment of what the Elizabethans might politely have called a paradise of dainty devices, though it would be more accurate to speak of an amusement park of rhythmical gadgets. Some of these latter are pleasant and readable enough: with others, one is strongly tempted to take the plangent tone of a couplet which appears on the opening page of one of the year's few published volumes:

> Last of the mighty oaks nurtured in freedom!
> Brambles and briars now supersede treedom.

However, here goes. The good book, of course, as the Governor-General's committee has this time recognized, is Jay Macpherson's *The Boatman*. . . . The book itself is one of the few physically attractive objects on my Canadian poetry shelves, and the fact is an appropriate tribute to its contents, for *The Boatman* is the most carefully planned and unified book of poems that has yet appeared in these surveys. It is divided into six parts. The first, "Poor Child," contains poems that appeared in a small pamphlet reviewed here some years ago: they form a series of tentative explorations of poetic experience, ranging in tone from the macabre "The Ill Wind" to the

From *University of Toronto Quarterly* 27, no. 4 (July 1958). © 1958 by University of Toronto Press.

plaintive "The Third Eye." The next two sections are called "O Earth Return" and "The Plowman in Darkness." The titles come from two poems of Blake that deal with "Earth" as the whole of fallen nature in female form, and the subjects are chiefly the more common mythical figures connected with this "Earth," including Eve, Eurynome, the Cumaean Sibyl, Mary Magdalene, and the bride of the Song of Songs, identified with the Queen of Sheba. Hence the subtitle, "A Speculum for Fallen Women." The two parts are, like Blake's lyrics, matched by contrast against each other, the relation often being marked by identical titles. The contrast is not so much Blake's innocence and experience, though related to it, as a contrast between a theme idealized by a kind of aesthetic distance and the same theme made colloquial and familiar. "Sibylla," whose fate is described in the motto to Eliot's *The Waste Land*, appears in "O Earth Return" thus:

> Silence: the bat-clogged cave
> Lacks breath to sigh.
> Sibylla, hung between earth and sky,
> Sways with the wind in her pendant grave

and in "The Plowman in Darkness" thus:

> I'm mercifully rid of youth.
> No callers plague me ever;
> I'm virtuous, I tell the truth—
> And you can see I'm clever!

In the last two sections the corresponding male figures appear. "The Sleepers," intensely pastoral in tone, is focused on Endymion and his moon-loved daze, with overtones of Adonis and Adam. Then the figures of Noah and his ark emerge, expanding until they become identified with God and his creation respectively. The creation is inside its creator, and the ark similarly attempts to explain to Noah, in a series of epigrams in double quatrains, that it is really inside him, as Eve was once inside Adam:

> When the four quarters shall
> Turn in and make one whole,
> then I who wall your body,
> Which is to me a soul,
>
> Shall swim circled by you
> And cradled on your tide,

> Who was not even, not ever,
> Taken from your side.

As the ark expands into the flooded world, the body of the Biblical leviathan, and the order of nature, the design of the whole book begins to take shape. *The Boatman* begins with a poem called "Ordinary People in the Last Days," a wistful poem about an apocalypse that happens to everyone except the poet, and ends with a vision of a "Fisherman" who, more enterprising than Eliot's gloomy and luckless shore-sitter, catches a "myriad forms," eats them, drinks the lake they are in, and is caught in his turn by God.

Such myths as the flood—and the apocalypse appear less for religious than for poetic reasons: the book moves from a "poor child" at the centre of a hostile and mysterious world to an adult child who has regained the paradisal innocent vision and is at the circumference of a world of identical forms. In the title poem the reader is urged to follow this process as best he may:

> Then you take the tender creature
> —You remember, that's the reader—
> And you pull him through his navel inside out.

The wonderland of this Noah's ark inside Noah, where the phoenix and the abominable snowman have equal rights with books and eggs and the sun and moon, is explored in the final section: "The Fisherman: A Book of Riddles." The riddles are not difficult, the solutions being thoughtfully provided in the title, and, like so many of the Anglo-Saxon riddles, they are circumferential rather than simply elliptical descriptions, hence the riddle on "Egg" symbolizes the poet's relation to her reader as well:

> Reader, in your hand you hold
> A silver case, a box of gold.
> I have no door, however small,
> Unless you pierce my tender wall,
> And there's no skill in healing then
> Shall ever make me whole again.
> Show pity, Reader, for my plight:
> Let be, or else consume me quite.

Miss Macpherson chooses strict metres and small frames: she is, as the blurb says, melodious, but her melody is of that shaped and epigrammatic quality which in music is called tune. Within her self-imposed limits there is an extraordinary tonal variety, from the delicate *ritardando* of "The Caverned Woman" to the punning *knittelvers* of "The Boatman," and from the whispered *pianissimo* of "Aiaia" (the island of Circe) to the alliterative thundering of "Storm." She can—a noticeable feat in Canada—write a sexual poem without breaking into adolescent pimples and cackles; she can deal with religious themes without making any reed-organ wheezes about the dilemma of modem man; she has a wit and an erudition that are free of wisecracks and pedantry; she can modulate in eight lines from "Philomel's unmeasured grief" to the human jay who

> Chatters, gabbles, all the day,
> Raises both Cain and Babel.

The elegiac poems are the most resonant, and they make the strongest initial impression, though the lighter ones have equal staying power. There are few dying falls: usually a poem ends with a quiet authority that has a ring of finality about it, leaving the reader nothing to do but accept the poem "Reader, take," as the riddle on "Book" says.

There is little use looking for bad lines or lapses in taste: *The Boatman* is completely successful within the conventions it adopts, and anyone dissatisfied with the book must quarrel with the conventions. Among these are the use of a great variety of echoes, some of them direct quotations from other poems, and an interest in myth, both Biblical and Classical, that may make some readers wonder uneasily if they should not be reading it with a mythological handbook.

One should notice in the first place that the echoes are almost invariably from the simplest and most popular types of poetry. They include Elizabethan lyrics ("While Philomel's unmeasured grief" sounds like the opening of a madrigal); the lyrics of Blake; hymns ("Take not that Spirit from me"); Anglo-Saxon riddles; Christmas carols ("The Natural Mother"); nursery rhymes ("Sheba"); ballads and newspaper verse ("Mary of Egypt" and the second "Sibylla"). The use made of these echoes is to create a kind of timeless style, in which everything from the tags of mediaeval ballad to modem slang can fit. One has a sense of rereading as well as reading, of meeting new poems with a recognition that is integrally and specifically linked with the rest of one's poetic experience. The echoes also enable the poet to achieve the most transparent simplicity of diction. There is little of the "density" of more intellectualized poetry, and ambiguities and ironies are carried very lightly:

In a far-off former time
And a green and gentle clime,
Mamma was a lively lass,
Liked to watch the tall ships pass,
Loved to hear the sailors sing
Of sun and wind and voyaging,
Felt a wild desire to be
On the bleak and unplowed sea.

The flat conventional phrases here, including the Homeric tag in the last line, would seem commonplace or affected if their context had not been so skillfully worked out for them. It is true that for many readers there is nothing so baffling as simplicity, but Miss Macpherson's simplicity is uncompromising.

As for mythology, that is one of poetry's indispensable languages: most of the major English poets, including the best poets of today, demand and expect a considerable knowledge of myth, and although Douglas LePan calls Canada a country without a mythology, the same thing is increasingly true even of Canadian poets. Miss Macpherson's myths, like her allusions, flow into the poems: the poems do not point to them. Knowing who Adam and Eve and Noah are will get one through most of the book, and although a glance at the opening page of Robert Graves's Penguin book on Greek myth might help with Eurynome, I find no poem that has the key to its meaning outside itself.

Oh wake him not until he please,
Lest he should rise to weep:
For flocks and birds and streams and trees
Are golden in his silver sleep.

For thousands of years poetry has been ringing the changes on a sleeper whom it is dangerous to waken, and the myths of Endymion, of the bridegroom in the Song of Songs, of Adam, of Blake's Albion, of Joyce's Finnegan, are a few of the by-products. Such myths in the background enrich the suggestiveness of the above four lines, but the lines are not dependent on the echoes, either for their meaning or for their poetic value. Or again:

The woman meanwhile sits apart and weaves
Red rosy garlands to dress her joy and fear.
But all to no purpose; for petals and leaves
Fall everlastingly, and the small swords stands clear.

The reader who remembers his Milton, however vaguely, will see how the fall of sex from love to lust belongs in a complex which includes the first efforts at clothing, the appearance of thorns on the rose, the coming of winter after fall, the angelic swords over Paradise, and the aggressive use of sex which the phallic image of "small swords" suggests. But none of this would have any point if the quatrain itself did not carry its own meaning.

I have glanced at the critical issues raised by *The Boatman* because it seems to me a conspicuous example of a tendency that I have seen growing since I began this survey eight years ago. With the proviso that "professional" in this context has nothing to do with earning a living, the younger Canadian poets have become steadily more professional in the last few years, more concerned with poetry as a craft with its own traditions and discipline. The babble of unshaped free verse and the obscurities of private association are inseparable from amateurish poetry, but they are emphatically not "modern" qualities: serious modem poets in Canada struggle hard for clarity of expression and tightness of structure. The second volumes of Douglas LePan, P. K. Page, and James Reaney (of whom more next year) show this markedly, as do the first volumes of Wilfred Watson and Anne Wilkinson, and all the volumes of Irving Layton since *In the Midst of My Fever*. It is consistent with this that the more amateurish approach which tries to write up emotional experiences as they arise in life or memory has given way to an emphasis on the formal elements of poetry, on myth, metaphor, symbol, image, even metrics. The development is precisely parallel to the development in Canadian painting from deliberately naive landscape to abstraction and concentration on pictorial form. As in 1890 with the Scot-Lampman-Roberts group, and again in the *New Provinces* generation, there seems to be once more in Canadian poetry, on a much bigger scale, a "school" in its proper sense of a number of poets united only by a common respect for poetry.

MARGARET ATWOOD

Jay Macpherson: Poems Twice Told

Whehen I was young, poetry reviewing in Canada was very ingrown. Poets reviewed the work of their friends and enemies then, partly because few others were interested in reviewing poetry at all, partly because the poetry world was so small that everyone in it was either a friend or an enemy. However, it was understood that anyone likely to read the review would know which was which.

Writers still occasionally review their friends and enemies, but it can no longer be assumed that the average reader knows it. So I feel it necessary to state by way of prelude that Jay Macpherson not only taught me Victorian literature back in 1960—like all good teachers, she behaved as if it mattered, thus converting my surly contempt for the subject into fascinated admiration—but is one of my oldest and most appreciated friends. Having said that, I will retreat to the middle distance, from which the reviewer's voice should issue impartial as God's (though it rarely does) and try to deal with the subject at hand.

Impossible, of course. Re-reading *The Boatman*, the first of the two books included in this volume, makes me remember Jay Macpherson as I first knew her. I was enormously impressed, not just by the fact that here in front of me was a real poet, and a woman at that, who had actually had a book published—no mean feat in the Canada of those days—but by her wardrobe.

From *Second Words*. © 1982 by O. W. Toad Ltd. House of Anansi Press Ltd. and Beacon Press, 1982.

She always wore clothes that were by no means "fashionable," clothes in fact that nobody else could get away with, but which seemed exactly right for *her*.

It's the same with the poetry. No one else writes like this. In fact, looking back, it seems that no one else ever did, and that all the fuss about a "mythopoeic school" of poetry was simply misguided criticism. If "mythopoeic" means that the poet lets on she knows about mythologies, the most unlikely among us would have to accept the label. (Daphne Marlatt, George Bowering and Frank Davey, for example.) Although a critic intent on the usual version of this theory might make a case for *The Boatman* and its involvement with the shapes of traditional stories, *Welcoming Disaster* would probably defeat him. Its personal and indeed sometimes notably eccentric voice carries the reader far beyond any notions of "school." Macpherson's poetry is one-of-a-kind, not in defiance of current convention so much as apart from it. It's a world unto itself, and from *The Boatman's* poem called "Egg" comes the best advice for approaching it: "Let be, or else consume me quite."

The Boatman has been much written about, but for the sake of those who may not be familiar with it I'll say a little about it. It appears to be a "sequence" of very short, condensed lyric poems. (I say "appears," because it was not planned that way; Macpherson is not a programmatic writer, and her work, when it falls into sequences, does so because her imagination is working with a certain body of material, not because she thinks she needs a poem of a certain kind to fill a gap and then composes it.) They are not an of the same kind: some are straight-faced lyrics, some are sinister or comic parodies on the same subjects (*pace* Blake's two sets of *Songs)* and some are puzzle-poems, or riddles. I tend to get on a little better with the straight lyrics. The others are adroit and clever, though they seem to me to exist, as many kinds of jokes do, for the purpose of defusing a profound uneasiness.

The central voice of *The Boatman* is one of a complex and powerful grief, and its central symbols revolve around separation and loss. Like all hermetic poetry, *The Boatman* offers the reader multiple choices about its true "subject." Is it "about" the relationship between two lovers, the relationship between Creator and fallen world, the relationship between author, book and reader, or dreamer and dream, or man and his imaginative world? Why not all? The most potent poems in the book, for me, are those in the small sequence-within-a-sequence, "The Ark," eight eight-line lyrics that are astonishing for their simplicity and grace, and for the amount of emotional force they can pack into sixty-four lines. They are "about" all of the above, and after more than twenty years of reading them I still find them devastating.

One of Macpherson's most exquisite poems is in the small section entitled "Other Poems"—post-*Boatman*, pre-*Disaster*. It's called "The Beauty of Job's Daughters," and I won't quote from it because you need to read the whole thing, but it's an excellent example of what an outwardly-formal, flexibly-handled lyricism can do. It also epitomizes one of the main themes of *The Boatman*: the "real" world, that of the imagination, is inward.

Between *The Boatman* and "Other Poems," and *Welcoming Disaster*, came a long pause. Macpherson's total output has been minute compared with that of most other Canadian poets of her stature, and she's about the farthest thing from a "professional" poet you could imagine. A young novelist said to me recently, "Poetry isn't an art, it's a circuit." For Macpherson, never a circuit-rider, poetry isn't a "profession" but a gift, which is either there or not there but can't be made to be there by exercise of will. In fact, the first poems in *Welcoming Disaster* are about the loss or absence of the imaginative world so beautifully evoked in "Job's Daughters," the failure of inspiration, and the futility of trying to conjure it up. As well as its redemptive qualities: "Breathing too is a simple trick, and most of us learn it. / Still, to lose it is bad, though no-one regrets it long." When the Muse finally shows up, what she reveals this time is not paradise regained.

If *The Boatman* is "classical" (which, in purity of line, simplicity of rhythms, and choice of myths and symbols, it is), then *Welcoming Disaster* is, by the same lights, "romantic": more personal, more convoluted, darker and more grotesque, its rhythms more complex, its main symbol-groupings drawn not only from Classical and Biblical mythology but from all kinds of odd corners: nineteenth-century Gothic novels (and their twentieth-century avatars, such as *Nosferatu* and Karloff movies), the Grimms' Goose Girl story ("What Falada Said"), Babylonian mythology ("First and Last Things"), lore of magicians, ghouls, mazes and crossroads. The main movement of the book concerns a descent to the underworld; and, as everyone knows, the most successful recipes for this include a plan for getting not only there but back, usually by means of the advice or actual company of a sybil, spirit guide or boatman. (The boatman in *The Boatman* is mainly Noah; in *Welcoming Disaster* it's his upside-down counterpart, Charon, who takes you not to the world renewed but to the world dead.) In this case the fetish-cum-spirit-guide-cum-God-cum-sinister-ferryman is a teddy bear, which—again—only Macpherson could get away with.

What's in the underworld? In Egyptian mythology it's the place where the soul is weighed; for Orpheus, it's the place where the lost love is finally lost; in Jackson Knight's book on Virgil (cited in Macpherson's notes) the underground maze leads to the king and queen of the dead, especially the queen: it's a place of lost mothers. There are echoes too of all those nineteenth-century ghosts, from Catherine Earnshaw on down, who come to the window at night, of vampiristic or sinister-double relationships which recall Blake's Shadow and Emanation figures; of Faustian pacts with darkness. Jungians will revel in this book, though it is hardly orthodox Jungianism. But the important thing is that in the process some poems emerge that would more than satisfy Houseman: they do make the hair stand up on the back of your neck. "They Return," for instance, or "Hecate Trivia," or "Some Ghosts and Some Ghouls."

Welcoming Disaster, like *The Boatman*, has its more playful moments, but on the whole its tone ranges between the eerie and the ruthless: poems of invocation or rigorous and sometimes bloody-minded self-analysis. Macpherson was never much of a meditative Wordsworthian, if such labels apply. She's much more like Coleridge: inner magic, not outer-world description or social comment, is her *forte*.

When I was asked to write this review it was suggested that I include an "appreciation" of Macpherson's "career." But what do we mean by a poet's "career," apart from the poems? Do poets even have "careers?" Some do, but it's a word that seems more appropriate when applied to politicians: something pursued, worked at, having to do with leverage and personal advancement and the media-created persona. Jay Macpherson is simply not career-minded in this way. There's nowhere she wants to get, in the sense of "getting somewhere." She reminds us that poetry is not a career but a vocation, something to which one is called, or not, as the case may be. She's still the best example I know of someone who lives as if literature, and especially the writing of poetry, were to be served, not used.

HAROLD BLOOM

Anne Carson: Eros, Irony, the Sublime

The Canadian poet Anne Carson is so original and authentic in her works that I can think of only two other poets of her eminence now alive and writing in English: John Ashbery and Geoffrey Hill, and they are a full generation older.

A classical scholar by profession, Carson is a learned poet, but always with a difference. She is like no one else alive. Emily Brontë and Emily Dickinson are her authentic precursors. Carson is a poet of the Sublime, in the sense that she revives in her "Essay with Rhapsody," *FOAM*. Longinus, the true origin of literary criticism, is her quarry, because his Sublime consists of quotations, "lustres," as Plutarch and Emerson called them. These come at us like volcanic eruptions, and clearly Carson is fond of active volcanoes, as Longinus must have been:

> Look this is the real Homer who storms like a wind alongside the fighting men, none other than Homer who "rages as when spearshaking Ares or ruinous fire in the mountains rages, in folds of deep forest, and foam is around his mouth."
> —Longinus, *On the Sublime* 9.11; Homer, *Iliad* 15.605-7

Appearing first in this publication ©2002 by Harold Bloom

Carson's genius is to spot that foam and elucidate it:

> Foam is the sign of an artist who has sunk his hands into his own
> story, and also of a critic storming and raging in folds of his own
> deep theory.

Carson's first book was *Eros the Bittersweet: An Essay* (1986), a meditation
upon a trope of Sappho (all of whose fragments Carson has now translated).
In the dance of Sappho's mind: "Desire moves. Eros is a verb." Invoking
Plato's *Phaedrus*, *Eros the Bittersweet* breaks off (it cannot end, or come to rest)
with a luminously resigned paragraph:

> From the testimony of lovers like Sokrates or Sappho we can
> construct what it would be like to live in a city of no desire. Both
> the philosopher and the poet find themselves describing Eros in
> images of wings and metaphors of flying, for desire is a
> movement that carries yearning hearts from over here to over
> there, launching the mind on a story. In the city without desire
> such flights are unimaginable. Wings are kept clipped. The
> known and the unknown learn to align themselves one behind
> the other so that, provided you are positioned at the proper
> angle, they seem to be one and the same. If there *were* a visible
> difference, you might find it hard to say so, for the useful verb
> *mnaomai* will have come to mean "a fact is a fact." To reach for
> something else than the facts will carry you beyond this city and
> perhaps, as for Sokrates, beyond this world. It is a high-risk
> proposition, as Sokrates saw quite clearly, to reach for the
> difference between known and unknown. He thought the risk
> worthwhile, because he was in love with wooing itself. And who
> is not?

The wisdom of Socrates was not to think that he knew what he did not
know. I suppose that the use of literature for life is reaching wisdom, not to
reach wisdom, which cannot be done. Carson is a wisdom writer of genius,
rather than a Socratic wise woman. She is an artist who has sunk her hands
into her own story, and she has a Homeric effect upon a critic (at least this
one), causing me to storm and rage in my own deep theory of influence. Her
strong reading of Emily Brontë and of Emily Dickinson is implicit in much
of her poetry, and sometimes emerges with fierce explicitness.

Carson's first book after *Eros the Bittersweet* was *Short Talks* (1992),
available now as Part II of *Plainwater* (1995). The scariest of these thirty-two
prose poems is "On Walking Backwards":

My mother forbad us to walk backwards. That is how the dead walk, she would say. Where did she get this idea? Perhaps from a bad translation. The dead, after all, do not walk backwards but they do walk behind us. They have no lungs and cannot call out but would love for us to turn around. They are victims of love, many of them.

With my own number of beloved recently dead, I have taken to turning around as I walk. Carson, more even than Geoffrey Hill, makes me uneasy. Her "Introduction" to *Short Talks* serves as prelude to everything she has written since:

Early one morning words were missing. Before that, words were not. Facts were, faces were. In a good story, Aristotle tells us, everything that happens is pushed by something else. Three old women were bending in the fields. What use is it to question us? they said. Well it shortly became clear that they knew everything there is to know about the snowy fields and the blue-green shoots and the plant called "audacity," which poets mistake for violets. I began to copy out everything that was said. The marks construct an instant of nature gradually, without the boredom of a story. I emphasize this. I will do anything to avoid boredom. It is the task of a lifetime. You can never know enough, never work enough, never use the infinitives and participles oddly enough, never impede the movement harshly enough, never leave the mind quickly enough.

This is the task of her lifetime, and since I am two decades older than Carson, one of my likely regrets when I depart is that I will not have absorbed her lifetime's work. I pass on here to what seem her first published verse poems, *The Life of Towns*, a sequence of thirty-six brief meditations, with overtones of Emily Dickinson, who receives the elliptical tribute of "Emily Town":

Riches in a little room.
Is a phrase that haunts.
Her since the mineral of you.
Left.
Snow or a library.
Or a band of angels.
With a message is.

Not what.
It meant to.
Her.

Dickinson favored no punctuation except dashes—Carson gives us ten periods for ten very short lines. Christopher Marlowe's "infinite riches in a little room" (*The Jew of Malta*) is echoed ironically by Touchstone's allusion to the murder of Marlowe in *As You Like It*: "it strikes a man more dead than a great reckoning in a little room." This becomes the room in her father's house in Amherst where Dickinson wrote her poems and letters. Where is Carson in this poem, or is this not her town, but then, none of the towns in the sequence is hers.

Carson's own story of the self is first told (more or less) in the long narrative essay, *The Anthropology of Water*, that concludes *Plainwater*, where she identifies herself as the only one of the fifty Danaides who did not slay her bridegroom, and thus drowned instead in the deep water:

Water is something you cannot hold. Like men. I have tried.
Father, brother, lover, true friends, hungry ghosts and God, one
by one all took themselves out of my hands.

The Anthropology of Water is eloquently memorable, but I prefer *The Glass Essay*, the narrative poem that leads off *Glass, Irony, and God* (1995), where Carson's greatness as a poet first fully emerges. Emily Brontë is Carson's daemon, as Heathcliff was Catherine Earnshaw's. Visiting her mother, who lives alone on a Brontë-like moor in the north of Canada, Carson confronts her main fear: "I feel I am turning into Emily Brontë,/ my lonely life around me like a moor."

The story of loss—of a man called Law—is perhaps the same as in *The Beauty of the Husband* (2001), but there the recital is harsh and direct, while here we are in an atmosphere of glass, where context would be shattered were the poet to express fury. Instead she meditates upon morning visions she calls Nudes: "naked glimpses of my soul." The central vision is the final night with Law, "a night that centred Heaven and Hell,/ As Emily would say." Law is no Heathcliff, only another cad, to the reader, but Carson effectively presents herself as a living wound of love, her own "pain devil," as Heathcliff was Emily Brontë's. The poet-novelist of *Wuthering Heights* and a handful of magnificent lyrics addressed a transcendental Thou in a few poems that seem to me Gnostic hymns to the Alien God, who is a stranger in this cosmos. All but identified with Emily Brontë, Anne Carson disengages from this relation to a Thou:

Very hard to read, the messages that pass
between Thou and Emily.
In this poem she reverses their roles,
speaking not as the victim but *to* the victim.
It is chilling to watch Thou move upon thou,
who lies alone in the dark waiting to be mastered.

It is a shock to realize that this low, slow collusion
of master and victim within one voice
is a rationale

for the most awful loneliness of the poet's hour.
She has reversed the roles of thou and Thou
not as a display of power

but to force out of herself some pity
for this soul trapped in glass,
which is her true creation.

Those nights lying alone
are not discontinuous with this cold hectic dawn.
It is who I am.

Mutually trapped in glass, the two poets again fuse. After a series of harrowing Nudes, *The Glass Essay* attains its majestic closure:

I saw a high hill and on it a form shaped against hard air.

It could have been just a pole with some old cloth attached,
but as I came closer
I saw it was a human body

trying to stand against winds so terrible that the flesh was
        blowing off the bones.
And there was no pain.
The wind
was cleansing the bones.
They stood forth silver and necessary.
It was not my body, not a woman's body, it was the body of us all.
It walked out of the light.

Overwhelming in context, this remains extraordinary even on its own. There is no consolation in this cleansing, yet there is also no pain. Since this is a vision, and not a privileged moment, we cannot speak of a secular epiphany. Nor can one find the spirit of Emily Brontë in this: it is Anne Carson transcending—momentarily—her own suffering, because erotic loss is universal, male and female. For this visionary moment, melancholia recedes, and we are given an exemplary figure for what Sigmund Freud brilliantly termed "the work of mourning."

The epilogue to *The Glass Essay* is a sequence of eighteen poems called *The Truth About God*. Two of them are astonishing: "Deflect" and "God's Name," both founded upon the early Kabbalah of Isaac the Blind. What is deflected is the light that emanated from the Adam Kadmon, the God-Man:

> From the lights of his forehead were formed all the names of
>   the world.
> From the lights of his ears, nose and throat
> came a function no one has ever defined.
>
> From the lights of his eyes—but wait—
> Isaac waits.
> In theory
>
> the lights of the eye should have issued from Adam's navel.
> But within the lights themselves occurred
> an intake of breath
>
> and they changed their path.
> And they were separated.
> And they were caught in the head.
>
> And from these separated lights came
> that which pains you
> on its errands (here my friend began to weep) through the
>   world.
>
> For be assured it is not only you who mourn.
> Isaac lashed his tail.
> Every rank of world
>
> was caused to descend
> (at least one rank)
> by the terrible pressure of the light.

Nothing remained in place.
Nothing was not captured except
among the shards and roots and matter

some lights
from Adam's eyes
nourished there somehow.

The intake of breath is the *zimzum*, God's withdrawal to permit creation, but the lights separate, and the *kelim* or vessels shatter into "shards and roots and matter." Carson adds her own lively touches; Isaac the Blind becomes a dragon of the Deep, lashing his tail and roaring, witnessing the catastrophe creation. "God's Name" also shows Carson as her own Kabbalist:

The name is not a noun.
It is an adverb.
Like the little black notebooks that Beethoven carried

in his coatpocket
for the use of those who wished to converse with him,
the God adverb

is a one-way street that goes everywhere you are.
No use telling you what it is.
Just chew it and rub it on.

Carson will not tell us that adverb but I suspect it is "endlessly," while the verb that goes with it is "suffers." "Book of Isaiah," which follows later in *Glass, Irony, and God* may be Carson's most disjunctive narrative, and the strongest so far. Guy Davenport accurately notes that Carson captures prophetic narrative with a peculiar felicity:

It was a blue winter evening, the cold bit like a wire.

Isaiah laid his forehead on the ground.

God arrived.

Why do the righteous suffer? said Isaiah.

Bellings of cold washed down the Branch.

Notice whenever God addresses Isaiah in a feminine
singular verb
                something dazzling is
about to happen.

Isaiah what do you know about women? asked God.

Down Isaiah's nostrils bounced woman words:

Blush. Stink. Wife. Fig. Sorceress—

God nodded.

Isaiah go home and get some sleep, said God.

Isaiah went home, slept, woke again.

Isaiah felt sensation below the neck, it was a silk and bitter
sensation.

Isaiah looked down.

It was milk forcing the nipples open.

Isaiah was more than whole.

I am not with you I am *in* you, said the muffled white voice
        of God.

Isaiah sank to a kneeling position.

New pain! said Isaiah.

New contract! said God.

Carson's comic Sublime evades bitterness, whether in Hebraic context
or in the classical convolutions of her extraordinary "novel in verse,"
Autobiography of Red (1998), too long and intricate for me to describe here. A
remarkable outburst of Carsonian fecundity gave us *Men in the Off Hours*
(2000) and *The Beauty of the Husband* (2001), from which I will draw a few
texts for consideration, only to suggest the expanding contours of her

achievement. But I cite, as her *intended* aesthetic, the opening paragraph of her "Note on Method" that preludes *Economy of the Unlost* (1999), her study of verbal economy in Simonides and Paul Celan:

> There is too much self in my writing. Do you know the term Lukács uses to describe aesthetic structure? *Eine fensterlose Monade.* I do not want to be a windowless monad—my training and trainers opposed subjectivity strongly, I have struggled since the beginning to drive my thought out into the landscape of science and fact where other people converse logically and exchange judgments—but I go blind out there. So writing involves some dashing back and forth between that darkening landscape where facticity is strewn and a windowless room cleared of everything I do not know. It is the clearing that takes time. It is the clearing that is a mystery.

I do not know what to do with this. Could one imagine Emily Brontë or Emily Dickinson or Gertrude Stein saying: There is too much self in my writing? Lukács, a Marxist, deplored too much self, since the single person is a myth, according to Marx. Why read Carson rather than a thousand other poets now writing, except that she sensibly goes blind in the absurd realm of "objectivity"? That mode or landscape is easy, vulgar, and therefore disgusting: authentic subjectivity is difficult, sublime, and inspiring. In any case, Carson's genius is to write on the self, not fashionably off it.

There is so much superb poetry available by reading *Men In the Off Hours*, that all I can do here is discuss the poem that most moves me, "Father's Old Blue Cardigan," the elegy for the loss of love to Alzheimer's disease:

> Now it hangs on the back of the kitchen chair
> where I always sit, as it did
> on the back of the kitchen chair where he always sat.
>
> I put it on whenever I come in,
> as he did, stamping
> the snow from his boots.
>
> I put it on and sit in the dark.
> He would not have done this.
> Coldness comes paring down from the moonbone in the sky.

His laws were a secret.
But I remember the moment at which I knew
he was going mad inside his laws.

He was standing at the turn of the driveway when I arrived.
He had on the blue cardigan with the buttons done up all the
way to the top.
Not only because it was a hot July afternoon

but the look on his face—
as a small child who has been dressed by some aunt early in the
morning
for a long trip

on cold trains and windy platforms
will sit very straight at the edge of his seat
while the shadows like long fingers

over the haystacks that sweep past
keep shocking him
because he is riding backwards.

If that *is* pathos, the control is so firm that I cannot locate the point where logos takes over. I reread Carson's poem and suddenly remember the day I encountered an old friend and Yale colleague sitting on the pavement in front of the Graduate School, shoe in one hand and the other hand counting his toes, over and over. A month before, we had encountered each other at the same spot, and enjoyed an intense discussion of American religion, about which he knew everything. The look on his face, as he counted over his toes, was the small child's expression so precisely caught by Carson's train-ride metaphor.

The Beauty of the Husband, dancing its twenty-nine death-tangos, has the remorseless drive of Freud taking us beyond the pleasure-principle. It would be grisly to select a favorite tango, but I cannot get no. XXII "Homo Ludens," out of my head, though I would like to. The nameless husband, after a three-year separation, takes his wife to Athens, supposedly for reconciliation. At night, in the hotel room, they dispute as ever concerning his serial infidelities, and suddenly his nose begins to bleed:

Then blood runs down over his upper lip, lower lip, chin.
To his throat.
Appears on the whiteness of his shirt.

Dyes a mother-of-pearl button for good.
Blacker than a mulberry.
Don't think his heart had burst. He was no Tristan
(though he would love to point out that in the common version
Tristan is not false, it is the sail that kills)
yet neither of them had a handkerchief
and that is how she ends up staining her robe with his blood,
his head in her lap and his virtue coursing through her

as if they were one flesh.
Husband and wife may erase a boundary.
Creating a white page.

But now the blood seems to be the only thing in the room.

If only one's whole life could consist in certain moments.
There is no possibility of coming back from such a moment
to simple hatred,
black ink.

Cold-heartedly, I might observe that I know no other moment like this, in literature, but that praise seems pointless in confronting Carson's eloquent immediacy. Our lives, even in retrospect, do not consist in certain moments, secular epiphanies that come back to us, glories or humiliations. That is part of the dark wisdom of a long poem that beings: "A wound gives off its own light" and ends with the former husband fictively saying: "Watch me fold this page now so you think it is you."

Yet I don't want to end this brief appreciation of Anne Carson with that voice, but with her own. She is a highly active volcano, and fascinates a critic who has been a Longinian all his long life. Somewhere in *Plainwater* she writes: "Language is what eases the pain of living with other people, language is what makes the wounds come open again." Not language, not at all language, I want to murmur, but only language's rare masters—like Emily Brontë, Emily Dickinson, Anne Carson.

Biographical Notes

ELIZABETH BISHOP was born on February 8, 1911, in Worcester, Massachusetts. Her father died eight months after her birth, and her mother was hospitalized for mental disorders several times in Bishop's very early life, and then from 1916 until her death in 1934. She grew up in the homes of various relatives: with her mother's parents in Nova Scotia, with her father's parents in Worcester, and finally with her Aunt Maud in Boston.

In 1934, during her senior year at Vassar, Bishop met Marianne Moore, and the two poets became very close friends. Bishop's first poems were published in 1935 in an anthology entitled *Trial Balances*. Her first book, *North & South*, was published in 1946; a year later she received a Guggenheim Fellowship. Other awards followed, from Bryn Mawr and the American Academy of Arts and Letters, and Bishop decided in 1951 to use some of her prize money to travel in South America and through the Strait of Magellan. She came to a halt in Brazil because of illness, but, after she recovered, decided to stay there. For the next twenty-three years she lived with her friend Lota Constenat de Macedo Soares in Rio de Janeiro and Ouro Prêto, Brazil.

Bishop's poems *North & South—A Cold Spring* appeared in 1955 and won the 1956 Pulitzer Prize, a *Partisan Review* Fellowship, and an Amy Lowell Traveling Fellowship. Her next book, *Questions of Travel*, was published in 1965. *Complete Poems* followed in 1969, winning a National Book Award. In the fall of 1970, she began a yearly one-semester appointment at Harvard, and when Lota died, Bishop moved to Boston. Coincident with the publication of her *Geography III* in 1976, she received the Neustadt International Prize for Literature. Three years later she died, and the last collection of her poetry, *The Complete Poems: 1927–1979*, was published posthumously.

MAY SWENSON was born in Logan Utah, in 1919, to Swedish Mormon parents. She graduated from Utah State Agricultural College with a B.A. degree in English, and went to work as a reporter for various newspapers in and around Logan. In 1937 she went to New York, where she worked as a secretary. She later became editor for New Directions Press. Her first poems were published by the *Saturday Review of Literature;* appearances in *The Nation, Poetry, The Hudson Review, Partisan Review*, and *Contact* followed. Her first book, *Another Animal: Poems*, was published in 1954. *A Cage of Spines* appeared in 1958, and she won an Amy Lowell Traveling Fellowship in 1961. *To Mix with Time* (1963) followed this journey, and in 1965 Swenson became the poet in residence at Purdue University. *Poems to Solve* was published in 1966, *Half Sun, Half Sleep* in 1967, and *Iconographs* and *More Poems To Solve* appeared in 1971. Her most acclaimed book, *New and Selected Things Taking Place*, was published in 1978 and nominated for the National Book Award in 1979. Swenson also won a $10,000 fellowship from The Academy of American Poets in 1979. She served as a Chancellor of The Academy of American Poets from 1980 to 1989. She died in 1989.

GWENDOLYN BROOKS was born on June 7, 1917, in Topeka, Kansas. She grew up on the South Side of Chicago, however, where she lives today. Strongly encouraged by her parents, she wrote poetry throughout her childhood, and, at sixteen, published her first poem in *The Defender.* She met her husband, aspiring writer Henry Blakely, at an NAACP Youth Council meeting, and they were married in 1939. Their son, Henry Jr., was born in 1940, and their daughter, Nora, in 1953.

Brooks's first book, *A Street in Bronzeville*, was published in 1945, and she received a grant from The National Institute of Arts and Letters, *Mademoiselle's* Merit Award, and a Guggenheim Fellowship. With the publication of *Annie Allen* in 1949, Gwendolyn Brooks became the first black woman to win a Pulitzer Poetry Prize. *Maud Martha* appeared in 1953, followed by *Bean Eaters* in 1960, *Selected Poems* in 1963, *In the Mecca* in 1968, and *The World of Gwendolyn Brooks* in 1971.

Brooks taught at various colleges in Illinois in the 1960s and in 1968 was named Poet Laureate of Illinois. Late in the 1960s, she became active in the Black Arts Movement; along with other black poets, she began to organize "neighborhood cultural events"—art exhibits, music festivals, and poetry readings—in Chicago's black neighborhoods. She also began to publish her books with black-owned and -operated presses. *Riot* (1969), *Family Pictures* (1970), *Aloneness* (1971), a children's book, and *Beckonings* (1975) were all published with the Broadside Press. Brooks was awarded her first honorary degree in 1970 from Northwestern University; which was followed by more than forty such degrees. She received two Guggenheim Fellowships, a Frost medal, a National Endowment for the Arts award, and the Shelley Award from the Poetry Society of America. From 1985–1986 Brooks was Consultant in Poetry to the Library of Congress, and she continued to publish with black presses: *Primer for Blacks* (1980) and *To Disembark* (1981) were published by The Third World Press. Among her other volumes of poetry are *The Near-Johannesburg Boy and Other Poems* (1986), *Blacks* (1987), and *Children Coming Home* (1991). She died December 3, 2000.

DENISE LEVERTOV was born on October 24, 1923, in Ilford, Essex, England. She began writing poetry as a child, and at twelve had the audacity to send a sample of poetry to T. S. Eliot. He responded, advising her to continue writing. "Listening to Distant Guns" was published in *Poetry Quarterly* in 1940, and thereafter, her work was frequently accepted by British literary magazines. Her first book, *The Double Image*, was published in late 1946.

While traveling in Switzerland after the war, Levertov met the American writer Mitchell Goodman and married him. They moved to the United States in 1948, when she was pregnant with their son, Nikolai Gregory. She became a citizen of the United States in 1955, and her first American book, *Here and Now*, was published in 1957 by City Lights Press. Other volumes followed quickly: *Overland to the Islands* appeared in 1958, and *With Eyes at the Back of Our Heads*, a collection that won the Bess Hopkin Prize from *Poetry* magazine, in 1960. In 1962, Levertov received a Guggenheim Fellowship; in the early 1960s she was also poetry editor of *The Nation*. From 1964 to 1966 she was an associate scholar at the Radcliffe Institute for Independent Studies in Boston. In 1965 she received a medal from the American Institute of Arts and Letters and, with Muriel Rukeyser and other poets, established an activist group called Writers and Artists Protest against the War in Vietnam. *The Sorrow Dance*, published in 1967, shows signs of this activism and the death of Levertov's sister, Olga. Other books, *To Stay Alive* and *The Freeing of the Dust*, written during the war years, are also strongly marked by these experiences of war and protest.

Levertov served as poetry editor for *Mother Jones* between 1975 and 1978, and taught at Stanford University from 1982 to 1993. He rother books of poetry include *Poems 1968-1972* (1987), *A Door in the Hive* (1989), *Evening Train* (1992), and *The Sands of the Well* (1996). Denise Levertov died in December 1997, her book *This Great Unknowing: Last Poems* was published posthumously in 1999.

ANNE SEXTON was born Anne Gray Harvey on November 9, 1928, in Newton, Massachusetts. On August 16,1948, she eloped with Alfred Muller Sexton II to North Carolina. The following year they moved to Massachusetts, where, after attending a modeling course, Anne Sexton was periodically employed as a model. Between the birth of her daughter, in 1953, and her son, in 1956, she was hospitalized for "emotional disturbance." In 1956, she was again admitted to a mental hospital, her children were sent to relatives, and she attempted to commit suicide.

With the encouragement of her psychiatrist, she began to write poetry; they both saw it as a way of allowing her unconscious to "speak." She began to take poetry classes with John Holmes at the Boston Center for Adult Education in 1957, and in 1958 she won a scholarship to the Antioch Writers Conference, where she worked with W. D. Snodgrass. She also developed friendships with Maxine Kumin, Sylvia Plath, and George Starbuck, and was given a place in Robert Lowell's graduate writing seminar at Boston University. Her first book, *To Bedlam and Part Way Back*, was published in 1960, and in 1961 she taught poetry and writing at Harvard and Radcliffe. The following year she was hospitalized again, in a pattern that continued to repeat itself: awards and publication, followed by suicidal depression. By the end of 1963, she had published eight books and received a number of awards which included a traveling fellowship from the American Academy of Arts and Letters, election as a Fellow of the Royal Society of Literature in London, a Pulitzer Prize for *Live or Die*, the Shelley Award from the Poetry Society of America, a Guggenheim Fellowship, and honorary degrees from Tufts and Fairfield Universities and Regis College. On October 4, 1974, she committed suicide by carbon monoxide poisoning.

ADRIENNE RICH was born in Baltimore on May 16, 1929. She wrote poetry throughout her childhood, and when she graduated from Radcliffe College in 1951 her first book, *A Change of World*, was published in the Yale Younger Poets series. The following year, she received a Guggenheim Fellowship, and traveled in Europe. When she returned in 1953, she married

Alfred H. Conrad, a professor at Harvard. Their first son, David, was born in 1955, the same year that *Diamond Cutters and Other Poems* appeared. Two other sons were born, Paul in 1957 and Jacob in 1959. In 1960, Adrienne Rich won The National Institute of Arts and Letters Award for Poetry and was the Phi Beta Kappa poet at William and Mary College. The following year she received another Guggenheim Fellowship and took her family to live in the Netherlands. The year 1962 brought her a Bollingen Foundation Grant for the translation of Dutch poetry, and the following year an Amy Lowell Traveling Fellowship.

Snapshots of a Daughter-in-Law won The Bess Hopkin Prize from *Poetry* magazine. In 1965 Rich was the Phi Beta Kappa Poet at Swarthmore College; the following year *Necessities of Life* was published and nominated for the National Book Award. In 1966 Rich was Phi Beta Kappa poet at Harvard, and from 1966 through 1968 she taught, variously, at Swarthmore, Columbia, and in the Open Admission and SEEK programs at City College of New York. *Selected Poems* was published in England in 1967, and *Leaflets* appeared in 1969.

In 1970 her husband died. Adrienne Rich remained in New York City with her sons, continuing to teach and write with an increasingly feminist focus. *The Will to Change* was published in 1971, winning the Shelley Award of The Poetry Society of America, and *Diving into the Wreck* appeared in 1973. She accepted the National Book Award for *Diving*, along with the other nominees, Audre Lorde and Alice Walker, "in the name of all the women whose voices have gone . . . unheard." Other works of poetry include *The Fact of a Doorframe: Poems Selected and New 1950-1984* (1984), the often-taught *Dark Fields of the Republic: Poems 1991-1995* (1995), and *Fox: Poems 1998-2000* (2001). Rich's nonfiction work includes *Of Woman Born: Motherhood as Experience and Institution* (1986), *What is Found There: Notebooks on Poetry and Politics* (1993), and most recently *Arts of the Possible: Essays and Conversations* (2001).

Rich has won the Ruth Lilly Poetry Prize, the Lenore Marshall Poetry Prize, the National Book Award, and a MacArthur Fellowship. In 1999 she received the Lifetime Achievement Award from the Lannan Foundation.

SYLVIA PLATH was born on October 27, 1932, in Boston. Her father died when she was eight years old. In August 1950, just before she entered Smith College, her short story "And Summer Will Not Come Again" appeared in *Seventeen* magazine. A poem, "Bitter Strawberries," was also published in the *Christian Science Monitor.* These small successes were followed by more short stories and reviews in *Seventeen*, and a prize-winning story published in

Mademoiselle. At the end of her sophomore year, Plath won a guest editorship on the staff of *Mademoiselle*, and for the month of June 1952 lived in New York in what seemed a fashionable whirl of celebrities. The month culminated in the publication of an article, an editorial piece, and a poem. Later that summer, after her return home, Plath attempted to commit suicide. She was rescued, however, and after several months of hospitalization and treatment, she returned to Smith and completed her degree with honors. Funded by a Fulbright Fellowship, she began a program of studies at Cambridge, and she continued to publish poems. She also met and married the British poet Ted Hughes in 1956. A year later the couple moved to the United States, Plath to teach at Smith, and Hughes at the University of Massachusetts. After a year of teaching, the two poets moved to Boston to try to live on the earnings from their writings.

In December 1959, Ted Hughes and Sylvia Plath returned to England; the following April their daughter, Frieda, was born. Later that year, Plath's first volume of poetry, *The Colossus*, was published. In 1961 she received a Saxton Fellowship, which covered her expenses while she wrote *The Bell Jar*, published in 1963 under the pseudonym Victoria Lucas. In 1962, a son, Nicholas, was born, Sylvia Plath finished a radio play entitled *Three Women: A Monologue for Three Voices*, and discovered that her husband was having an affair. The dissolution of their marriage was explosive and catapulted Plath into a deep depression. She and the children moved to London and lived in a tiny apartment during the winter of 1962–1963, the period when she composed most of the poems which comprise the *Ariel* volume. On the morning of February 11, 1963, Sylvia Plath committed suicide by inhaling gas from her oven. Most of her work was published posthumously, and *The Collected Poems*, edited by Ted Hughes and published in 1981, won a Pulitzer Prize for poetry.

AUDRE LORDE was born on February 18, 1934, in New York. As a young adult in the 1950s, she held several jobs and attended night school at Hunter College. When her father died in 1953 and left her a small inheritance, she decided to go to Mexico, where she attended the National University of Mexico for a year. Upon her return, she was hired as an assistant to the librarian in the Welfare Department; she also continued to take classes at Hunter and completed her degree in 1959. Two years later she received a Master of Library Science from Columbia University, and began to work in New York libraries. Her first publishing success was also in 1961: Langston Hughes included some of her poems in his anthology, *New Negro Poets, USA*. Throughout the 1960s her poetry was anthologized, for the most part by editors in Holland, Italy, and England. Her poetry also began to appear in black magazines such as *Black World* and *Harlem Writers Quarterly*.

Although Lorde has identified herself throughout her life as a lesbian, she married Edwin Ashley Robbins in 1962. They had two children and were amicably divorced within seven years. Finally, in the late 1960s, Lorde began to receive recognition for her work. In 1968 she received an award from the National Endowment for the Arts, held a visiting professorship at Atlanta University, and was the Poet in Residence at Tougaloo College in Mississippi. Her first book of poetry, *The First Cities*, also appeared that year. *Cables to Rage* was published in 1970 by Broadside Press, and *From a Land Where Other People Live* (1972) was nominated for a National Book Award in 1974.

In the 1970s, Lorde taught at Lehman College, John Jay College of Criminal Justice, City College of New York, and was eventually appointed a professor at Hunter College. *Coal*, published in 1976, was her first book to be published by a major publisher, W.W. Norton. Lorde's other works include *The Black Unicorn* (1978), *Chosen Poems Old and New* (1982), *Our Dead Behind Us* (1986), and several volumes published after her death in 1992. Lorde has also written *The Cancer Journals* and *Zami: A New Spelling of My Name*, both autobiographical prose, and *Sister Outsider*, a collection of essays.

In the 1980s, Lorde co-founded with writer Barbara Smith Kitchen Table: Women of Color Press, a press dedicated to publishing the works of women of color. Lorde won a National Book Award for her work *A Burst of Light* (1988), and served as Poet Laureat of New York from 1991–1992. She died of cancer in 1992.

AMY CLAMPITT was born in the first half of the twentieth century in New Providence, Iowa, and graduated from Grinnell College. In 1978, her poems began to appear in literary magazines and periodicals, including *The New Yorker*, *The Kenyon Review*, *The New Republic*, *Prairie Schooner*, *Poetry*, and *The Yale Review*. She was awarded a Guggenheim Fellowship in 1982, and her first highly acclaimed book, *The Kingfisher*, was published in 1983. Her other works include *What the Light Was Like* (1985), *Archaic Figure* (1987), *Westward* (1990), and *A Silence Opens* (1994). In 1992 Clampitt was made a MacArthur Foundation Fellow. She died in September 1994.

VICKI HEARNE was born in 1946. A horse and dog trainer for some years, she also wrote poetry. Her first book, *Nervous Horses*, was published in 1980, and in 1982 she coauthored *Horse Breaking: The Obedience Method*. She taught poetry and fiction at the University of California at Riverside and was a visiting fellow at the Institution for Social and Policy Studies at Yale University from 1989 to 1995. Her second volume of poetry, *In the Absence of Horses*, was published in 1983, and her third volume, *The Parts of Light*, was published in 1994. Hearne's other work includes numerous essays, and several books on animal training. She was a frequent contributor to *The New York Times Book Review*, and *Harper's* where she served as a contributing editor. Vicki Hearne died in August 2001.

JAY MACPHERSON, born in 1931, is a Canadian, reportedly descended from the 18th-century Scottish poet Macpherson who wrote under the name Ossian. She has taught English at Victoria College in the University of Toronto. Her critical work includes a major study of the nineteenth-century prose romance, *The Spirit of Solitude*, and her poetry has appeared in three volumes: *The Boatman* (1957), *Welcoming Disaster* (1976), and *Poems Twice Told* (1981) which earned her the Governor General's Award. She has also written on mythology for children.

ANNE CARSON, born in 1950, is a Canadian poet, essayist and scholar trained in the classics. She has taught at the University of Calgary, Princeton University, and Emory University, and is currently the Director of Graduate Studies, Classics at McGill University in Montreal. Her books of poetry include *Glass, Irony, and God* (1995), *Plainwater* (1995), *Autobiography of Red: A Novel in Verse* (1998), *Men in the Off Hours* (2000), and most recently *The Beauty of the Husband: A Fictional Essay in 29 Tangos* (2001). Carson, a MacArthur Fellowship recipient, has also been awarded the T. S. Eliot Prize for Poetry, the Lannan Literary Award for Poetry, the Pushcart Prize for Poetry, and a Guggenheim Fellowship.

Contributors

HAROLD BLOOM is Sterling Professor of the Humanities at Yale University and Henry W. and Albert A. Berg Professor of English at the New York University Graduate School. He is the author of over 20 books, including *Shelly's Mythmaking* (1959), *The Visionary Company* (1961), *Blake's Apocalypse* (1963), *Yeats* (1970), *A Map of Misreading* (1975), *Kabbalah and Criticism* (1975), *Agon: Toward a Theory of Revisionism* (1982), *The American Religion* (1992), *The Western Canon* (1994), and *Omens of Millennium: The Gnosis of Angels, Dreams, and Resurrection* (1996). *The Anxiety of Influence* (1973) sets forth Professor Bloom's provocative theory of the literary relationships between the great writers and their predecessors. His most recent books include *Shakespeare: The Invention of the Human*, a 1998 National Book Award finalist, and *How to Read and Why*, which was published in 2000. In 1999, Professor Bloom received the prestigious American Academy of Arts and Letters Gold Medal for Criticism.

HELEN VENDLER has taught English at Boston University and at Harvard University, and served as President of the Modern Language Association in 1980. She is a prolific critic whose works include *Part of Nature, Part of Us: Modern American Poets* (1980), *The Harvard Book of Contemporary American Poetry* (1985), and *The Art of Shakespeare's Sonnets* (1997).

LEE EDELMAN is a professor of English at Tufts University. He writes poetry and has published criticism on Hart Crane, John Ashbery, and

Elizabeth Bishop. His books include *Transmemberment of Song: Hart Crane's Anatomies of Rhetoric and Desire* (1987), and *Homographesis: Essays in Gay Literary and Cultural Theory* (1994).

RICHARD HOWARD is a poet, critic of poetry, and translator. His books of poetry include *Fellow Feelings* (1976), *Misgivings* (1979), *Lining Up* (1984), *Like Most Revelations: New Poems* (1994), and *Trappings: New Poems* (1999) He also translated Baudelaire's *Les Fleurs du Mal*, as well as many books by Roland Barthes.

GARY SMITH has taught English at Southern Illinois University at Carbondale. He co-edited *A Life Distilled: Gwendolyn Brooks, Her Poetry and Fiction* (1987) with Maria K. Mootry.

PAUL A. LACEY is provost and professor of English at Earlham College in Richmond, Indiana. His books include *The Inner War: Forms and Themes in Recent American Poetry* (1972), and *Revitalizing Teaching Through Faculty Development* (1983).

J. D. McCLATCHY is both a poet and a critic of poetry. His works include four books of poetry, and numerous critical essays. Among those works are *Stars Principal* (1986), *The Rest of the Way* (1992), and *Ten Commandments* (1998). He has also edited numerous books including *Anne Sexton: The Artist and Her Critics* (1978), *The Vintage Book of Contemporary American Poetry* (1990), and *The Vintage Book of World Poetry* (1996).

MARGARET HOMANS is a professor of English at Yale University and the author of *Women Writers and Poetic Identity: Dorothy Wordsworth, Emily Brontë, and Emily Dickinson* (1980), *Bearing the Word: Language and Female Experience in Nineteenth-Century Women's Writing* (1986), and *Royal Representations: Queen Victorian and Victorian Culture, 1837-1876* (1998).

BARBARA HARDY has taught in the History and Literature Program at Harvard University as well as at Birkbeck College in London. Her books include *Forms of Feeling in Victorian Fiction* (1985), *Shakespeare's Storytellers: Dramatic Narration* (1997), and *Dylan Thomas: An Original Language* (2000).

R. B. STEPTO teaches English and African-American Studies at Yale University. His books include *From Behind the Veil: A Study of Afro-American Narrative* (1991) and *Blue as the Lake: A Personal Geography* (1998). He has co-edited such volumes as *Afro-American Literature: The Reconstruction of*

Instruction (1978), and *Chant of Saints: A Gathering of Literature, Art, and Scholarship* (1979).

JOHN HOLLANDER is a poet, critic, and professor of English at Yale University. His numerous books include *Vision and Resonance: Two Senses of Poetic Form* (1975), *Power of Thirteen* (1983), *The Work of Poetry* (1997), *Figurehead* (1999), and *Rhyme's Reason: A Guide to English Literature* (3rd edition 2000). He has also edited *The Oxford Anthology of English Literature* (1972) with Frank Kermode.

NORTHROP FRYE taught English at the University of Toronto. Through his writing and speaking, he has done much to contribute to and encourage Canadian letters. Several of his many books are *Fearful Symmetry: A Study of William Blake* (1947), *The Bush Garden* (1971), *The Secular Scripture: A Study of the Structure of Romance* (1976), and perhaps most notably *Anatomy of Criticism* (1957).

MARGARET ATWOOD is a Canadian writer, poet, and critic. She is the author of numerous books of poetry, several novels, and several works of criticism. Her novel *The Blind Assassin* (2000) won the 2000 Booker prize, and her newest work *Negotiating with the Dead: A Writer on Writing* (2002) will be published by Cambridge University Press.

Bibliography

Abel, Elizabeth, ed. *Writing and Sexual Difference*. Chicago: The University of Chicago Press, 1982.

Benstock, Shari, *Feminist Issues In Literary Scholarship*. Bloomington: Indiana University Press, 1987.

Case, Sue-Ellen. *Performing Feminisms: Feminist Critical Theory and Theatre*. Baltimore: Johns Hopkins University Press, 1990.

Dearborn, Mary V. *Pocahontas's Daughters: Gender and Ethnicity in American Culture*. New York: Oxford University Press, 1986.

Evans, Mari, ed. *Black Women Writers (1950–1980): A Critical Evaluation*. New York: Anchor Press/Doubleday, 1984.

Freeman, Barbara C. *The Feminine Sublime: Gender and Excess in Women's Fiction*. University of California Press, 1995.

Gilbert, Sandra M. *No Man's Land: The Place of the Woman Writer in the Twentieth Century*. New Haven: Yale University Press, 1988.

Gilbert, Sandra M., and Susan Gubar, eds. *Shakespeare's Sisters: Feminist Essays on Women Poets*. Bloomington: Indiana University Press, 1979.

Jacobus, Mary, ed. *Women Writing and Writing About Women*. London: Croom Helm in association with The Oxford Women's Studies Committee, 1979.

McConnell-Ginet, Sally, Ruth Barker, and Nelly Furman, eds. *Women and Language in Literature and Society*. New York: Praeger Publishers, 1980.

Moers, Ellen. *Literary Women*. Garden City, NY: Doubleday and Company, 1979.

Rich, Adrienne. *On Lies, Secrets and Silence*. New York: W. W. Norton and Company, 1979.

Vendler, Helen. *Part of Nature, Part of* Us. Cambridge: Harvard University Press, 1980.

Winders, James A. *Gender, Theory, and the Canon*. Madison, Wis.: U of Wisconsin P, 1991.

ELIZABETH BISHOP

Blasing, M. Konuck. "Mont d'Espoir or Mount Despair, The Re-Verses of Elizabeth Bishop." *Contemporary Literature* 25, no. 3 (Fall 1984): 341–53.

Bromwich, David. "Elizabeth Bishop's Dream Houses." *Raritan* 4, no. 1 (Summer 1984): 77–94.

Costello, Bonnie. "Vision and Mastery in Elizabeth Bishop." *Twentieth Century Literature* 28 (Winter 1982): 351–70.

———. *Elizabeth Bishop: Questions of Mastery*. Cambridge: Harvard University Press, 1991.

Dodd, Elizabeth. *The Veiled Mirror and the Woman Poet: H. D., Louise Bogan, Elizabeth Bishop, and Louise Gluck*. Columbia: University of Missouri Press, 1992.

Doreski, Carole. "Elizabeth Bishop: 'All the Conditions of Existence.'" *Literary Review* 27 (Winter 1984): 262–71.

———. *Elizabeth Bishop: The Restraints of Language*. New York: Oxford University Press, 1993.

Goldensohn, Lorrie. Elizabeth Bishop: *The Biography of a Poetry*. New York: Columbia University Press, 1992.

Handa, Carolyn. "Elizabeth Bishop and Women's Poetry." *South Atlantic Quarterly* 82 (Summer 1983): 269–81.

Lombardi, Marilyn M. *Elizabeth Bishop: The Geography of Gender*. Charlottesville: University Press of Virginia, 1993.

McCabe, Susan. *Elizabeth Bishop: Her Poetics of Loss*. University Park: Pennsylvania State University Press, 1994.

Millier, Brett C. *Elizabeth Bishop: Life and the Memory of It*. Berkeley: University of California Press, 1993.

Parker, Robert D. *The Unbeliever: The Poetry of Elizabeth Bishop*. Urbana: University of Illinois Press, 1988.

Schwartz, Lloyd, and Sybil P. Estess, eds. *Elizabeth Bishop and Her Art*. Ann Arbor: University of Michigan Press, 1983.

World Literature Today. Special issue on Elizabeth Bishop (Winter 1977).

MAY SWENSON

Smith, Dave. "Perpetual Worlds Taking Place." *Poetry* 135, no. 5 (1980): 291–96.

Stanford, Anne. "May Swenson: The Art of Perceiving." *The Southern Review* 5, no. 1 (January 1969): 58–75.

Stepanchev, Stephen. "May Swenson." *American Poetry Since 1945.* New York: Harper and Row, 1965.

GWENDOLYN BROOKS

Callahan, John F. "'Essentially an Essential African': Gwendolyn Brooks and the Awakening to Audience." *North Dakota Quarterly* 55.4 (Fall 1987): 59-73.

Dawson, Emma W. "Vanishing Point: The Rejected Black Woman in the Poetry of Gwendolyn Brooks." *Obsidian II* 4.1 (Sprg 1989): 1-11.

Furman, Marva Riley. "Gwendolyn Brooks: The 'Unconditioned' Poet." *College Language Association Journal* 17, no. 1 (September 1973): 1–10.

Hansell, William H. "Aestheticism versus Political Militancy in Gwendolyn Brooks's 'The Chicago Picasso' and 'The Wall.'" *College Language Association Journal* 17, no. 1 (September 1973): 11–15.

Horvath, Brooke K. "The Satisfactions of What's Difficult in Gwendolyn Brook's Poetry." *American Literature* 62.4 (Dec 1990): 606-16.

Hudson, Clenora F. "Racial Themes in the Poetry of Gwendolyn Brooks." *College Language Association Journal* 17, no. 1 (September 1973): 16–20.

Hull, Gloria T. "A Note on the Poetic Technique of Gwendolyn Brooks." *College Language Association Journal* 19, no. 2 (December 1975): 280–85.

Kent, George E. *A Life of Gwendolyn Brooks.* Lexington : University Press of Kentucky, 1990.

Madhubuti, Haki R., ed. *Say That the River Turns: The Impact of Gwendolyn Brooks.* Chicago: Third World Press, 1987.

Melhem, D. H. *Gwendolyn Brooks: Poetry and the Heroic Voice.* Lexington : University Press of Kentucky, 1987.

Mootry, Maria K. and Gary Smith. eds. *A Life Distilled: Gwendolyn Brooks, Her Poetry and Fiction.* Urbana : University of Illinois Press, 1987.

Smith, Gary. "The Black Protest Sonnet." *American Poetry* 2, no. 1 (Fall 1984): 2–21.

Stetson, Erlene. "*Songs After Sunset (1935–1936):* The Unpublished Poetry of Gwendolyn Elizabeth Brooks." *College Language Association Journal* 24, no. 1 (September 1980): 87–96.

Taylor, Henry. "Gwendolyn Brooks: An Essential Sanity." *Kenyon Review* 13.4 (Fall 1991): 115-31.

Werner, Craig. "Gwendolyn Brooks: Tradition in Black and White." *Minority Voices 1*, no. 2 (Fall 1977): 27–38.

DENISE LEVERTOV

Block, Ed, Jr. ed. "Spirit in the Poetry of Denise Levertov." *Renascence* 50.1-2 (Fall-Winter 1997-98).

Brooker, Jewel S. *Conversations with Denise Levertov*. Jackson, MS : University Press of Mississippi, 1998.

Gilbert, Sandra M. "Revolutionary Love: Denise Levertov and the Poetics of Politics." *Parnassus* 12-13.2-1 (Spring-Winter 1985): 335-51.

Howard, Richard. "Denise Levertov." In *Alone with America*. New York: Atheneum, 1980.

Little, Anne C., and Susie Paul. eds. *Denise Levertov: New Perspectives*. West Cornwall, CT : Locust Hill, 2000.

MacGowan, Christopher. *The Letters of Denise Levertov and William Carlos Williams*. New York: New Directions, 1998.

Marten, Harry. *Understanding Denise Levertov*. Columbia: University of South Carolina Press, 1988.

Ostriker, Alicia. "In Mind: The Divided Self and Women's Poetry." *The Midwest Quarterly 24*, no. 4 (Summer 1983): 351–65.

Rodgers, Audrey T. *Denise Levertov: the poetry of engagement*. Rutherford, N.J.: Fairleigh Dickinson University Press, 1993.

Sautter, Diane. "Tacit and Explicit *Tulips*." *Pre/Text: Interdisciplinary Journal of Rhetoric 1*, no. 1/2 (1982): 45–59.

ANNE SEXTON

Bixler, Frances. ed. *Original essays on the poetry of Anne Sexton*. Conway, Ark.: University of Central Arkansas Press, 1988.

Colburn, Steven E. ed. *Anne Sexton: telling the tale*. Ann Arbor: University of Michigan Press, 1988.

Hartman, Geoffrey. "Les Belles Dames Sans Merd." *Kenyon Review 22*, no. 4 (Autumn 1960): 691–94.

McClatchy, J. D., ed. *Anne Sexton: The Artist and Her Critics*. Bloomington: Indiana University Press, 1978.

Middlebrook, Diane W. *Anne Sexton: a biography*. Boston: Houghton Mifflin, 1991.

Wagner-Martin, Linda. ed. *Critical essays on Anne Sexton*. Boston: Mass.: G.K. Hall, 1989.

Zollman, Sol. "Criticism, Self-Criticism, No Transformation: The Poetry of Robert Lowell and Anne Sexton." *Literature and Ideology 9* (1971): 29–36.

ADRIENNE RICH

Altieri, Charles. "Self-Reflection as Action." In *Self and Sensibility in Contemporary American Poetry.* Cambridge: Cambridge University Press, 1984.

Atwood, Margaret. "Adrienne Rich: *Poems, Selected and New.*" In *Second Words.* Toronto: House of *Anansi* Press, 1982.

Cooper, Jane R. ed. *Reading Adrienne Rich: reviews and re-visions, 1951-81.* Ann Arbor: University of Michigan Press, 1984.

Estrin, Barbara L. "Space-Off and Voice-Over: Adrienne Rich and Wallace Stevens." *Women's Studies* 25.1 (Nov 1995): 23-46.

Gelpi, Barbara Charlesworth, and Albert Gelpi, eds. *Adrienne Rich's Poetry.* New York: W. W. Norton and Company, 1975.

Gilbert, Roger. "Framing Water: Historical Knowledge in Elizabeth Bishop and Adrienne Rich." *Twentieth Century Literature* 43.2 (Sumr 1997): 144-61.

Howard, Richard. "Adrienne Rich." In *Alone with America.* New York: Atheneum, 1980.

Hudgins, Andrew. "'The Burn Has Settled In': A Reading of Adrienne Rich's *Diving into the Wreck.*" *The Texas Review 2,* no. 1 (Spring 1981): 49–65.

Kalstone, David. *Five Temperaments.* New York: Oxford University Press, 1977.

Keyes, Claire. *The aesthetics of power: the poetry of Adrienne Rich.* Athens: University of Georgia Press, 1986.

Martin, Wendy. *An American triptych: Anne Bradstreet, Emily Dickinson, Adrienne Rich.* Chapel Hill: University of North Carolina Press, 1984.

McCorkle, James. "Adrienne Rich: A Common Language of Self-Definition." *Notes on Modern American Literature* 9.3 (Winter 1985): Item 15.

McDaniel, Judith. *Reconstituting the World: The Poetry and Vision of Adrienne Rich.* Argyle, NY: Spinsters Ink, 1978.

Vivley, Sherry Lute. "Adrienne Rich's Contemporary Metaphysical Conceit." *Notes on Contemporary Literature 12,* no. 3 (May 1982): 6–8.

SYLVIA PLATH

Alexander, Paul, ed. *Ariel Ascending: Writings About Sylvia Plath.* New York: Harper and Row, 1985.

————. *Rough Magic: A Biography of Sylvia Plath*. New York: Penguin Books, 1991.

Axelrod, Steven G. *Sylvia Plath: The Wound and the Cure of Words*. Baltimore: Johns Hopkins University Press, 1992.

Broe, Mary Lynn. "Recovering the Complex Self: Sylvia Plath's Beeline." *Centennial Review 24* (Winter 1980): 1–24.

Bundtzen, Lynda K. *Plath's Incarnations: Woman and the Creative Process*. Ann Arbor: University of Michigan Press, 1983.

Dickie, Margaret. "Sylvia Plath's Narrative Strategies." *Iowa Review 13*, no. 2 (Spring 1982): 1–14.

Guber, Susan. "Prosopopoeia and Holocaust Poetry in English: Sylvia Plath and Her Contemporaries." *Yale Journal of Criticism* 14, no. 1 (2001): 191-216.

Meyering, Sheryl L. *Sylvia Plath: A Reference Guide*. Boston: G.K. Hall, 1990.

Newman, Charles, ed. *The Art of Sylvia Plath: A Symposium*. Bloomington: Indiana University Press, 1970.

Perloff, Marjorie. "Sylvia Plath's *Collected Poems:* A Review Essay." *Resources for American Literary Study 11* (Autumn 1983): 304–13.

Simpson, Louis. *A Revolution in Taste*. New York: Macmillan Publishing Company, 1978.

Stevenson, Anne. *Bitter Fame: a life of Sylvia Plath*. Boston: Houghton Mifflin, 1989.

VanDyne, Susan. "Fueling the Phoenix Fire: The Manuscripts of Sylvia Plath's 'Lady Lazarus.'" *Massachusetts Review 24* (Summer 1983): 395–410.

————. *Revising Life: Sylvia Plath's Ariel Poems*. Chapel Hill: University of North Carolina Press, 1993.

AUDRE LORDE

"Audre Lorde: A Special Section." *Callaloo* 14.1 (Winter 1991): 39-95.

De Veaux, Alexis. "Searching for Audre Lorde." *Callaloo 23*, no. 1 (2000): 63.

Dhairyam, Sagri. "'Artifacts for Survival': Remapping the Contours of Poetry with Audre Lorde." *Feminist Studies* 18.2 (Summer 1992): 229-56.

Holland, Sharon P. "'Which Me Will Survive?': Audre Lorde and the Development of a Black Feminist Ideology." *Critical Matrix* 1 (Spring 1988): 1-30.

Keating, AnaLouise. *Women reading women writing: self-invention in Paula Gunn Allen, Gloria Anzaldua, and Audre Lorde*. Philadelphia: Temple University Press, 1996.

———— "Audre Lorde (1934-1992)." *Contemporary African American Novelists:*

A Bio-Bibliographical Critical Sourcebook. Ed. Emmanuel S. Nelson. Westport, CT: Greenwood, 1999. 284-88.

Lorde, Audre, and Adrienne Rich. "An Interview." In *Sister Outsider.* Trumansburg, NY: The Crossing Press, 1984.

Olson, Lester C. "On the Margins of Rhetoric: Audre Lorde Transforming Silence into Language and Action." *Quarterly Journal of Speech* 83.1 (Feb. 1997): 49-70.

———— "Liabilities of Language: Audre Lorde Reclaiming Difference." *Quarterly Journal of Speech* 84.4 (Nov 1998): 448-70.

Steele, Cassie P. *We Heal from Memory: Sexton, Lorde, Anzaldua, and the Poetry of Witness.* NY: Palgrave, 2000.

AMY CLAMPITT

Fenton, James. "*The Kingfisher* by Amy Clampitt." *Poetry Review 74*, no. 1 (April 1984): 27–29.

McClatchy, J. D. Review of *The Kingfisher* by Amy Clampitt. *Poetry 143*, no. 3 (December 1983): 165–67.

Spiegelman, Williard. "What to Make of an Augmented Thing: The Collected Works of Amy Clampitt." *The Kenyon Review 21*, no. 1 (1999): 172.

Vendler, Helen. "On the Thread of Language." *The New York Review of Books*, March 3, 1985, 19–22.

White, Edmund. "Poetry As Alchemy." *The Nation*, April 16,1983,485–86.

JAY MACPHERSON

Berner, Audrey. "The 'Unicorn' Poems of Jay Macpherson," *Journal of Canadian Poetry 3*, (1980): 9-16

Bromwich, David. "Engulfing Darkness, Penetrating Light." *Poetry 127*, no. 4 (January 1976): 236–39.

Djawa, Sandra. "Letters in Canada 1981." *University of Toronto Quarterly 51*, no. 4 (Summer 1982): 344–45.

Namjoshi, Suniti. "In the Whale's Belly: Jay Macpherson's Poetry." *Canadian Literature 79*, (1978): 54-59.

Reaney, James. "The Third-Eye: Macpherson's *The Boatman.*" *Canadian Literature 3*, (1960): 23-34

ANNE CARSON

Jennings, C. "The Erotic Poetics of Anne Carson." *University of Toronto Quarterly 70*, no. 4 (2001): 923–936.

Laughlin, James. "Anne Carson: Epiphany, Trying to Please, Spring Comes Again (fivers)." *Parnassus 23*, no. 1–2 (1998): 309.

Padel, Ruth. "Seeing Red." *The New York Times Book Review*, May 3, 1998: 23.

Rehak, Melanie. "Things Fall Together." *The New York Times Magazine*, March 26, 2000: 36–39.

Ward, David C. "Anne Carson: Addressing the Wound." *PN Review 27*, no. 5 (May–June 2001): 13–16.

Acknowledgments

"Elizabeth Bishop: Domestication, Domesticity, and the Otherworldly" (originally entitled "Elizabeth Bishop") by Helen Vendler from *World Literature Today 51*, no. 1 (Winter 1977), © 1977 by University of Oklahoma Press. Reprinted by permission. This essay also appeared in *Part of Nature, Part of Us: Modern American Poets* (Harvard University Press, 1980).

Edelman, Lee. "The Geography of Gender: Elizabeth Bishop's 'In the Waiting Room'" *Contemporary Literature* Vol. 26, No. 2. © 1985. Reprinted by permission of University of Wisconsin Press.

"May Swenson: 'Turned Back to the Wild by Love'" by Richard Howard from *Alone with America: Essays on the Art of Poetry in the United States since 1950* by Richard Howard, © 1980 by Richard Howard. Reprinted by permission.

"Gwendolyn Brooks's *A Street in Bronzeville*, the Harlem Renaissance and the Mythologies of Black Women" by Gary Smith from *MELUS: The Journal of the Society for the Study of the Multi-Ethnic Literature of the United States* 10, no. 3 (Fall 1983), © 1983 by MELUS. Reprinted by permission.

"Denise Levertov: A Poetry of Exploration" (originally entitled "A Poetry of Exploration") from *The Inner War: Forms and Themes in Recent American Poetry* by Paul A. Lacey, © 1972 by Fortress Press. Reprinted by permission of Augsburg Fortress.

211

"Anne Sexton: Somehow to Endure" by J. D. McClatchy, excerpted from a longer essay in *Anne Sexton: The Artist and Her Critics*, edited by J. D. McClatchy, © 1978 by J. D. McClatchy. Bloomington: Indiana University Press, 1978. Reprinted by permission.

Homans, Margaret; *Women Writers and Poetic Identity:Dorothy Wordsworth, Emily Bronte, and Emily Dickinson* ©1980 by Princeton University Press. Reprinted by permission of Princeton University Press.

"Sylvia Plath: Enlargement or Derangement?" (originally entitled "Enlargement or Derangement") by Barbara Hardy from *The Advantage of Lyric: Essays on Feeling in Poetry* (Indiana University Press, 1977). © 1977 by Barbara Hardy. Reprinted by permission of the author.

"Audre Lorde: The Severed Daughter" (originally entitled "The Phenomenal Woman and the Severed Daughter") by R. B. Stepto from *Parnassus: Poetry in Review* 8, no. 1 (Fall/Winter 1979), © 1980 by Poetry in Review Foundation. Reprinted by permission of the author

"Amy Clampitt: 'The Hazardous Definition of Structures'" (originally entitled "The Hazardous Definition of Structures") by Richard Howard from *Parnassus: Poetry in Review 11*, no. 1 (Spring/Summer 1983), © 1984 by Poetry in Review Foundation. Reprinted by permission.

"Tremors of Exactitude: Vicki Hearne's *Nervous Horses*" (originally entitled "Tremors of Exactitude") by John Hollander from *Times Literary Supplement*, no. 4061 (January 30, 1981), © 1981 by John Hollander. Reprinted by permission of the author.

"Jay Macpherson: Poetry in Canada, 1957" (originally entitled "Letters in Canada: 1957") by Northrop Frye from *University of Toronto Quarterly* 27, no. 4 (July 1958), © 1958 by University of Toronto Press. Reprinted by permission of the author and University of Toronto Press Incorporated.

"Jay Macpherson: *Poems Twice Told*" from *Second Words* by Margaret Atwood © 1982 by O. W. Toad Ltd. Reprinted by permission of House of Anansi Press, Toronto.

Index

213